Doing Theology at the Grassroots

Copyright 2018

All rights reserved. No part of this publication may be reproduced, stored in a retrieval system, or transmitted in any from or by any means, electronic, mechanical, photocopying, recording or otherwise without prior permission from the publishers.

Luviri Press
P/Bag 201
Luwinga, Mzuzu 2
Malawi

ISBN 978-99960-98-20-8

eISBN 978-99960-98-21-5

Luviri Press is represented outside Malawi by:

African Books Collective Oxford (orders@africanbookscollective.com)

www.africanbookscollective.com

Layout und Index: Marvin Esau

First published by Kachere Series, Zomba, 1999

Doing Theology at the Grassroots

Theological Essays from Malawi

Patrick A. Kalilombe

Luviri Press

Luviri Reprint no. 2

Mzuzu

2018

Luviri Reprints

Many books have been published on or in Malawi that are no longer available. While some of these books simply have run their course, others are still of interest for scholars and the general public. Some of the classics have been reprinted outside Malawi over the decades, and during the last two decades, first the Kachere Series and then other publishers have achieved "never out of stock status" by joining the African Books Collective's Print on Demand approach, but there are still a good number of books that would be of interest but are no longer in print.

The Luviri Reprint Series has taken up the task to make those books on or from Malawi, which are out of print but not out of interest, available again, through Print on Demand and therefore worldwide.

While the Luviri Reprint Series concentrates on Malawi, it is also interested in the neighbouring countries and even in those further afield.

Luviri Reprints publish the books as they originally were. Usually a new Foreword is added, and where appropriate, new information has been added. All such additions, mostly in footnotes, are marked by an asterisk (*).

The Editors

Contents

Series Editors' Preface	6
Introduction: My Life, My Faith, My Theology, and My Country:	8
1 Christ's Church in Lilongwe Today and Tomorrow	44
2 Evangelization and the Holy Spirit	74
3 The African Local Churches and the World-wide Roman Catholic Communion	87
4 The Salvific Value of African Religions	109
5 Lessons from African Traditional Religion: Unity from Below	126
6 Black Theology	143
7 Doing Theology at the Grassroots: A Challenge for Professional Theologians	172
8 The Bible and Non-literate Communities: A Malawian Example	203
9 Spirituality in the African Perspective	220
Index	220

Series Editors' Preface

The Kachere Series is an initiative of the Department of Theology and Religious Studies at the University of Malawi. It aims to promote the emergence of a body of literature which will enable students and others to engage critically with religion in Malawi, its social impact and the theological questions which it raises. An important starting point lies with the publication of essays and theses which until now have been inaccessible to all but the most dedicated specialist. It is also hoped, however, that the development of theological scholarship in Malawi will stimulate the writing of many new books. General works with popular appeal can be published as Kachere Books. Documents and essays, which are of value as sources for the study of religion in Malawi, can be published as Kachere Texts. Full-length treatises, the fruit of sound primary research which meet rigorous academic standards, are published as Kachere Monographs. The Editors intend the Series to contribute substantially to the growth of a body of knowledge in the area of theology and religious studies in Malawi. As important resources for study related to this field, we are confident that they will come to be prized not only within Malawi but in every academic centre concerned with religion and society in Africa.

Patrick Kalilombe has been distinguished for more than twenty-five years as a pioneering theologian and ecclesiologist. Circumstances have determined that much of his best work has been produced and published outside Malawi and through such a diversity of outlets that it is very difficult for students and others to have access to his work as a whole. Hence we are convinced that this collection of his essays will have a very wide appeal, both in Malawi and beyond. The chapters are quite varied in their origins and subjects but the reader will not take long to notice recurrent themes: the author's missionary vocation, the critical role of the "grassroots" in theological construction, the integrity of Chewa traditional belief, the combination of Catholic commitment with radical openness to all religious and cultural traditions. The text is accompanied by a series of photographs which lead progressively through the events of Bishop Kalilembe's 25th Jubilee celebration at Mua in 1997. It is fitting that this milestone should be marked also, even if a little belatedly, by the publication of this book which we believe will attain an important place in contemporary African theological literature.

Kachere Series Editors
Advent 1998

Introduction: My Life, My Faith, My Theology, and My Country:

"In the Footsteps of the Incarnate and Missionary Cosmic Christ"

On 27 August 1997 I celebrated 25 years of my Episcopal ordination. It was a consolation that this celebration could take place while I was on leave in my country, Malawi, and that a large number of relatives, friends, and well-wishers were able to join me in thanking God for the past twenty-five years of pastoral and academic ministry. But at the same time there was a poignancy in the thought that, of these 25 years, only the initial four had been spent in active service in the Diocese of Lilongwe of which I had been made bishop on 27 August 1972. The remaining twenty-one years have been lived outside the country, in a sort of "exile" that started in 1976 when I was asked to leave Malawi and my diocese. Thus the most intensive and prime years of my life and ministry have been spent in other lands: in Africa, in the USA, in Jerusalem, and then in Britain. Can one discern any sense or meaning in such a life?

The Jubilee was certainly an appropriate occasion for pausing a moment and looking back over the past years to try and understand what has been God's purpose and design for me. Some day I may want to write a full autobiography. That time has not yet arrived. But I might just as well begin now to trace an outline of such a life story and thereby share with others my present understanding of what God has been doing with me so far. The Scriptures exhort us always to "be prepared to make a defense to any one who calls (us) to account for the hope that is in (us)", adding: "yet do it with gentleness and reverence"! (1 Pet. 3:15-16). I could do this by merely tracing the course of events in my life. But that would not be of much use. I have chosen to accompany the narrative with some interpretation of the events by presenting them as

God's purposeful interventions and also as challenges that asked for appropriate responses from me.

Inculturation ist he key to the progress of the Church

Looking back over the past years, I seem to sense that all along it was my Faith in Christ that was being exercised. Events have contributed to the development of a certain way of life, certain convictions and dispositions, a way of feeling, thinking, acting and reacting, which for want of a better word I would call a "spirituality" or a Theology. I try to identify the guiding principles, the intuitions and visions that have been dominant in my life and ministry. This is best done, I think, by tracing the line of involvements and encounters, on the occasion of which I was led to express myself in writing. I have therefore selected a number of articles written since 1973, which I hope will shed some light on the development of my faith and theological thinking, especially in so far as these were related to my commitment to serve the people of Africa generally, and those of my country Malawi in particular, both in the Church and in society as a whole. Hence the title of this introductory chapter: "My Life, My Faith, My Theology, and My Country".

The rather awkward subtitle: "In the Footsteps of the Incarnate and Missionary Cosmic Christ", attempts to express in a nutshell the salient motivational and inspiring thoughts in these articles. Although there have been some editorial changes, for the most part these articles retain their original shape and structure. Each one is best understood within the context of the time and occasion when it was first written. In order to give the reader a better understanding of the themes and motifs that appear in these articles of later years, I have described in some detail the earlier period of my life: from infancy to the year 1976 when I finally left Malawi and began to live and work abroad. I do not think anyone is in a position to describe the full significance of his or her own life. After all, the real meaning of our lives comes out as a result of our interaction and relationships with other people. For a more balanced and realistic appraisal of our life, those "others" should be allowed to give their opinion. Nevertheless, there are important points in one's life that he or she alone, is able to express authentically.

The Early Years: 1933-1938

I was born at Mua on 28 August 1933, the ninth of the eleven children of Pierre Mangulenje Kalilombe and Helena Mzifei, of whom six were girls and five boys; but at the time of my birth, the family had already lost five of the girls. Two more boys were born after me; and so I grew up in the company of two elder brothers and an elder sister, and two younger brothers. Until 1938 our family lived in the compound of the Roman Catholic mission of Mua where my father had been working since 1916 in the mission carpentry shop. When he retired in 1938, we moved to a plot in the nearby Chewa village of Kanchamba, which is where I really grew up. But my father and mother had come originally from two neighbouring "Ngonised" villages near Mtakatalca Mission, some 10 miles from Mua. We have not forgotten, therefore, that at Mua we are really a family of "immigrants" from Mtalcataka where most of our relatives still live. And yet we have come to regard ourselves as part and parcel of Mua and are conscious of having been deeply marked by our links with that mission or parish.

Mua, situated near the south-western end of Lake Malawi at the bottom of the escarpment of the Kirk Range, in the lakeside Rift Valley, is in Dedza District. Although until recently it was a relatively isolated locality and a bit out of the way of modern developments, it lies in an area that has. deep connections with centuries of the social, cultural, political and religious history of the people of Malawi. Mua lies within easy reach of Mankhamba, the ancient "capital" of the Maravi paramountcy of the Karongas, which continued to function until it was dismantled in the late 19th century during the Yao invasions, and was effectively replaced by the Ngoni chieftaincy of Kachindamoto at the turn of the century. Just as in past centuries this whole area had been the scene of interaction and rivalries between the proto-Chewa Banda clans and the invading Phiri/Maravi groups, so also in later years the coming of the Yao and the Ngoni at the same time that European influence was beginning to be felt in the country (both colonial and missionary), intensified the process of cultural and religious interaction among the inhabitants.

The early Livingstonia Missionaries had established a mission post in 1875 at Cape Maclear, not far from Mua.[1] In 1894 missionary responsibility for this area was transferred to the Dutch Reformed Church whose bases were at Mvera in the north, Livulezi in the south, and Malembo some few miles from Mua and Mtakataka. Catholic missionaries were relatively late comers on the scene. After the Montfort Fathers had started a mission at Nzama in 1901 in the Ntcheu area, the White Fathers arrived in 1902 to establish themselves at Mua with an eye on Chief Kachindamoto's headquarters at Mtakataka. Thus Mua was the second Roman Catholic mission post in Malawi. It developed into an important place with its church and Fathers' house, its schools and hospital (including, for a long time, a leprosarium), its gardens and orchards, and especially its mechanized carpentry shop. A group of

---

[1] Cf. Christoff Martin Pauw, "Mission and Church in Malawi: The History of the Nkhoma Synod of the Church of Central Africa, Presbyterian 1889-1962", D.Th, University of Stellenbosch, 1980, pp. 21-26.

"White Sisters" (Missionaries of Our Lady of Africa) had come early on to join in the missionary enterprise. They ran the hospitals and a school for girls; but their influence was much wider in the area especially among women. After all, in this rather remote place, they were the only white women with whom the people came regularly into contact, just as the Fathers and Brothers were the only white men living so closely with the local people.

In his important book on the history of Catholic missions in Malawi, Ian Linden found it appropriate to devote a whole chapter to a description of Mua as a portrait of a typical mission station.[2] His main point is that Mua offers the chance to discover and study layers and networks of diverse historical, cultural and religious interactions which have been involved in the missionary enterprise. His analysis and description help to elucidate some attitudes that seem to mark my life profoundly. Our family was among those local people, typical products of the area's long history, who came under the influence of Mua Catholic Mission and have been deeply affected by that experience. As I have explained in one of the articles appearing in this collection,[3] by the time I was born, our family was undoubtedly Roman Catholic. We, the children, were all born on the mission compound, were baptized as infants, and were brought up in the mission schools from an early age. This explains how the sense of belonging to the Catholic Church has remained so naturally part of me: something I was born with, and which I have never even contemplated abandoning! Just as for my natural family, it happens to be what God wanted for me. It is not as if I have had to sit down and examine various options, and then fmally decided to become a Catholic! Moreover, my belonging is not dependent on any reasoned conviction that this is necessarily the best of churches in the world, or (as some like to put it) that it is "the only true church". That might well be the case (ask God!); but the reason why I am so attached to that church, and love it, warts and Al, is just because it is where God wanted me to

---

[2] Ian and Jane Linden, *Catholics, Peasants, and Chewa Resistance in Nyasaland 1889-1939*, Berkeley and Los Angeles: University of California Press, 1974.

[3] P.A. Kalilombe, "Unity from Below: Lessons from African Traditional Religion", reproduced in this volume, pp.122-137.

be. This attitude seems to explain another conviction which has been with me all along: I do not see any valid reason why the same God should not want others to belong to other churches, - or to other religions for that matter. If he did, that would be because of the same love for them that he has for me.

Does this explain why many of my commitments in the ministry have been within what are called "ecumenical"- or "inter-faith" contexts? Perhaps. In any case, I often wished to find out whether this attitude could be explained by my early influences. The article mentioned above was written in .1992 when I was invited to reflect on what contribution the "young churches" could make in the area of mission and ecumenism. It starts off with a reflection on what I can remember about our family: how we lived as committed Roman Catholics in the rather religiously "pluralistic" context of our environment, especially in relation to our extended family. As I recalled the past, I realized that my father had made such a profound impression on me in the way he practised his faith, and that it may be from his praxis that I absorbed these ecumenical and inter-faith attitudes. Although Mua was a Catholic mission, we did not live enclosed and isolated in the mission compound, but were constantly exposed to and interacting with elements of traditional culture and religion, and with members of other churches and faiths. My deep and sincere appreciation of African, and especially Malawian, history, culture and traditional religion is most likely due to experiences in those early contacts.

Early Schooling: 1938 -1943

There were two schools at the mission. One was at the White Sisters *(kwa Amai),* for the very young of both sexes and for more advanced girls. It was run by the nuns and a number of lady teachers. The other was at the White Fathers *(kwa Abambo),* for more advanced boys. It was run mainly by male teachers (among them my eldest brother). My earliest recollections of school are from around 1938 when I was attending classes at the Sisters' school. But my elder sister remembers taking me with her to school even earlier than this, and that it was customary for older girls to bring their smaller brothers and sisters (of kindergarten age) into their own class and keep watch over them while lessons were in progress. Perhaps this explains why I do not remember when exactly I first learnt to read and write: it must have been during those moments of *ersatz* kindergarten. But by the year 1939 I had been at school long enough to attempt to join the group being prepared for First Communion and Confirmation, though the Sister in charge sent me back then as being too young, and said I should come the next year when I would be 7. In 1941 I must have gone as far as the Sisters' school could take boys, and should have proceeded to the school at the Fathers. Instead, I joined a group of small kids whom the Sisters were sending to a preparatory seminary at Kasina. We were told, however, that this "pre-seminary" was not yet ready. My father decided then to send me to the boarding school at Mtakataka Mission, ten miles from Mua. And so, at the tender age of 8, I left home for my first experience of boarding school, and spent two years there in what was the equivalent of the "middle primary school", where everything was taught in the vernacular (at that time most Catholic primary schools deliberately refused to teach English, for fear, we learnt later on, that their pupils might end up being lost to the Catholic Church!). My desire to join the Seminary in order to become a priest continued; and so at the end of 1943 I applied and was accepted to go to Kasina Minor Seminary.

This decision, at such an early age, to train for the priesthood may seem surprising. But it just came quite naturally. After all, I had grown up literally in the shadow of the church, attending Mass almost daily, and serving the priests at the altar from the age of 6 or 7 years. Moreover Father J.B. Champmartin *(Bambo Chamare)*, who was Superior of Mua for endless years, was notorious for his zeal in recruiting candidates for the seminary. He would suggest the idea to a large number of boys and then send them on to Kasina in droves, chuckling wryly: "I know, most of them will return; but there is always the possibility that the odd crazy one will persevere!" I must have been one of those crazy ones! Fr Champmartin loved to invite the young seminarians of Kasina to come to Mua for holidays, when he would ply them with bananas and sugar canes and other goodies, and have them visit the villages and meet people. He would invariably take such occasions to impress on his parishioners the importance of having local priests. In actual fact, he had much success: quite a number of Mua boys became priests (two of them later became bishops!). In my case, though, it was my elder sister who seems to have had the most decisive influence in my choice. I remember her telling me one day: "Pat, look at those seminarians! ... They are going to become priests - just like Bambo Chamare. A pity I am just a girl. Had I been a boy, I would have gone to the seminary long ago!" (She had wanted to become a nun, but had had to renounce it as, being the only and elder sister of several younger brothers, she felt she should hang around to, help mother with the children). That was a real challenge! I told myself: if she cannot become a priest, I *can* and I shall! Strange how "vocation" actually works out.

When I went to Mtakataka in 1941, it meant indeed "leaving home". From then on I would come back to my family only on rather short holidays: at the end of term while at Mtakatalca, and at the end of the school-year while at Kasina. When I went on to Kachebere Major Seminary in 1949, I was not to see home until 1954 (and even then, only for a day or two!) when I was on my way to North Africa to join the White Fathers. Understandably, once abroad in Algeria and Tunisia between 1954 and 1958, I did not come home until July 1958 when I was given a one-month home leave before going on to Rome for another four years of study. This, I am sure, accounts for the fact that all my life I have not had the feeling of having a stable "home" anywhere, but have had to learn to "make myself at home" in different places. People sometimes ask me whether there are moments when I feel "home-sick". The honest answer is: not really, if you mean genuine home-sickness. Only once, in 1976, when it dawned on me that there was a real possibility that I might never return to Malawi and Africa, did I experience the gripping gloom of not having a home to call my own. But otherwise, I seem to have developed the attitude of a "pilgrim", someone like Abraham and the patriarchs who moved about "living in tents ... like strangers and exiles on the earth ... seeking a homeland ... desiring a better country, that is, a heavenly one" (Heb. 11:8-16). I suppose God was preparing me for the kind of life of a "wanderer" or an "exile" which has become my lot.

At Kasina Minor Seminary: 1943-1949

I went to Kasina Minor Seminary (Dedza District) towards the end of 1943. At that time the full course of the Minor Seminary, an equivalent of the upper primary school (and a bit later, junior secondary school), was over seven years. Its distinctive characteristic was that it sought to give the young aspirants to the priesthood an education and formation that would prepare them for the Major Seminary. Over and above the human and intellectual education, special attention was paid to appropriate spiritual training and behaviour formation for teenagers and adolescents looking forward to the priestly life and ministry, especially in view of the celibate life which priests promise to follow until death. It was impressed on the seminarians that they were "separated from the world", and that holiness was a basic objective in the formation. At this stage it is expected that there will be a process of discerning the genuineness of the aspirant's vocation to the priesthood. The candidate himself, or the formation staff, may come to the conclusion that there is no genuine vocation after all, and so the candidate will be asked to leave the seminary. There are bound to be moments of anxiety and fear, doubt and hesitation, as one asks himself whether indeed he is really called to be a priest. I had my fair share of such moments, but also a great deal of affirmation.

All in all, I enjoyed my years at Kasina, including the studies, especially of Latin. It was a time when I came to interact with boys from different parts of Malawi, Zambia, and even Mozambique, and learnt the art of understanding and even appreciating people's diversities and differences; for it was never easy for boys from different tribes, languages and cultures to live together in harmony. I came to know many fellow students who became great friends in later life, among them Bishop G. Chisendera and Archbishop M. Mazombwe who were my classmates, as well as Archbishop E. Milingo who was a year ahead of me at Kasina, but whose group I joined when we went to Kachebere at the end of 1949. That year, it had been decided that our "class" would have to continue at Kasina for a further two years as the seminary course was being extended to include the Junior Certificate. But for some reason, I was told to leave my classmates in Kasina and go on immediately to Kachebere joining the class ahead of us, after only 6 years at the minor seminary. It was rather painful to leave Kasina in this way. And the feeling of being made to step into the unknown was made even more ominous when, on my bus trip to Kachebere, my luggage was stolen. And so I finally made my appearance at the Major Seminary, walking on foot, as a dirt-covered, tired and "destitute" teenager, who found it difficult to convince people that he was coming as a candidate for the Major Seminary!

At Kachebere Major Seminary: 1949-1954

In 1949 Kachebere was celebrating 10 years of its existence as a Major Seminary. Until 1939 candidates for Philosophy and Theology, coming from Zambia and Malawi, had been going to Kipalapala in Tanzania for the ten-year period of Major Seminary. It was only in 1939 that Kachebere started to function as the Major Seminary for candidates from the then Northern Rhodesia and Nyasaland. 1949 was an auspicious year as 10 of the first Kachebere students were ordained priests that year. The ten-year course was divided in this way: Years 1-3: Philosophy; Years 4-7: Dogmatic and Moral Theology; Year 8: Probation in home Vicariate (later, Diocese); Year 9-10: Pastoral Theology: ordination to Subdiaconate and then Diaconate, and at the end to the Priesthood. This was certainly a lengthy period of training. When our group arrived in 1949 consultations were in course to shorten it a bit: the first 7 years were reduced to 6 (with 3rd year of Philosophy and ist year of Theology joined into one). Other changes were to come in later years, until the present course of 6 years became established.

The Major Seminary is the equivalent of the Theological and Ministerial College of other churches. But while academic studies do indeed figure prominently on the programme, a higher priority is the spiritual and priestly ministerial formation. The time-table is shot through with periods of prayer and liturgy, spiritual reading and conferences, and spiritual direction in which students are helped by members of staff to develop their spirituality and pastoral attitudes, and to continue the discernment of their priestly vocation. These years are seen in the image of a spiritual journey, the ideal being that candidates should keep growing humanly, academically, psychologically and spiritually towards the standard desirable in a priest and pastor. In the years I was at Kachebere the custom was still followed of marking this progress through liturgical rituals. After the first year of Theology, the candidate received the Tonsure to mark his entry into the "clerical state". At the end of the second year of Theology he received the first two of what were called "Minor Orders": 'Porter' and Lector'; and after the third year, those of 'Exorcist' and 'Acolyte'. He would then be looking forward to the "Major Orders" of 'Sub-deacon', 'Deacon', and 'Priesthood', after he had done his Probation year. The preoccupation with spiritual life and its growth is one of the important seeds that my stay in Kachebere has planted in me. It was going to be nurtured and strengthened during my years of novitiate and scholasticate in North Africa. But the roots were certainly planted at Kachebere.

In the same way Kachebere set me firmly on the road towards serious academic studies. The philosophy course did help to build up a habit of rigorous and orderly thinking. I also enjoyed the initiation into various areas of Theology, Church History, Catechetics, Liturgy, and Pastoral Theology, although Canon Law never really fascinated me! But most of all, it was at Kachebere that I first fell in love with Holy Scripture. Since that time I always hoped some day to get the chance of studying it properly. Our group of 8 (six became priests, out of whom three have become bishops) which came to Kachebere in 1949 consisted of very remarkable and brilliant students from both Zambia and Malawi, among whom were Emmanuel Milingo (from Chipata, Zambia, later Archbishop of Lusaka) and Allan Chamgwera (later Bishop of Zomba). We developed into a cohesive and warm fraternity, mutually supportive and stimulating. Among other things, we decided to embark on extra-curricular researches, wherein each one would specialize in a particular discipline. The results of our research were to be compiled regularly into a kind of digest-review, typed by one of us, and then distributed (clandestinely!) among ourselves. This is how "The Spark" originated, which later on was made open to the whole seminary and became the college magazine (changing its form radically in the process!). Since at that time Kachebere catered for all the dioceses of Malawi and Zambia, it was an exciting place for meeting and interacting with brethren from all corners of these two countries. This helped to broaden one's horizons in all sorts of ways. I am convinced that the ease with which later on I have been able to live with people from diverse nationalities and cultures is again one of the fruits of my stay at Kachebere.

Strangely enough, this stay was cut short rather suddenly in May 1954, in the course of my 5th year (second year of Theology). That year I decided to join the Society of Missionaries of Africa, known as the "White Fathers". When I told my friends about this decision, they could not understand. And it was not easy to explain. The fact, however, is that the thought had started several months ,earlier, when the Rector, Father Bel-trand Peltier, himself a White Father, had told us in passing that the headquarters of the White Fathers in Rome had just sent a communication saying the Society was now willing to accept candidates from Africa (which had not been the case in the past). Somehow or other, this suddenly set me thinking. Was it not time our young churches in Africa began sending missionaries to other lands? We have received the faith because churches from overseas were generous enough to send some of their own people to other parts of the world in order to share their faith with those who had not yet received it. A church that knows only to receive, but does not know how to share what it has (however little that may be), is not yet mature. By definition Church is missionary. Why should we in Nyasaland not begin to send missionaries? ... and so on and so forth. In short, the reflection ended with the challenge: Why don't you yourself become a missionary? At first I could not believe myself, and thought: This is just one of those crazy thoughts! Just ignore it. But then the thought kept coming back. In the end I took the matter up with my spiritual advisor and we discussed it and prayed over it. I also wrote to my Bishop (or, at that time, Vicar Apostolic) in Lilcuni: Bishop J. Fady, whom, incidentally, I was to succeed later on as Bishop of Lilongwe. He was most encouraging and said he was prepared to support my application, if and when I made my decision. My letter of application was answered positively by the Superior General himself, who at the same time decided that I was to join the French-speaking novitiate in Maison-Carrée, Algeria, and gave directives about my travelling there. I was to travel to Mozambique and there join one of the White Fathers going on home leave, via Portugal. He would take me along and make sure that from Portugal I flew to

Algeria. And so, in May 1954 I said goodbye to Kachebere, and again "left home", this time on a long journey towards a far-away country.

From Novitiate to Priesthood: 1954-1958

Was it meant by God as a significant "portent", - just like my arriving at Kachebere after having been robbed of my luggage and having had to walk and wait for several days on the road? Well, this time again something happened to mark my going to the novitiate. When I came to Zobue Seminary in Mozambique to join Fr Prein who was to take me to Portugal, I needed to present my passport (my first ever) to the Portuguese immigration officials in order to obtain a visa for "Portugal" (including the colonies!). After doing so, we waited in vain for many days; by the time we were to leave for Beira to catch the boat for Portugal, the officials said they did not have my passport at Zobue: they did not even know where it could possibly be: in Beira? Lourenco Marques (Maputo)?, Angola?, or even Lisbon! But then, we asked, what should we do? The officials said we might try at those places, but added ominously: "But one does not move about without passport and visa! It's dangerous: you may be caught and sent to prison!" Obviously there was a sinister plan somewhere. We decided, nevertheless, to proceed to Beira (passport not there!) and took the boat, making the two-day trip (in First-class!) to Lourenco Marques. We went straight to the Archbishop, Cardinal De Gouveia, and explained my case. After phoning the authorities, it was clear to him that my passport had been impoundded, with the intention of preventing this potentially subversive "Mau-Mau" guy from Nyasaland from circulating freely within colonial Portuguese areas! They were intent on imprisoning me at the earliest possible occasion ... So, he decided to take me in his car to the far-off Namaacha Seminary on the Swaziland border, and instructed me to stay put there until further notice, telling any enquirers that I was one of His Eminence's seminarians! I spent a week at Namaacha, using the time to brush up my French and acquire a smattering of Portuguese.

One fine day, lo and behold, I found my passport had been brought to my room - nobody seemed to know by whom. All I had to do was collect it, go back to Maputo, jump on the plane (for the first time in my life), and return to Blantyre after having lost a whole month in Mozambique. From there I was back at Kachebere, just in time to take part in the ceremony of the blessing of the new buildings. This was my first brush with imprisonment! Did it mean I should renounce my intention of going to the novitiate? Many friends thought so, but I did not interpret the events in that way. After. the ceremony, I was allowed to accompany the Superior-General's Assistant who was returning to Rome. I spent a month in the Eternal City, and then they put me on the plane for Maison-Carrée, Algiers; and thus I joined the novitiate towards the endnf August 1954.

Until it was closed by the newly independent nation of Algeria in the early 1960s, Maison-Carrée had been an important place in the history of the White Fathers. Up to 1950 it was the Mother House and Generalate of the Society. There, too, was the novitiate where generations of early White Fathers were formed. Coming to it was therefore like touching base with the venerable and authentic roots of the Society's traditions and history. For religious congregations (and many religious-like societies like ours) the novitiate is a time of intense spiritual formation for the future members. It is also the time when they are initiated into the special "charism" and orientation of the group they are joining, learning about its history, constitutions, customs and traditions, and absorbing its ethos and spirituality. In our case, the year of novitiate serves to train members in the Society's specific missionary life of commitment to the evangelization and service of Africa and African peoples. The White Fathers understand themselves as called to a commitment to an apostolic and missionary ministry, very much in line with the Jesuits' Ignatian spirituality centred on discerning the will of God for the coming of his Kingdom on earth, and then following it with total dedication in the spirit of religious obedience. Their special characteristics are a commitment to Africa and to living and working in international communities.

I can only thank God that this year of novitiate widened and deepened my understanding-of what "mission" is all about. It also started me reflecting on what "evangelization" can mean. For in Algeria, and later on in Tunisia, I was living in a totally Muslim environment. Our missionnary Society had been founded by Cardinal Charles A. Lavigerie in 1868 precisely to work among North African Muslims (even imitating their traditional dress of white gandoura and bournous - hence the nickname of "White Fathers"!). And although soon afterwards the larger section of the Society has been evangelizing black 'pagan' Africa where 'conversions' to Christianity were taken for granted, there has always been a significant number of us engaged in faith dialogue with the Muslim world. Very early on in our history, the Cardinal had warned his missionaries that "mission" and "evangelization" in such a context had to be understood less in terms of proselytism or bringing the Muslims into communion with the visible Christian Church, and much more in terms of a Christian presence through a life of genuine evangelical witness and service. As I watched our confreres doing their "mission" in this rather austere and humanly unrewarding way, I was challenged to reflect on what is meant by the dialogue of faiths. What are the objectives in such a dialogue? What theological issues are being raised here about God's dealings with peoples and communities of other faiths; what convictions and attitudes should Christians have about and towards other faiths? In our Society there has always been a running joking relationship between those who work in black Africa ("they thrive on ever-growing statistics of converts, and take pride in how their arms become regularly numbed through baptizing crowds of babies and adults!") and those "arabisants" who spend their time in interminable learned "dialogues" with Muslims and die without ever baptizing a single one of them! But I feel it is a singular blessing for a missionary society like ours to have members on both sides: it keeps the Society on its theological toes as the two groups continue to raise mutually challenging questions about what it means to "evangelize" and to work towards the coming Kingdom of God. One of the essays included in this book: "Evangelization and the Holy Spirit", was written after my participation in the 1974 Synod of Bishops (with the title of "Evangelization in the Modern World"). It touches on several of these theological questions. No doubt that my life in Algeria and Tunisia helped to alert me to the need for raising them.

Typical of the Society's houses of formation, our group of novices comprized candidates of many nationalities: French, Germans, Spanish, Italians, Belgians, Dutch, Swiss, British, Canadians, and then myself as the only black African. Our novice master once jokingly remarked to me: "You think you have seen tribalism at work in your native Africa: well, you will be watching your white friends struggling with other types of 'tribalism'!" And in fact, if I as the lone black person had a hard time struggling with differences in culture and sensitivities, my friends too were engaged in a similar struggle to overcome traditional national and regional prejudices (the more so as this was a generation that had been growing up during World War II!). We were, forced to face up to all sorts of family and national conditionings, and bravely bear with one another as we struggled to learn how our diversities could be accepted mutually, not as insurmountable obstacles to fraternity but as a challenge to build a richer community. I must admit that I went through the painful crucible of experiencing how different my history, culture, sensitivities and feelings were from those of my friends, and then striving to understand and accept theirs. In my later ministry this experience has stood me in good stead.

The year of novitiate ran from September 1954 to September 1955. Then it was time to move on and go to the Scholasticate (or Theological College) of the Society to resume my interrupted theological studies. At that time, the French province had two sections for the four-years theology course, one (for years 1 to 3) at Thibar in the Tunisian countryside, and another at Carthage near Tunis, for the final year. Since I had already done two years of theology at Kachebere, I could have gone straight into the third year at Thibar. But I asked to join the second year. My wish was to take in as much as possible of the Society's theological programme. Behind this was, among other things, the desire to check how the study programme which the White Fathers were given in their own colleges compared with the one they ran in their seminaries for African students. So I did two years at Thibar (1955 to 1957, repeating in the process some of the things I had already learnt at Kachebere) at the end of which I took the Oath as a White Father and was ordained priest on 3 February 1958, although (as was then customary) the course continued in Carthage until July when we returned to our homes for holidays before going on to our first missionary assignments.

As a community, Thibar was in many ways like the novitiate, with a similar international mix of students; only that here the numbers were greater (about 200) and so there was a wider and more exciting interaction among the students who actually came from various novitiates. There was also a greater scope for interacting with the outside than had been the case in the novitiate. We had regular contacts with people in the surrounding "villages" as we went on various 'pastoral experiences', or for walks and picnics. For me this contact with local people was quite an experience! The Arabs seemed quite intrigued to see a black man passing for a member of a group of Christian future priests. Was I really an equal member in this group of white folk, or was I simply a slave at their service?! And indeed was I a Christian *(roumi)* when everybody knows that all blacks are Muslims? I do not think many of them ever became quite convinced that I was a *bona fide* Christian: they suspected that I was a clandestine Muslim spy sent in by some African community, and they wanted to know what exactly my 'mission' was, and why my attempts at speaking Arabic were so pathetic! For my part, I was fascinated as I watched from such close quarters how the struggle for emancipation from colonialism was actually working in Africa in those years, and what it was like to live in a newly independent nation. The year of our novitiate in Algeria saw the beginning of what was going to be the long drawn out Algerian War of Independence. Even at the novitiate we had echoes of the FLN and their bitter confrontation with the French, especially with the *Pieds Noirs* or local French colonists. At the end of the novitiate we felt lucky to have been able to travel safely by train from Algiers to Thibar. And when we arrived there, Tunisia had just obtained its independence from France under its "Father of the Nation", President Bourguiba. In the Thibar countryside, as in the whole of the new nation, there was an atmosphere of nationalist and patriotic enthusiasm, a mixture of naive optimism about the future of the nation and a rather nervous suspicion of anything foreign, especially French. All this must have increased in me the desire to follow more closely the "Winds of Change" blowing at that time all over Africa, even in my home country of Nyasaland.

I enjoyed my studies in Thibar and Carthage. It is of course invidious to compare the level and style of studies at these colleges (which after all were part of the 'metropolitan' academic set-up) with those of Kachebere in the backwaters of Africa. It struck me, though, that here the level was decidedly higher and more demanding. I was astonished that the students were "allowed" to exercise freely their critical faculties and to examine any topic of the course in ways which seemed, to me, surprisingly radical. The students demanded and expected the best from their lecturers, and had no hesitation in engaging them in debate, offering criticism, and volunteering suggestions, - without feeling that they were thereby lacking in respect. It should, of course, be remembered that, at least in Europe (and in France particularly), this was a time when there was a radical questioning of all accepted traditions, in the Church as well as in the whole of society. World War II seems to have shattered much of the former self-assured sense of certitude and complacency about traditional Western civilization and culture. In ecclesiastical centres of learning, the conviction (normally held especially after the Councils of Trent and Vatican I) that the Church possessed a definitive and certain deposit of its Faith and that its shape and structures as a perfect society were God-given and unchangeable had started to be questioned. There was, in some quarters, a growing feeling that the One, Holy, Catholic, and Apostolic Church was in need of renewal, "updating" *(aggiornamento),* and even reform. These were the years when the atmosphere was being created that was to lead towards the Second Vatican Council.

In Thibar and Carthage influences of this growing movement of renewal were being felt at that time, especially since contacts with the European (and American) centres of research and re-thinking in the biblical, liturgical, catechetical, ecumenical and theological fields were inevitable. We were exposed to those new ideas and had to re-examine many things which hitherto had been accepted unquestioningly as being the unchanging tradition of the Church. Historical research in these fields was a decisive factor in the rethinking, along with the conviction that historical developments were in many ways responsible for much of the shape and structure that doctrines and ethical, legal and liturgical customs had taken in the Church.

Whether this rethinking was a blessing or a curse, one may wish to discuss. But I am convinced that this period of my intellectual and spiritual development has left indelible marks in my life. While being very much attached to and respectful of the Church's rich and constant traditions, I am also convinced of the historical and cultural relativity of many of them, and am consequently suspicious of any tendency to absolutize them.

Post-graduate Studies in Rome: 1958-1962

After graduating in Carthage, I was given a two-month holiday in my home country, and arrived in Malawi at the beginning of July 1958 (significantly at the same time that Dr H. Kamuzu Banda was also arriving to take charge of the nationalist struggle). It was important to meet my family and friends again after four years of absence abroad, and to become acquainted with the revolutionary changes going on at the time, especially with the struggle for national independence and the fight against the Federation of Rhodesia and Nyasaland. But by the beginning of September I left home again, this time to go to Rome for further studies. I had been appointed for post-graduate studies in Theology at the Gregorian University in Rome as a preparation for studies at the Pontifical Biblical Institute. So I spent two years at the Gregorian and obtained my Licentiate in Theology (equivalent to Masters) at the end of 1960; after which I joined the Biblical Institute and received my Licence in Holy Scripture at the end of 1962.

These were interesting years to be a student in Rome. It was only four years before Vatican II was to begin. Already the atmosphere of radical rethinking and discussion was in the air, and among the several universities in the Eternal City there were differences of attitudes and opinions. The Gregorian and the Biblicum, both in the hands of Jesuits, were reckoned among the more progressive schools which were likely to attract suspicions and even condemnation from rival institutions which prided themselves on being more faithful to tradition. There were funny scenes, like the one when this university in the city published grave accusations of "modernism" against a number of professors at the Biblicum, which the accused did not hesitate to refute in the press, a kind of public debate that excited and amused us students. But such accusations were not so funny when they came from higher places: from one of the Vatican congregations, for example. I can remember times when one or the other of our professors was not available for lectures, and we were made to understand that he was "not feeling well". Only later on did we learn that he had been "under investigation" and had had to appear before the 'authorities'. Significantly, most of these accusations were about points of doctrine (for example, concerning the Church) which were later to receive the seal of approval from Vatican II. It is an open secret also that quite a few members of staff from the Roman universities figured among the more influential *periti* of the coming Council.

One important bonus of studying in Rome is that one meets with fellow students from all over the world who are likely later on to occupy important posts in the Church. There are many occasions when students from various colleges and universities in the city meet and interact. They become acquainted with one another and build life-long friendships with people from different nations and cultures. As far as Africa is concerned, the Pontifical Urbanian University, which caters for students from the so-called 'Mission territories', has always been a place where African students from other colleges can meet and exchange ideas and concerns. In my time, there was an association, based in that university, the St Augustine's Association, which served to bring African students together and to promote studies and research of special interest for Africa. It used to publish its own review: LUX, through which interesting ideas were shared, among them, the development of African theology. It is not unusual for past students, who in the meantime have become cardinals, bishops, or seminary professors, to meet one another again on the African soil and renew networks of friendship and collaboration.

I arrived in Rome in the last months of 1958, just in time for the funeral of Pope Pius XII, and the process whereby Pope John XXIII became his successor. It was not immediately apparent then that this represented an important watershed in the history of the Church and the Papacy. When one lives long enough in Rome, one gets the chance of observing how the Roman centre relates with the Church and society world-wide. It has become clearer now how much has been changing in these relations ever since Pope John XXIII came to the throne and convoked the Second Vatican Council. Observing matters from the centre at such close range enables one to appreciate the divine aspects of the government of the Church, and how it is indeed the Holy Spirit that guides it through the storms of human history. But you also witness very much of the human and less edifying side of Church life. Sometimes people ask: Does this darker side of the Church not pose a risk to make you lose your faith? In my case, the answer is: No! The mistakes and failures of fellow human beings, however high up they may be in the Church, simply make it clearer that the Church is indeed run by God, who is quite capable of 'writing straight with crooked lines'. We human beings are only 'unworthy servants'. The Church is not our 'possession': it is God's and Christ's. I thank God that one of the most important results of my stay in Rome has been the capacity to continue loving and serving the Church in spite of its human deficiencies.

Pastoral Ministry in the Local Church: 1962-1964

At the end of my studies in Rome I received my first official missionary appointment from our Generalate. I was quite surprised, not to say disappointed, when I was told I would be going back to Malawi to work in Dedza, my diocese of origin. I had been hoping that, like most of my newly ordained colleagues, I would be sent to work away from home and feel that my desire to work as a missionary was at last going to be fulfilled. Nevertheless I gladly obeyed and returned home in July 1962. Very soon afterwards I was sent by my ordinary, Bishop Cornelius

Chitsulo, first to help out temporarily in Mtakataka Parish (our family's place of origin, not far from Mua my birthplace), and then soon afterwards to go to Bembeke Parish (up on the plateau, a mere ten miles away) where a team of us White Fathers was going to take over from local diocesan priests.

Bembeke is where I was initiated into the 'ordinary' parish ministry in rural areas and where I experienced the traditional community life of the White Fathers' missionary. congregation. The parish is small in size but densely populated. The northern half is typical of a fairly old mission (founded in 1908) which is now predominantly Catholic, while the southern section was, until quite recently, an almost exclusively Protestant fief. For the next two years I enjoyed working as a curate and member of a pastoral team within which I soon became acquainted with the usual routines of pastoral activities and administration. It was exciting to find out how the rather theoretical studies of so many years were now being tested through contact with the real life of people at the village level. I learnt quickly to appreciate the importance of starting from where the people are, rather than from my nice ideas of a scholar and church functionary. In this area where Roman Catholics and Protestants kept interacting with one another, I was struck by the persistence of denominational attitudes and rivalries inherited from our respective missionary pioneers. The Second Vatican Council had just started in Rome in the second half of 1962, and echoes of the ideas of ecumenism being discussed there were already reaching us. But it was clear that getting these ideas across to people at the grassroots level was going to be a long drawn out uphill struggle.

This was also the time when in the Catholic Church of Malawi, as indeed of other countries of Africa and abroad, there was a burst of renewal activity in all areas of church life: liturgy, catechetics, lay apostolate, youth movements, religious life, and even Bible study. The Episcopal Conference was striving to be in line with the on-going Council in Rome; so the bishops had set up diocesan and national commissions to coordinate and animate activities in all these areas. My bishop asked me to be director of the diocesan commissions for liturgy and catechetics, and later on also for lay apostolate. The Episcopal Conference was keen on following the Council's recommendations about promoting the Bible among Catholics and also the active participation of the faithful in the liturgy. So they commissioned me to undertake the translation of the Missal and the Ritual from Latin into Chichewa and also to revise and edit the manuscript of a Bible translation started some years back by a European missionary. Eventually the new Catholic Bible version was published and printed as *Malembo Oyera,* and for the first time Catholics could claim to have their own Bible alongside the venerable traditional *Buku Lopatulika* of long standing which had been available within non-Catholic Christian communities but had tended to be kept off limits for Catholics because of official suspicions and fears. The uanslation of the Missal and Ritual developed into a joint international undertaking when the Nyanja speaking Catholic dioceses of Zambia were drawn in and asked to contribute quite substantially towards the fmal texts which are widely used today.

These additional responsibilities gave me the chance to become acquainted with church life at the wider levels of the diocese, the country, and the extensive territory of Eastern and Central Africa. Along with this vernacular-ization, there was also a great push to contextualize church life, especially in the area of liturgy. As liturgical texts were being translated into the vernacular, logically there was the need to search for appropriate local cultural forms of expression to accompany the new liturgical and cate-chetical creations. Local tunes and ritual gestures of celebration began to be used, while at the same time people went for what they felt were 'African' liturgical vestments and utensils. I still recall, with some amusement now, the first tentative local tunes which I helped the students at the Teacher Training College of Bembeke to compose, and the Bishop's hesitation to authorize their use in the church! Today this 'Africanization' (or 'inculturation', in the new parlance) has been receiving a much wider acceptance in the church, both in Malawi and Zambia. Interest in and promotion of such localization has remained a significant feature of my church commitment.

At Kachebere Major Seminary: 1964-1972

Towards the end of 1964 I was appointed to Kachebere Major Seminary where, as member of staff, I was going to teach Holy Scripture, Liturgy, and Catechetics and share in the wider task of training and preparing future priests for the more than 16 dioceses of Malawi and Zambia. This was like returning to my *Alma Mater* of 10 years ago, but this time as member of staff. The eight years I was to spend at Kachebere were going to make a lasting impression on my whole subsequent life. Academic pursuits at the service of pastoral ministry: this has become like second nature to me.

The seminary staff was, at that time, still composed of only White Fathers. But I happened to be the first and only black staff member. The students were, understandably, quite excited. They expected that this was going to be their chance for new developments in the study regime. They invited me to be animator of their study club: 'Our African Way of Life', which they had just formed in order to give more substance to the recently introduced course called 'African Affairs' which I was also going to take over. Through that study club and the course we slowly developed a consistent programme of research and study on the history, traditional religions, social anthropology, politics and economics of African societies as the basis for the ever-growing endeavours for **Africanization**. In various degrees this search for Africanness did influence the other parts of the study programme. But there was a second overarching directing principle which was to influence the study and formation activities: implementing **Vatican II.**

The fact that in Rome the Vatican Council was in full swing had a peculiar impact on the study courses. Both staff members and students were quite aware that at that Council lively discussions were going on concerning what hitherto had been accepted as the perennial, immutable traditions of the Church in doctrinal matters as well as in discipline and legislation. There was a widespread foreboding that, by the time the Council ended, things would not be the same as before. In light of this situation, the traditional manuals on which seminary studies had been based until then lost their character of definitiveness. Students kept questioning the validity of whatever they were being taught; and in many cases the teachers could only give provisional answers adding that we all had to wait and see what came out of the Council! In the meantime there was ample scope for discussion. In a way, this was a rather unhealthy predicament: on the one hand you needed to feel sure of the basis on which you were preparing future ministers, and yet on the other, there seemed to be no such easily available solid ground! We muddled along as best we could, trying to take in the changes that were happening, while we hoped and prayed that the Holy Spirit would not stop guiding our steps. Nevertheless you do end up abandoning the idea of possessing a complete ready-made baggage of clear absolutes. You learn to live with areas of uncertainty where further inquiry is perfectly in order, while clinging faithfully to those basic orientations that you know are dependable. In the wake of the Second Vatican Council a lot of people in the Church have been feeling quite lost in the midst of so many changes; they look back with nostalgia to what they think was a time of certitude and clarity, and would like to forget Vatican II as a bad dream and recreate the certainties of that idealized past. My experience at Kache-bere taught me to be a bit more realistic. Vatican II is here to stay. What we leaders and pastors need to do is to develop the kind of skills and spirituality that can equip us to serve as dependable guides of God's People even in times of disconcerting changes.

In 1968 I was made rector of the Seminary, at a time when the membership of the staff was changing to include other than White Fathers. As leader of a formation team that was anything but homogeneous, I learnt to aim for a spirit of honest but mutually open exchange of ideas and viewpoints so that out of divergent traditions and orientations we could forge a coherent and commonly agreed formation programme. The position of rector of a major seminary tended to create endless involvements in meetings and consultations within the country and also abroad. It was also at this time that I was asked to join an ecumenical team which was to work on a new translation of the Bible into modern Chichewa likely to be acceptable to all the Christian churches. Although being rector of the seminary involved heavy work, I genuinely loved it and felt that it was a privilege to dedicate one's life to the formation of future church leaders. It came as a surprise when suddenly in 1972 I had to leave Kachebere for a new job.

Bishop of Lilongwe Diocese: 1972-1976

Rome had appointed me to succeed Bishop Joseph Fady of Lilongwe Diocese. This was a bit surprising. At that stage of intense localization of leadership in the African Church one did not expect Rome to appoint bishops from among the members of missionary congregations, but rather from the local diocesan clergy. I was not sure how the diocese, especially its clergy, was going to react to my appointment. There was also cause to wonder how I was going to fit in with my fellow bishops if my way of thinking and acting proved to be a bit different from theirs. And what about Rome? Was I the kind of personality that understood how the system works and could easily toe the official line? Friends with a biz. of experience were heard to wonder how long a biblical intellectual, unaccustomed to the juridical procedures of Canon Law and the complications of ecclesiastical politics, was going to survive. I too was wondering; but then what else could I do but move forward, trusting in the Lord? Lilongwe is a fairly large and populated diocese (around 200,000 Catholic members at the time). It is two-thirds coterminous with the Central Region, the heartland of the Chewa population and the principal base of Dr H. Kamuzu Banda's Malawi Congress Party, at that time the country's only political party, which was then at the height of its power. Lilongwe City itself was going to become the national capital in 1975. It was clear the diocese was right at the centre of national and political developments: a scary prospect for a 39-year old ingenious young bishop coming in from the ivory tower of academic life!

I embarked on my pastoral ministry with quite a lot of enthusiasm. During my time at the seminary I had been taken up with reflections as to how the Church in Africa could effectively renew itself in line with Vatican II. The Association of Member Episcopal Conferences of Eastern Africa which comprises the countries of Ethiopia, Sudan, Kenya, Uganda, Tanzania, Zambia and Malawi, had already embarked on a project of study called: "Planning for the Church in Eastern Africa in the 1980s". On suggestions from a number of missionaries and local clergy in the country the Episcopal Conference of Malawi had commissioned, in the late 1960s, a Pastoral Survey with the aim of finding out what could be done to "update" the structures and ministry of the Church. And although the resulting report and recommendations were not generally received with particular enthusiasm, in one of the dioceses (Chikwawa) a team of young missionaries got their bishop to authorize a process which resulted in the formulation of a "Diocesan Pastoral Plan". While at Kachebere, I had been fascinated by the idea, and was rather disappointed when it seemed to run into trouble. Now that I was bishop I decided to try it out in our diocese of Lilongwe. Almost immediately after my ordination in August 1972, the diocese launched what we chose to call a 'Mini-Synod' with the aim of eventually working out a Pastoral Plan for the diocese.

One of the articles in the present collection reproduces the pastoral letter *Christ's Church in Lilongwe Today and Tomorrow,* written early in 1973 as a sort of position paper for the Mini-Synod. It shows clearly what the leading ideas were: If we wanted the Church to have a sustainable future, we must aim at building a **self-reliant Church**: a Church that is self-ministering, self-supporting, and self-propagating (Henry Venn's `missiological principle'!). In order to achieve this, the whole Church membership, but especially the laity, must become (according to Vatican II's basic principles) actively involved in the whole life and mission of the Church, co-responsible, and working together in subsidiarity. In the particular circumstances prevailing in our part of the world, this can happen only if we base the Church's life and activity on the **small communities** in which the overwhelming majority of church members live and function. In theological terms the kind of Church we were after was along the ecclesiological model that Vatican II had deliberately chosen to propose: the model of **People of God and Mystical Body of Christ,** a Church that sees itself as the evangelical Light, Salt, and Leaven planted in the midst of the world in order to minister as the "Sacrament of the coming Kingdom of God". The insistence here is not so much on the Church being the (only authentic) instrument of salvation to which all must visibly belong if they want to be saved. It is rather on the Church as the embodiment of Christ the Servant of Yahweh, a visible, challenging, attractive, and imitable Sign of that redeemed, transformed and divinized humanity according to which God has always been intending to make the world. The efficacy of that Sign or Sacrament depends above all on how well the Christian community, living as fully as possible the life of the Gospel, becomes inserted into the rest of the world and spreads effectively the Gospel values by which it lives.

The Mini-Synod was designed as a process of conscientization for the whole diocese through interlocking sessions of reflection, discussion and planning at diocesan, deanery, parish, and outstation levels. The most ambitious aspect of the project was the decision to actively involve the ordinary people at the grassroots and make them co-responsible in the formulation of the pastoral plan. It was hoped that the methodology itself of the process, and also its rhythm and duration (two and half years) would help to transform the diocese into the kind of Church described above. In fact .the conviction was that the coming into being of a church based on grassroots small Christian communities would be the natural result of the Mini-Synod process itself.

Conflict with the State

It is only right and proper for me to insist that my objective all along was purely religious and ecclesiastic, and not narrowly political as some people were going to claim. Nevertheless I was not so naive as not to realize the public and "worldly" implications of the diocesan pastoral project. The mission of a Church like the one we were trying to build up cannot confine itself to "purely spiritual matters", but must encompass the whole of people's life: individual as well as societal, spiritual as well as secular. It must touch on such aspects of civil life as individual, family, and public morality, human rights, justice and peace, education, health, employment, development, and general politics. And given the fact that the population in the Diocese of Lilongwe, as indeed in the rest of Malawi, consisted predominantly of peasant cultivators living in villages in the rural areas, the main concern was with the life of ordinary people at the grassroots level as they struggle with the problems of transition from traditional culture to the complex challenges of modern living. However poor and vulnerable these people may be, they have the dignity of God's children. They do not deserve to be treated as just a mass of second-class citizens who may be dominated and exploited at will by their more powerful and privileged brothers and sisters. The Church's mission is to build up the faithful, as individuals but more so as communities, into a prophetic people who act as a ferment in society enabling all members to be critically aware of and actively involved as co-responsible participants in all that is going on.

In a society where, as is the case in a despotic one-party system, the ordinary citizens are likely to be deprived of their freedom and to be oppressed and exploited by a powerful and self-seeking minority, such a church will be seen as subversive. It will be accused of "meddling in politics". For it is typical of a one-party system to invoke the ambiguous principle of separation of spheres of influence and responsibility between the "spiritual": religious or ecclesiastic, and the "secular": politics, economics, and social. Even at the village level where local party activists were accustomed to impose on everyone the directives from on high, church members were expected to follow without question whatever was commanded by the political leaders. But the theology of Small Christian Communities which the diocese was inculcating among its faithful did not allow them to submit sheepishly to that kind of imposition. In the regular meetings of the small communities the faithful developed the habit of freely examining and evaluating according to Christian principles whatever was being asked of them, and then deciding to follow what they felt was their duty before God.

It did not take long before conflict flared up, especially in the remote rural areas, between party activists and members of the small Christian communities. The party accused the church of forming clandestine subversive groups which were working against the party and did not show respect and obedience to the Life President. When this was first reported to me, I thought it was simply a case of misunderstanding on the part of some overzealous minor party members. But I soon realized that the issue was much more serious than I had thought, and that higher authorities were behind what was happening. In several areas of the diocese leaders of Christian communities were arrested and charged with subversion; some were detained and beaten up. When they protested that they were merely following the directives of the diocesan mini-synod, they were told that, in the eyes of the government, the mini-synod was nothing but a clever plot of the Bishop to organize a political opposition party, and that serious measures were being taken to put an end to it. And sure enough, in March 1976 I myself was summoned to a meeting in Lilongwe with the Regional Minister (of the Central Region) and a delegation of ministers and members of parliament and was interrogated for six hours about this "confusion" in the diocese. It is clear for me that this matter was at the centre of the events that were to take place in the following weeks, when my fellow bishops were summoned by the President and instructed "to do something about Lilongwe and its Bishop, or else the government itself was going to do something"! Following that meeting, I was soon instructed to leave the diocese and Malawi in April and go to Rome where my 'case' would be heard and decided upon.

I had wondered all along how Rome and the other dioceses in Malawi really felt about the Mini-Synod and the diocesan pastoral project of Lilongwe. Theoretically there should not have been any reason why this project, which was nothing but an attempt to implement Vatican II, would not be fully acceptable to and even encouraged by the Church. And in fact, there were, on the official level, all the signs of approval and encouragement. Nevertheless, I sometimes wondered whether that approval was straightforward and unconditional. The project of "Small Christian, Communities" resembles in many ways that of "Basic Christian/Ecclesial Communities" as found in Latin America and elsewhere. Experience has shown that official sentiment in Rome is quite suspicious of these communities and of the movement of Liberation Theology that is associated with them. They are accused of representing an ecclesiology that is anti-rebelliously "popular", and leaning towards Marxism.

In the case of our Small Christian Communities, the accusation of Marxism/Communism did not come from Church authorities, but rather from the political establishment. And yet, why did the Church not seem willing to take up the case of the diocese and try to dissipate the misunderstandings? Instead, the Episcopal Conference together with the Apostolic Nuncio, at a special session following their meeting with the President, simply recommended that I quickly leave for Rome while back in Malawi the Church would do its best to make reconciliation with the state. For the Church the real issue was not anymore that of Small Christian Communities, but rather had to do with the conflict I had at the same time with the leadership of one of the diocesan Sisters' congregations, which conflict had been brought to the attention of the Apostolic Nuncio and the Episcopal Conference. The questions involved were really of an internal ecclesiastical nature, and should not have had anything to do with the government. Strangely enough, the two sides: the Church and the State, somehow joined forces in such a way that, while the Church could claim I was being sent out of the country because of my conflict with the state, the government was declaring that it was Rome and the Church that wanted me out. The whole affair developed in a strange atmosphere of secrecy, where accusations were never clearly stated and discussed, and people were left wondering what was really going on, while all sorts of rumours and innuendos kept circulating without anyone daring to discuss matters openly. I myself was never given clear explanations of the reasons for which I had to leave the diocese and Malawi, nor did I ever get the chance to give my side of the story.

The Life of an Exiled "Missionary"

The sub-title of these reflections on "My Life, My Faith, My Theology and My Country" is formulated rather cryptically as: **"In the Footsteps of the Incarnate and Missionary Cosmic Christ".** This is how I understand the meaning of my life ever since I left my diocese and country. I left Lilongwe on 27 April 1976, and flew to Nairobi, and then to Ghana for a meeting of the Symposium of the Episcopal Conferences of Africa and Madagascar (SECAM) of which I had been the representative for the AMECEA region (on which I was the current Vice-president). I had been commissioned by SECAM in 1975 to head a committee of 4 bishops from English-speaking Africa to work on plans for the establishment of a Catholic Institute of Higher Religious Studies for Anglophone Africa. In that capacity I visited Abidjan (Ivory Coast) and Kinshasa (Zaire) to observe the Institutes that the French-speaking countries had already set up. It had been agreed that our committee would report on our findings at the AMECEA Conference which was to take place in Nairobi in July that year. In the meantime I flew to Rome to appear, in June, at the offices of the Sacred Congregation for the Evangelization of Peoples for a discussion about my leaving Lilongwe and Malawi. It was then that I understood that Rome's intention was that I should not return to Africa, but should tender my resignation as Bishop of Lilongwe. When, in defiance of that instruction, I nevertheless returned in July to Nairobi for the AMECEA conference (at which I had been asked to give the keynote address on "Small Christian Communities" and to give the report on the Institute), Rome's disapproval was expressed in no uncertain terms. The Malawi government must have been aware of this disapproval; for when, during my stay in Nairobi, I ventured to fly to Malawi just to say goodbye to my dying mother, the Malawi government had me detained and kept under house arrest for a couple of days (16-18 July). When at last I was able to leave Malawi for Nairobi in the evening of 18 July 1976, I knew that my time of "exile" outside my country had indeed started.

Our (White Fathers') Generalate in Rome agreed to arrange that I would eventually go to the USA and spend some time on a sabbatical while working on a Ph.D. at the University of California in Berkeley. In the meantime, however, I flew from Rome to Jerusalem to join a group of my fellow White Fathers on a programme ,of spiritual and biblical renewal till the end of 1976. My studies at Berkeley were from 1977 to 1979. Then I went back to Jerusalem on a fellowship at the Ecumenical Centre of Tantur (1979-1980) while working on my Ph.D. dissertation and also setting up in Jerusalem an Ecumenical Centre for African Students and Pilgrims. It was while I was there that I received an invitation from the Mission Department of **Selly Oak Colleges in Birmingham, England,** to spend the year 1980-1981 as the William Paton Fellow of the Colleges. I was to return to Selly Oak Colleges at the end of 1982 (after my Ph.D. at Berkeley), but this time as Third World Lecturer in the Mission Department. Little did I know that Selly Oak was going to be the place where I would spend the next 14 years: the most productive years of my life: first as Third World Lecturer (1982-1987) then as Director of the Ecumenical Centre for Black and White Christian Partnership (1987-1996). Looking back over these years, I have come to believe that my ministry at Selly Oak represents what, in God's plan, must have been the most significant missionary activity of my life. It is as if all my experiences before 1980 were a preparation for my life and work as a **Missionary, an Ecumenist, and a Third World Theologian.**

An African Missionary Promoting Ecumenism in Europe

When I left Rome in 1962, after my studies there, and was sent back to Malawi to do pastoral work in my diocese of origin in Dedza, and went on from there to teach at Kachebere Major Seminary, and was then appointed as Bishop of Lilongwe, the feeling was that the missionary vocation I had chosen as a young seminarian was not being taken seriously. Would I ever satisfy my desire to work as a missionary? After four years of service as Bishop of Lilongwe, there I was: being sent into exile, and eventually ending up in Britain as Third World Lecturer and then director of the Ecumenical Centre for Black and White Christian Partnership in Selly Oak! What was happening? It then dawned on me that, at long last, I had begun to work as "missionary of Africa", but in the unforeseen context of Europe. This was God's own way of answering my desire. Here I was going to fulfill my missionary vocation. As a member of a Roman Catholic missionary congregation, I was going to help mainly "non-Catholic missionaries" to prepare themselves for their ministry in the Third World. And then I would go on and spend eight more years directing a centre that aimed at building bridges of mutual understanding and cooperation between the mainline "White-led, White-majority churches" and the independent "Black-led, Black-majority churches" of Britain and Europe.

My long experience in this kind of ministry has developed in me a widened understanding of what the "missionary" vocation is all about. A missionary is someone who, like the Incarnate Word of God, is called to promote the "gathering into one of the children of God who are scattered abroad" (Jn. 11:52). He/she becomes a Bridge and Bridge-builder, making it possible for God's children, who feel separated by all sorts of human differences and barriers, to begin to communicate and share the diverse endowments that each one has received from the same Creator God. In so doing, they proclaim that God, who is infnütely rich, keeps distributing his gifts among his children in such a way that no one group, on its own, has all that it takes to build a convincingly adequate picture of their heavenly Father. They all need one another in all sorts of ways in order to be able, together to produce an optimum manifestation of their being made in the image of their Father. By communicating and sharing with one another, they are able to complete and enrich one another, while at the same time mutually challenging and correcting one another in what is defective in all of them. The ideal is the building up of a New World (God's Kingdom) where varieties and differences do not separate and oppose, but come together to form a richly endowed Family or Body of God's children.

This vision of an "oecumene" that includes everyone is possible if the capstone is that "Word of God" proclaimed in John 1:1-5, 9-13, who, on becoming incarnate (Jn. 1:14) did not thereby lose his "cosmic" mission and efficacy and become a "tribal idol" appropriated exclusively by a section of humanity (be it Christians, Catholics, Protestants, or any one of the many possible rival confessional groups). This is the "Cosmic Christ" of Ephesians 1:3-10 and Colossians 1:15-20, the "one mediator" through whom is fulfilled the plan of the "one God our Saviour who desires all people to be saved and to come to the knowledge of the truth" (1 Tim. 2:3-6). It is in the footsteps of this "Cosmic Christ" that I feel I have been walking my missionary journey.

Theologian of the "Third, or Two-Thirds World"

When I left Malawi in July 1976 I had been invited to attend the inaugural conference of a group of theologians from Latin America, Asia, Africa, the Caribbean, and the USA which was to take place in Dar-es-Salaam in August of that year. Those who had taken the initiative to call this meeting explained that there was an urgent need for theologians from what was then known as the Third World to meet and begin to consciously work together towards the development of a way of doing theology that could meet the crying needs of their peoples. This resolve was motivated by a double constatation. On the one hand: by the mid-1970s the situation in the so-called "underdeveloped" or "developing" nations was becoming desperately tragic. Their relation of dependency vis-à-vis the powerful industrialized nations of Europe and North America, instead of helping to bring development and progress as had been hoped for, was actually creating more and more poverty and powerlessness for the majority of the people. If things were to change, the Third World would have to fmd ways of "liberating" and empowering itself. Could the Church, which is charged with a message of liberation (cf. Lk. 4:17-21) be depended upon to help in this process of liberation and empowerment? The second constatation was that the standard theologies from the West are generally not adequate for equipping the Church for such a mission in favour of the poor and the oppressed. Hence the need for theologians from the poor nations to work out appropriate theologies for the Third World.

The Dar-es-Salaam conference (6-11 August 1976) intended to take up the challenge. The delegates took time to analyze the social, political, economic and ideological situation in the Third World, and then asked themselves what kind of theology could address that situation in the name of the Gospel. At the end of the conference they decided to form an association which would serve as an on-going forum for carrying forward the task of developing and "practising" theologies appropriate for the needs of the Third World. It was called the "Ecumenical Association of Third World Theologians" (EATWOT). I was privileged to be included among its first group of officers and elected as Vice President. One of the articles included in this book: "Doing Theology at the Grassroots: A Challenge for Professional Theologians", recalls some of the main characteristics that participants agreed should inform theologies from the Third World. For me, this conference was a powerful eye-opener It impressed on me how much the major part of humanity today is suffering under various forms of oppressive systems, many of which are of human creation and need to be fought against in the name of the God of the Oppressed and of his Liberating Christ and Saviour. I suppose that the terrible suffering which I was experiencing personally at that time helped me to identify naturally with fellow victims of oppression and exploitation everywhere in the world, and to commit myself irrevocably to the struggle for full human liberation. Since that conference I have considered working as a Third World Theologian to be an essential part of my ministry and mission.

Conclusion

The foregoing pages have attempted to highlight some of the events and experiences in my life which, I think, can help to explain my faith and my theological thinking. Hopefully, too, they will serve as a sort of background to the articles which have been collected in this book. Most of these articles were written after 1976, in the period which, in these introductory pages, has received only a summary description. They are reproductions of my contributions at various conferences or workshops. Understandably they reflect my preoccupations and state of thinking at the time they were published. And so it is possible that some of the views and opinions expressed in them have changed over the years, and that today I might want to express myself differently. But it is fair to leave them as they are, assuming that readers will prefer to follow me as I struggled with issues that were of great importance at the different stages of my life and ministry.

1 Christ's Church in Lilongwe Today and Tomorrow

Our Diocesan Pastoral Planning Project

This is a slightly edited reproduction of the Pastoral Letter written in 1973, and printed by Likuni Press. It was meant to serve as the Bishop's Keynote Address, introducing the Diocesan "Mini-Synod" of Lilongwe, which was held from 1973 to 1975 and resulted in the Pastoral Guidelines: Lilongwe Diocese Mini-Synod: 24 November 1973 - 24 August 1975 (Likuni: Likuni Press and Publishing House, 1975) booklet containing conclusions from the 5 sessions of the Mini-Synod which laid down guidelines and regulations for the running of church life and activities at the "Small Christian Community" (m'phakati) level.

The main ideas in this Pastoral Letter were taken up in the course of the sessions of the Mini-Synod at diocesan, parish, and outstation levels. They can be traced back in the several Booklets in Chichewa ("Mabvu" booklets) which served as discussion guides for the Mini-Synod sessions. It will be noticed that the letter is based on teachings from the Vatican II documents. The "diocesan Pastoral Planning Project" was set up as a way of implementing Vatican II in Lilongwe Diocese.

To the Priests, Brothers, Sisters, Lay-Missionaries, and Faithful of Lilongwe Diocese.

My dear Brethren,

As you know, sometime back I asked all of you to join me in the task of rethinking our common ministry in this Diocese in view of rendering it more enlightened, realistic, efficient and adapted to the conditions of our times here in Malawi. Christ is calling us to his own Mission so that as his Body we may bring the Salvation that his Father intends for all His dear children in the world. This is the call and challenge that has been thrown to the whole Church. We take it up in a spirit of faith and

Christian hope, humbly confiding in Christ's own Spirit that is at work in us, slowly transforming the world through love into God's own Kingdom.

Such a rethinking is an adventure leading to a courageous questioning not only of existing structures and activities, but more so of our basic assumptions, vision, and attitudes. You will understand that where a common rethinking is called for there must also be the sharing of a common vision and basic assumptions. This questioning is aimed at formulating plans for our common apostolate. And this can only come about if we start from an agreed vision of what God is calling us to do.

I would like to share with all of you my own personal vision, the way I look at the task that is being offered to the Church today. I need not stress the point that my intention is far from trying dogmatically to impose such a personal vision on you all. Rather I feel it is fair to you that I lay my cards on the table and frankly let you see how I look at the task lying ahead of us. This will enable you to enter into the spirit that initiated this project, so that you can better collaborate with me through your suggestions and even criticism. The Holy Spirit is present not in me alone, but also in you. Just as I ask you to listen to Him, so also am I prepared to receive from you whatever He is saying, in diverse ways, through your own reactions and thinking.

1. Our starting point: Vatican II

I am convinced that what God wants of us today has been adequately shown in the conclusions of the Second Vatican Council. In the documents issuing from this Spirit-guided Council we find the basic vision and principles that should guide us in our humble efforts to answer God's challenge today. I have found most helpful and enlightening especially these four documents.

> The Church (Lumen Gentium) (L.G.)
> The Church today (Gaudium et Spes) (G.S.)
> The Laity (Apostolicam Actuositatem) (A.A.)
> The Missions (Ad Gentes) (A.G.)

But the other documents (v.g. on Religious life, Bishops, Priests, and Non-Christians) also contain much that is likely to guide us. May I franldy let you know that, so far as I am concerned, Vatican II is basic to the whole exercise that we intend to undertake. This may sound rather obvious: still it needs to be clearly stated, since, it is by no means certain that everybody is ready to *be* guided by the conclusions of Vatican II. Sometimes people are put off by aberrant or exaggerated applications of these conclusions, and they would simply like to throw overboard all that has been acquired through Vatican II, and return to the "peaceful pre-Vatican II conditions". I do not find this wise: it is not being docile to the Spirit. "The lion roars: who can help feeling afraid? The Lord Yahweh speaks: who can refuse to prophesy?" (Amos 3:8).

2. Observing the signs of the times

But as you very well know, Vatican II was not meant to be a detailed or ready-made blue-print for Church renewal. The Council merely put down basic guidelines and orientations. Its recommendations are a call and a task. They need to be worked out and applied to fit concrete circumstances of place, people and time.

The Catholic Church subsists in a variety of countries, peoples, cultures and places. It is called upon by the Lord to meet problems and needs that arise in times and places of unending diversity. Loyalty to Christ and his Church demands openness to concrete reality because God's call is made known in the context of such circumstances.

Our project of Pastoral Rethinking and Planning will need to be made with as adequate an understanding as possible of the conditions in the country today and tomorrow. We are dealing with the Church as it is called by God to face the world of today and prepare itself to serve faithfully that of axnorrow. In our rethinking and planning, therefore, let us constantly observe the signs of the times, ascertain the reality as it is, the real problems that we face, the needs that have to be met, the resources at our disposal in terms of personnel, finances, opportunities and talents. Let us not fear to take fully into account the limits of our possibilities, but also the ange of our capacities. In the name of our fidelity to Christ and the Church we must avoid making irrealistic or irrelevant plans.

3. Understanding the Church

Our Diocese of Lilongwe is a portion of the Universal Church; or rather, it is the Church itself as rendered present and operative in this part of the world. The Church is not a human creation. It is God-given, God-structured, God-led, and God-animated. We have no freedom to make of it what we want, but must simply accept it as it has been given by its founder, the Lord. Our task is to be faithful to its constitution and its mission. Our project of Pastoral Planning is therefore just a humble attempt to be as faithful as possible to Christ's will for the Church today and tomorrow. But then we need to have a clear and adequate understanding of what the Church is and what its mission is. Such an understanding is evidently basic and important; it should be the foundation of all our work of rethinking and planning.

4. A community of salvation

When we ask the Bible what the Church is, we are given a list of images that strive to give us a certain understanding of the Mystery of the Church. It is a "Sheepfold", a "Flock", the "field of God's tilling", a "household", a "vine", a "holy temple", a "Body", "the bride of Christ", "God's Kingdom" or simply "The People of God". All these images suggest a group of people, united or organically structured, with an in-built capacity for life, growth and multiplication. And indeed we are told that this is a People called specially by God, whom he has saved and has called into his own family by assimilating them to his Son Jesus Christ through Baptism and the Spirit (cf. 1 Pet. 2:9-10). They are one with Christ, since with him they form one Body, of which Christ is the head and they are the members (1 Cor. 12). Through them flows the saving life that is supplied by Christ in his mystery of death and resurrection. Christ is their Pastor: feeding and caring for them especially through his

Sacraments. He is their Leader to guide them safely towards the Father. They rally around him and are therefore assured of effective leadership on their way home to the Father (Jn. 10). Christ is also their Teacher because he, who alone really knows the Father and his plans (Jn. 1:18), keeps teaching them the truth which is the light showing the way to the Father. The Church is thus a community of salvation. It groups together those chosen people to whom God offers His life and salvation in Christ. It offers them all the help to grow in this divine life, and the leadership and guidance towards God. The Church is thus a community where salvation is made possible. That is why it is like an open house ready to welcome any new members. It even goes out to the cross-roads to invite as many people as possible to the Wedding Feast (Mt. 22), since God's call is universal.

5. The Sacrament of Christ's presence in the world

A deeper understanding of these images offers us a further insight into the nature of the Church. It is the Body of Christ (Rom. 12:4-8; 1 Cor. 12; Eph. 4). That is: its members, through faith and baptism, are incorporated into Christ. He is in them, they are in Him. This presence is evidently different from the earthly one that Christ had while on earth. That one was a physical presence, enjoying the privileges of sensible proximity and availability, but also hampered by the limits of time and space. But ever since Christ has passed through death and resurrection and has ascended to the Father, he is present in the world in a new way, a mystical one. Having become a "vivifying Spirit" (1 Cor 15:45-49) he lives on and operates through the members of his Church. Christ is in the Church. He is one with it since he is the head of the Body, of which all those attached to him by faith and baptism are members.

These members, individually and in their various categories, are endowed with a diversity of charisms, entrusted with all sorts of duties and responsibilities, and called to a variety of complementary services in the Body (cf. Rom. 12:4-8; 1 Cor. 12; Eph. 4:3-13): But it is one and the same Spirit, the Spirit of the Risen Lord, that expresses himself in all these gifts and services. They are the gifts of Christ himself. In each and every authentic ecclesial charism the Lord is present and at work in order to structure the Body proportionately and equip it for all the services that God asks of the Church. And so, in and through the whole Church, Christ is present in the world and is carrying on, in his members, the mission given him by the Father. The presence of the Church is the presence of Christ in the world. The Church is thus a sort of Sacrament of Christ (cf. L.G. no. 1): signifying him and rendering him present and operative.

6. A community with a mission

No member of the Church is a merely passive one, but all are called to be the instruments of Christ's salvific work in the world. The Church is thus not just a community where people come to find their own salvation. It is above all the instrument whereby God is at work bringing Salvation to the world. Just as Christ himself is the light of all nations (Lk. 2:32) so also his Body the Church is called upon to be the salt of the earth and the light of the world (Mt. 5:13-14), the yeast that has to transform humanity (Mt. 13:33). What is this mission of the Church in the world?

7. The champion of God's plan of salvation

It is Christ's own mission: that of being the new Adam (Rom. 5:15-21) the first-born of all God's creation (Col. 1:15-20). In other words, the Church is that little family of God's children that strives to answer fully the call of God to humankind, and to help all their fellow human beings to do the same. God's call to humanity is what we call the Plan of Salvation. The Church, because of Christ, is led towards an ever-growing understanding of this Plan and is helped by the power of Christ's Spirit to fulfill progressively this Plan. It does not do this as a ghetto community, closed in on itself. It has been chosen by God, like Abraham of old, so that in it all humankind may find God's blessing. This is why its full mission is not just to answer God's call, but also to help the whole world to do the same. Through its life of conformity to God's will, the Church enters into a dialogue with the rest of humanity and fulfills a prophetic role by promoting love and fighting sin. As the Church gives perseveringly this witness, the world is slowly transformed, until some day will come when the whole of humanity will live according to God's will. The Kingdom of God - His Kingship over people's lives - will thus have come. This is the task of the Church: it is the mission it has from its Lord.

8. What is this plan of God?

The first chapters of Genesis help us to understand what God intended when he created the world and humanity. Human beings have been .made "in the image, in the likeness of God", in the way that a child takes after its parents and is expected to express this similarity in its way of life: sharing with its parents the same culture, the same set of values, language, and even traits of character and physiognomy. Every human being coming into this world is called to this likeness with God, expressed in a way of life that becomes children of God's family. Now "God is love" (1 Jn. 4:8) and his children, his family, behave like him when their life and work is regulated by love: love of their common Father, and love of all their brothers and sisters, since they are all related. "Love is always patient and kind, it is never jealous (1 Cor. 13:4-7).

In other words, God's plan is for a society of his children where love, peace, justice, mutual concern, prosperity, happiness for all are the ruling honour, and everything that can be thought virtuous or worthy of praise" tenets. It is a society where there is "everything that is true, everything that is noble, everything that is good and pure, everything that we love and come: the earth becomes a paradise, a worthy dwelling place for God's children. People will live in happy brotherhood, peace, justice, prosperity, and happiness. (Phil. 4:8). When this is the case among people, then God's Kingdom has come: the earth becomes a paradise, a worthy dling place for God's children. People will live in happy brotherhood, peace, justice, prosperity, and happiness.

But God's ambition for humanity does not end there: He has made our heart too big for that. The Father is constantly pulling us to a far fuller union with Himself, to a fuller realization of this peace, joy and prosperity. The Kingdom of God which is to cover the world and transform it, is the first, the preliminary phase, of the full plan of God. "For there is no eternal city for us in this life, but we look for one in the life to come" (Heb. 13:14). God is calling us towards that full union with him, beyond the grave, when He himself will be all in all. This life on earth is meant to lead us to that final stage. And so the two stages are not opposed; the earthly paradise does not cancel or replace the heavenly one, but is meant to lead up to it. Both stages are part and parcel of God's plan for the world.

9. The need for salvation

Unhappily, humanity refused this Plan of God. Sin and egoism stand out as obstacles to its fulfillment. The Bible presents this sad state in dramatic terms. Humanity broke away from God through the futile attempt to become the equal of God and to assert themselves as complete and independent master of their own destiny. But this pathetic attempt succeeds only in destroying the harmony of the world. It creates egoism, greed, hatred, injustice, oppression and cruelty. Human beings do not recognize themselves anymore as brothers and sisters, but as rivals and enemies: wars spring up, exploitations of all sorts, oppressions, jealousies, etc. All these change the picture: instead of an earthly paradise, the world tends to become a valley of tears. But though humanity has the power to bring this destruction on themselves, they lack the capacity to pull themselves out of the mess: they cannot save themselves. God has to intervene once more and save them. God intervenes to put order again and make it possible for humanity to enjoy what He had planned for them.

10. Christ the Saviour, and the Church his Body

Jesus-Christ, God made man, is the agent of this salvation. In Him, God Himself comes into the world to save it. He comes as light to chase away the darkness of ignorance in which the world is plunged. He comes as life to quicken humankind. He comes as the way leading people back to God. Jesus is Prophet, Priest and King.

The Church, we said, is the Body of Christ. In it, Christ himself is present and operative, slowly transforming the world into the image of God. This is the full mission of the Church. Wherever it exists, it carries God's call and challenge: to render present and effective Christ the Saviour of the World. The Church of God here in Lilongwe should strive to discern this call and to answer it fully.

11. The Existential presence of the Church in the world

The Church is Christ's Body: it is his presence to the world. But then how exactly is the Church present in and to the world? We should distinguish, as it were, several levels or "modes" of the Church's existence in the world.

The Church exists first of all as the world-wide Catholic communion, grouping in unity (not uniformity!) of faith, hope and love, all the local churches of the world, presided over and led by their Pastors who together form the College of Bishops, successors of the Apostles. The source and effective sign of this unity is the Bishop of Rome, the Pope, successor of St Peter. As head and source of unity in the Episcopal College, he effectively 'strengthens his brothers" (Lk. 22:32) and leads them in "shepherding the Flock of God entrusted to them" (1 Pet. 5:2). Thus is assured in the Church the presence of Christ the Head, as Teacher, Sanctifier and Leader. And the unity of the whole Body becomes real and operative - harmonious communication and mutual strengthening and support runs through the churches in spite of their diversity, tongues, customs, and cultures and their dispersion in space and time.

This Catholic unity is basic and real. Thanks to it, the Church is present in and to the world as the Sacrament of Christ's saving presence. But this presence is rendered concrete and operative through the other level of the Church's existence.

12. The local Church

The Church exists concretely in local communities grouping members of Christ's Body as they live and work in their natural, geographical, cultural and human milieu. Just as Christ was present to the world through incarnation in a particular people, culture, place and time, so also is the Church present by being incarnated in given human situations. The Church universal subsists in and through these local churches. As Vatican II says: "This Church is truly present in all legitimate local congregations of the faithful which, united with the pastors, are themselves called churches in the New Testament. For in their own locality these are the new people called by God, in the Holy Spirit and in much fullness. In them the faithful are gathered together by the preaching of the gospel of Christ, and the mystery of the Lord's Supper is celebrated "that by the flesh and blood of the Lord's body the whole brotherhood may be joined together" (L. G. no. 26).

"The local Church is not simply a fragment - as though we had to add together all the fragments before we could arrive at the 'Church'. The local church is the Church for and in this place, whether it be Camden Town or Harlem. This is the Church which is within our range, our experience, within our grasp. It is here that Christ is present, in the gospel read and expounded, in the Eucharist which is shared and in the love which results from both".[1]

Ladies welcome the cortege as they approach the sanctuary

13. Dimensions of the local Church

Existential incarnation is the criterion of the Church's "locality". Wherever and to the extent that the Church is structurally inserted into a valid and identifiable human society, to that same extent it can be called local. It is clear, therefore, that we can speak of "local church" at various dimensions because the natural human society exists locally also at varying dimensions. We have the nation dimension, the culture dimension, the tribe, the clan, the village, and the family society dimensions. All these are valid and identifiable human societies, but they exist at different dimensions. And yet each one of them possesses a realistic factor: language, culture, administration, geographical proximity, kinship, etc. that commands its unity and identity. It is possible thus to have wider or narrower societies.

And yet there is a law whereby the vitality and functioning of the wider society is in proportion to the vitality and functioning of its narrower or component sub-societies. A country cannot function properly at a national level if its regional or district levels are ineffective or non-existent. At best it would be a theoretical "nationality" corresponding to nothing that really exists.

In the same way the Church becomes localized on different levels. When Vatican II speaks of "local churches", it may be referring to different levels of locality: Patriarchates, larger groupings of Episcopal Conferences according to geographical or cultural homogeneity, National Episcopal Conferences, Dioceses, or Parishes. In the last analysis "local church" means any stable group of Christians assembled around the Eucharistic table: In our case here in Lilongwe Diocese, this can mean the Parish community, but more realistically so the outstation or sub-parish communities. It is legitimate to refer to the SECAM (Symposium of Episcopal Conferences of Africa and Madagascar) as the local church in our case. But even so could the AMECEA region be called local church. Similarly the ECM region (the Church in Malawi) has all the right to be called the local church in Malawi since its unity is based on the Church's insertion in the Malawian nation. Our diocese of Lilongwe is part of the wider Malawian local church, because by reason of geographical and national homogeneity it is necessarily in fraternal intercommunion, collaboration, mutual support, and unity with the sister-dioceses in Malawi.

14. The Diocese of Lilongwe, our local church

But the locality that concerns us immediately in the Diocesan Pastoral Planning project we have here in Lilongwe is the one on the diocesan level. It is a real and authentic locality since it is based on the bond linking the bishop with his presbyterium and the whole People of God living in the geographical and administrative part of the country that is ours. Vatican II reminds us that "a Diocese is that portion of God's people which is entrusted to a Bishop to be shepherded by him with the cooperation of the presbytery. Adhering thus to its pastor and gathered together by him in the Holy Spirit through the gospel and the Eucharist, this portion constitutes a particular church in which the one, holy, catholic, and apostolic Church of Christ is truly present and operative." (C. D. no. 11).

But here again we must realize that the diocese itself is "local church" only in a wide sense. The diocese is made up of parishes, and these are usually still subdivided into smaller church entities (outstations, sub-parishes, etc.). These are also "local churches" at a more basic and real level. What we are saying about Church applies more, in fact, to these basic local churches than to the wider levels of parish and diocese.

All that has been said in the foregoing pages may sound like vain and idle theory, an exercise in empty theologizing that has no practical import for our project of Diocesan Pastoral Planning. But it is not! It was necessary for me to share with you at some length the vision I have of the Church and its role in the world. It was important too that I let you see how I look at the presence and operation of the Church. Because now you will be able, I hope, to understand, from my point of view, where our project comes in.

15. The aim of our project

As far as I am concerned, the purpose of the Diocesan Pastoral Planning project is to enable us to make of Lilongwe Diocese a living and effecttive local church.

The underlying conviction is that, unless we work - and immediately! - towards the building up of a really dynamic local church we are not answering God's call to us today: we are not preparing for the Church of tomorrow, and we are rendering useless the heroic work of the pastoral workers who have preceded us.

16. What is our objective?

What do we mean by saying "a living and effective local church"? We mean exactly what Vatican II says in its decree on "the Church's missionary activity" (A.G.).

The work of planting the Church in a given human community reaches a kind of milestone when the congregation of the faithful, already rooted in social life and considerably adapted to the local culture, enjoys a certain stability and firmness. This means that the congregation is now equipped with its own supply, insufficient though it be, of local priests, religious, and laymen. It means that it is endowed with those ministries and institutions which are necessary if the People of God is to live and develop its life under the guidance of its own bishop. (A.G. no. 19)

In other words, the local church becomes living and effective in the measure in which it becomes basically self-reliant in its internal life and its external mission; when all the basic structures and resources for its life and work are found in it, even if a measure of reliance on external help may still continue.

It is extremely important that we today realize that it is high time our Church reached this stage. Events all over the world, and especially in parts of our Continent, should serve as a timely warning that perhaps time is not on our side. We owe it to the Church and to our people to do all we can in the time that Providence may still kindly grant us to build up a Church that stands the chances of survival and growth even in the worst imaginable hazards. Such a Church will have to be:

- self-ministering,
- self-propagating,
- self-supporting.

17. A self ministering Church

For the nurturing and constant growth of the People of God, Christ the Lord instituted in His Church a variety of ministries, which work for the good of the whole Body (L.G. no. 18). In a broad sense these ministries are those "services" that need to be present and active in the Christian Body for the two functions of the Body:

1. That of living and growing: keeping the Body healthy and increasing it with living, new members. This is done through preaching (faith), and feeding (Sacraments and liturgy), and ordering of the community (government).

2. That of witnessing to and serving the world (apostolate). This is assured through all sorts of Church involvement in the world whereby it is called to serve as Leaven, Light and Salt of the world and to bring about God's Kingdom in the world.

We can say that in this broad sense all Christians are called to be "ministers" since through Baptism they participate in Christ's own Mediatorship as Prophets, Priests and Leaders. In this sense there is indeed a great variety of services and ministries, and all members are called to exercise their own "ministries", each one according to their calling.

A local church is self-ministering when all the essential services needed for the life and work of the Church are actively assumed by members of that local church, and not mainly by helpers from outside. As long as these services are heavily dependent on missionary or external aid, the Church is not yet self-ministering; and this is a situation that has to be changed as soon as possible if the Church is to feel secure in facing the hazards of history.

Our Diocesan Pastoral Planning project has to aim at setting up realistic structures whereby such self-ministering will be hastened and facilitated. *This is a priority.*

18. An adequate and adapted local clergy.

When we talk of ministry we usually refer, in a rather narrower sense of the term, to the Ordained Ministry: Bishops, priests, deacons. And this is quite correct, for as Vatican II says: "With their helpers, the priests and deacons, bishops have therefore taken up the service of the community, presiding in place of God over the flock whose shepherds they are, as teachers of doctrine, priests of sacred worship, and officers of good order (L.G. no. 20).

There can be no thriving Church without the leadership of the clergy. The hierarchical service, which represents the feeding, coordinating and animating leadership of Christ, is a most basic service in the Church. All the rest depends on it.

Our project has to take the question 'of Clergy as a major priority. The question is not simply that of making sure that today we have enough priests to serve the Church. It rather is to find out ways and means of assuring a realistically planned availability of priests from local resources. As it is, we are still relatively well off as far as priests are concerned, even if we already feel the pinch. But then the main assurance comes from an overdose of missionary personnel: the kind gift of our elder Sister Churches from overseas. The local clergy is just a handful, and the immediate prospects (number of seminarists, rate of ordinations, proportion of perseverance up to priesthood) are not reassuring. The more so as the priest's work is increasing rapidly in quality (v.g. growth of Christian communities) and complexity.

I know that the solution here will not be simply in heroic efforts to increase the number of local priests. For one thing, whatever our efforts, there is a sort of in-built ceiling to the increase of the type of priests that we are striving to produce. Could there be ways of making conditions such that a greater production of priests than is actually the case is rendered possible, without lowering standards? What standards are we talking about? These are questions that we are to face courageously. The Church has to be assured of an adequate supply of ordained ministers, that is certain. Any rethinking or adjustment in methods to make this possible is capital for the survival of the Church.

19. Strengthening non-ordained ministries

On the other hand, what we might tend to forget is that the real objective is not as large a number of priests as possible. The objective is adequate ministry in the Church to meet the needs that are there. By itself an increase in the number of priests would not automatically solve our problems. The ordained ministry is just one (the most basic, I grant) of the indispensable ministries in the Church. But there are many other ministries needed for the proper functioning of the Body of Christ. And these ministries are not necessarily "ordained": they can be exercised by lay-people - often even better by them! Thus we have ministries of teaching religion, organizing and executing liturgical functions and prayer, leading and ordering Christian communities, sanctifying Christians in all sorts of ways, including the celebration of some sacraments, taking care of the material side of Church administration, etc. For these and other ministries, the clergy is admittedly mainly responsible because of their role in the Church. But Christ's will is such that the clergy alone cannot fulfill them adequately. And that, not just due to their small number, but because the proper running of these services calls for a variety of charisms and gifts that are not found among the clergy alone. And so "the laity can also be called in various ways to a more direct form of cooperation in the apostolate of the hierarchy ... further, laymen have the capacity to be deputed by the hierarchy to exercise certain church functions for a spiritual purpose (L.G. no. 33). Is it not true that to a large extent, the shortage of priests is felt more acutely due to the fact that a large number of non-ordained ministries tend to fall on the shoulders of priests alone? An enormous reserve of potential non-ordained ministers lies untapped among the lay people. If we are to accelerate the advent of a self-ministering Church, it is imperative that a realistic redistribution of ministries, ordained and non-ordained, be established. We must stop the trend whereby the ordained ministry has tended to swallow up other ministries in the Church. We should revalorize these ministries and associate as many trained people as possible in these ministries.

20. The charism of religious life

In the Church there is an extremely important charism that should not be confused with either the ordained ministry or those non-ordained ministries to which I have just been alluding. This is the charism of "religious life".

In a way, we are fully entitled to call it a "ministry", a "service" within the Church, because religious life exists, not primarily for the proper good (sanctification and salvation) of the Christian members who are called to embrace it, but for the good of the whole Church. The Church, and indeed the whole world, needs this service.

We tend to value the religious mainly because of the admirable help they give in all sorts of services undertaken by the Church: education, health, social services, catechetics, etc. While we are grateful that different religious communities take a lion's share in these essential services, we might forget that these services are not the aims of the religious life, but the means whereby the specific aim of religious life is rendered.

The religious charism is essentially one of Prophetism and witness. Their service in the Church is precisely this "witness".

Religious should render visible the real aim of Christ's Church as Light of the world (showing visibly the full Plan of God for the world: a plan of love) and as Salt of the earth (showing visibly that this Plan is realistic, possible, already realized in a certain way). The life and work of the religious are meant to show visibly what salvation in Christ really means: liberation from the slavery of sin, and full liberty to live a life of love, and invite all people to it.

The service of the religious consists therefore in rendering visible and understandable, challenging and inviting, the Plan of God which the whole Church is called upon to realize. All its members are called to be

Light, Salt and Leaven of the world. But this is not always very visible and challenging. We need a group of "professionals" whose role is to render this visible in the name of the whole Church. This especially through witnessing communities, visible and concrete images of the saved humanity. Thus the concrete services that religious render in all sorts of ways are a means for them to render their service of witness. If this witness is not visible anymore, these concrete services have to be reviewed.

You are well aware that a major part of the religious (both male and female) consists of missionaries from overseas. They have implanted in our church the seed of religious life, active and contemplative. But their sincere aim has been that local Christians will join them and become the nucleus of a future local religious life. Indeed, already a good number of local young men and women have embraced this religious life.

Our efforts must be to increase the number of these dedicated persons, so that the religious vocation becomes really part and parcel of our church. Our church will be very much the poorer if religious life dies down.

But one thing that needs stressing is that, if religious life is to be the kind of "service" that the church needs, it has to be "localized". By this I do not just mean that more and more local Christians should come forward to join the ranks of the religious. By itself this is not enough. What I mean is that the way of living religious life in this country should be such as to meet the real needs of the people. If indeed religious life is meant to be a witness, then this witness must be such that it is rightly understood by the ordinary local people and affects them in the right way. There are ways of living religious life that may be valid witnessing in other parts of the world, but that would not be effective witnessing in this country. We do not need them. Our religious must tailor their life to speak to us and to prophesy to us. This is a challenge thrown to the religious communities. It asks for a courageous rethinking and reform.

21. A self-propagating church

A church that is self-ministering is by the same token a self-propagating one. It is equipped to assure the growth of the church by the acquisition of new members. By its very nature the Church is missionary. It should not become a sect or a ghetto, closed in on itself, and not concerned about those many others whom God may be wishing to call into the Church. Were it to become a ghetto, it would be vowed to slow extinction and a weakening of its vitality through lack of new blood. A living and effective local church should possess the outgoing dynamism for attracting new members. A self-propagating church is one that does not rely for this attracting of new members only or mainly on outside missionaries, but on its own members, its own initiatives, its own methods and means.

Our Christians have been trained in this spirit since the beginning. We know that many members have been attracted to the Church through the missionary spirit of the neophytes. But our project must devise ways and means of strengthening and organizing this apostolic energy. We must learn more and more how to entrust to our faithful the responsibility of the Church's growth. It would be a pity if, with the waning of the missionary personnel, the missionary spirit of our Christians were to decrease too.

22. A self-supporting church

"A church that depends for its existence and essential services upon the continuous charity of other churches is not a healthy, properly established church. Basic economic self-reliance is as much a part of the establishment of the Church, which is the specific purpose of missionary work, as is the indigenization of its hierarchy". I do not think that anyone of us would dispute the truth of these words of Fr A. Hastings.[2] We all have had ample proof of what he says earlier: "The People of God are an earthly, eating, drinking, buying, selling people. It is not only

---

[2] Adrian Hastings, *Mission and Ministly,* London: Sheed and Ward, 1971, p. 14.

practically advantageous, it is theologically necessary that a local Church be itself an economically viable unit".[3]

Let me repeat: we all agree with this - theoretically! But do we take seriously the logical consequences of such principles? By tradition, our church has depended for its economic viability on continuous outside help. For a long time this was both inevitable and beneficial. We have to acknowledge with sincere gratitude all the outside help that has been forthcoming. It is thanks to this help that we were able to build our missions, initiate and run essential but expensive services like hospitals and schools, maintain a large number of pastoral workers, quite a few of whom have been living well above the standards of the majority of the local population. The material organization and network of services in our church is clearly such that it cannot continue, let alone develop, without an ever increasing flow of outside help. How many buildings, means of transport, instruments of work, schools, hospitals, and dispensaries, etc. have been rendered possible only through kind grants from Rome or other international or national organizations, and from the generous sacrifices of individual missionaries, their Congregations, or their relatives and friends from abroad. We have grown accustomed to taking all that for granted, and to act in a way that seems to presume that these grants will always be forthcoming. But suppose the grants stopped or dwindled: suppose these generous missionaries left us, what would become of our admirable structures? I tremble when I ask myself such questions.

A really strong local church cannot afford to bask in such a false assurance. We can sit back and look to the future with a sense of security only when the situation is such that our church can feel it is realistically self-supporting. Our Diocesan Pastoral Planning project will be valuable only if it can devise ways and means of bringing about a sufficient measure of self support. What does that involve?

---

[3] *Ibid.*

23. Training towards finding local resources

It involves, in the first place, a bold plan to train local members of our church towards supporting their own church: finding money and other material goods to maintain and run its essential services, to support and maintain its pastoral workers, and to expand and develop those services that need developing.

To achieve this, everything must be done to make the Christians realize that the Church is theirs: they are the Church. The feeling that the priests or missionaries own the Church must stop. A new sense of responsibility should grow whereby everybody feels that the life and work of the Church depends on him or her. We have made untiring efforts to create such a feeling through involvement of our Christians in *Mtulo* and other systems of Church support. And in quite a few parishes this sense is growing. But have we gone really far? Do we take this question seriously enough? Do we realize that here too perhaps time is not on our side? Perhaps our way of doing gives the impression that the contribution of our people is not indispensable: we can do very well without it. Perhaps we often want to achieve grandiose projects and are not ready to wait for participation and involvement from our people. The Catholic Church has created for itself the reputation of infinite economic possibilities. Are we sometimes loath to fall short of people's expectations on this point?

From now on, let the rule be that the running of the church is not done without a serious involvement and participation of the local people. No new projects should be initiated without a direct involvement of the people. We have indeed inherited, through no fault of ours, establishments and services that are expensive and complicated to run. In all fairness we have so maintain and run them. But wherever possible, let us rather hand these over to those (v.g. government) who can run them efficiently. We may dare to start new projects of a grandiose magnitude only when and where we are sure we shall be able to hand them over when we feel the church is unable to run them. You will pardon me for saying this so bluntly: we have no right to start anything today that involves the church in the future, without making certain that it will continue with reasonable local resources. Doing otherwise is being unjust to the local church which may later on be left with an impossible task.

24. Realistic standards of living

If we are serious in wanting to build a self-supporting church, and want our people to take us seriously, then there is a basic condition. We must be prepared to come down to a realistic standard of living and working. Our people are what they are: a basically poor community, just emerging from the subsistence level of economy. Even if they were heroically generous, there is definitely a limit to what they can contribute towards the support of their church. It is not realistic to make giant projects and then expect them to realize them with their limited resources. It would not be fair to ask them to support a church tailored to fit opulent overseas standards!

You will realize that this is a challenge to all of us. Are we prepared to come down to a standard of life and service that is within reach of the ordinary person in Lilongwe Diocese? This will be very demanding, the more so as we have been used to living on an "expatriate level". But if we really want our church to work towards self-support, we have to pay the price! I grant that we cannot come to the ideal overnight. We are still victims of systems that are not easily modified. But may I hope that our Pastoral Planning project will generously take this into account?

25. Building up a committed laity

I need not point out that the programme just described (a self-ministering, self-propagating and self-supporting church) is a very ambitious programme indeed. There will be people who will think that it is an irrealistic one. It is my conviction, however, that there can be no hope for the future of our church unless this programme is seriously implemented.

May I be allowed to go on here and say something of extreme importance to my way of thinking? If we really want to realize what has been described, then there is a condition: *our church must be de-clericalized.* I hope I shall be rightly understood here. What I mean is that the vision of the Church presented here cannot materialize unless we arrive at building up a *Committed Laity.* As you can see, the essential in this plan depends on the involvement of the lay people. And that is just as it should be.

The Church is first of all the Lay People. They are the Church; they are by far the majority. The tonality of Church life and work is determined by the tonality of the lay people's presence in the Church. The hierarchy, the clergy, and even the religious are only a minor group in the Church, and what is more: their *raison d'être* is the service of the larger Church membership. Any plan for the Church has to take the laity into first-place consideration.

26. The double involvement of the laity

From what I said in the foregoing pages, you will rightly conclude that the laity is included in the Church's mission on a double level. Vatican II says:

> Christ's work, while of itself directed to the salvation of men, involves also the renewal of the ‚whole temporal order. Hence the mission of the Church is not only to bring to men the message and grace of Christ, but also to penetrate and perfect the temporal sphere with the spirit of the gospel. In fulfilling this mission of the Church, the laity therefore, exercise their apostolate both in the Church and in the world, in both the spiritual and the temporal orders. These realms, although distinct, are so connected in the one plan of God that He Himself intends in Christ to appropriate the whole universe into a new creation, initially here on earth, fully on the last day. In both orders, the laymen, being simultaneously a believer and a citizen, should be constantly led by the same Christian consciousness. (A.A. no. 5)

The first level is that of *helping the hierarchy or the clergy in those services that are the main responsibility of the clergy:* the task of teaching, sanctifying and organising the Christian Community. As I said, even in these services, the clergy need the collaboration of a large number of lay-people, v.g. Catechists, Church elders, Pious Associations, and other lay helpers in the organization and administration of Church affairs. Without this cooperation of the laity, clergy would find it difficult, not to say impossible, to serve their communities properly.

There is a responsibility in the Church that is special to the layman. Vatican II describes it as "bringing the gospel and holiness to men ... penetrating and perfecting the temporal sphere of things through the spirit of the gospel". It goes on to say: "Since it is proper to the lay man's state in life for him to spend his days in the midst of the world and of secular transactions, he is called by God to burn with the spirit of Christ and to exercise his apostolate in the world as a kind of Leaven". (A.A. no. 2)

I earnestly ask all of you to pay special attention to that point. The Church is there for a mission: to bring about the kingdom of God in the world by helping all men live by the standards of Christ's Gospel. This asks that the Church becomes involved in the world, but involved in a particular way. What I mean is this: There is no hope for the Church to transform the world unless she, in a *way, identifies herself with the world.* The Church ins to be part and parcel of mankind. She can not be *leaven* in the human dough, *light* in the dark world, or *salt* of the earth, if she keeps aloof and uninvolved in the general march of mankind.

But her presence is not that of passive assimilation, but of *prophetic transformation* of the community. While being integrated into the natural community and espousing its aspirations, problems, hopes, joys and sorrows, the Church is called by God to transform the world through the power of God's Word.

This work can be realized only through the apostolate of the committed layman. But the conditions must be such that the layman is in a position to fulfill his role.

27. Strengthening and adapting lay movements

The first pre-requisite is to help the layman to realize this role of his. In all sorts of ways we must let him see that he is the active wing of the church. He must come to see that we take this responsibility of his seriously and expect him to answer the call of God.

It would be no use the layman realizing his responsibility if he did not have at his disposal the instruments to get trained and organized for the work. A wide variety of Lay Movements have sprung up in the Church for this purpose. In our diocese we know of a number of Lay Movements: Legion of Mary, YCW, YCS, Family Movement, etc. Time has come when we should make full use of these movements in order to make it possible for the laity to be active. The clergy (and the religious) are called to cooperate here, just as the laity is called to cooperate in what is the clergy's specific responsibility. The clergy do not run the lay movements, nor do they bear the responsibility in them. But they are called upon to help as advisors, animators, coordinators and supporters. Let the clergy then show full but respectful interest. This will encourage and push the laity.

28. Formation of leaders

You know very well how the Lay Apostolate functions. All members of the Church are expected to be apostles. But the majority witness in a general non-specialized way. The Lay Movement, however, group individuals who volunteer to exercise their apostolate in an organized way, pursuing specific aims, and employing special methods. In those movements the members are given the aid to explicit training, organized control, and group encouragement.

In order that such movements work efficiently they need to be led, animated and controlled by leaders within their own groups. These leaders must be very carefully trained, trained in general leadership and in the leading and animation of their particular movement. The *Lay Movements* are extremely important because they are the *back-bone of lay apostolate.* All efforts put into the training of Lay Movement leaders are well spent.

The results may be slow or they may not be readily visible. But we should be prepared to give of our best in this work. Some may be surprised at the special attention paid to Lay Movements. The reason is easy to understand. Our objectives - and also a major priority in our planning - is the formation of a conscious and committed Laity. *All* our lay people in the Church, even those who do not belong to any specialized Lay movement, must be made conscious of their role and be helped to assume it. But if we want the laity at large to become conscious of their responsibility, the most powerful instrument is first to strengthen the specialized Lay Movements. Why? Because these *Lay Movements serves as leaders of the whole Lay Aposto-late;* they are what we might call the spearhead of the Laity. If you allow me the comparison, they are among the Laity what religious are in the Church. As we said, the religious ideal is basically the same general Christian ideal of perfection. But religious are a group of Christians who are called and given the special charism to pursue in a particular and "professional" way, with a way of life designed to make them visible signs and spearheads of Christian perfection. Their role is a *service* to the whole Church: to pull her and push her towards an ever-growing pursuit of this perfection.

So also the Lay Movements have as ideal the self-same call of the whole Laity. But these organized movements answer that call in a special way: in an organized specialized way, using definite methods and ways of living and working. They are called to stand out among the rest of the laity as a clarion call to their fellow lay people, urging them, each according to his 'or her own situation, to rise up and become involved in the total mission of the Church. They are models and pushers; they serve as a sort of leaven among their fellow laity, to animate, encourage, and direct the total lay involvement in the Church. You see then that if a Church really desires to arouse the laity, the best way is to strengthen the specialized Movements of Lay Apostolate.

29. The formation of basic Christian communities.

As I said, the whole Christian Body is called to live fully the Christian life received at Baptism so that all members are living cells in the Body and not dead branches and dead weight. Secondly, these living members are commissioned by Christ to work in the world as leaven, salt and light of the earth.

The existential conditions of the Church must therefore be such that this double call is rendered possible and easy. Now, the Church is not just a haphazard collection of baptized individuals. If she were that, she could not fully answer the double call. The Church is a community, a Body, and her life and work depend on her living as concrete community involved as such in the total human community.

I said earlier that the Church exists concretely on different levels. But I added that there is a law whereby the functioning of the wider levels is governed by the vitality of the narrower levels of Christian communities. For in everyday life where real living and work take place, people do not live consciously as wide communities, but as cells, basic, manageable social entities, cells whose members can experience constantly a real face-to-face relationship and feel a sense of communal belonging both in living and working. These are what we might call basic communities.

The Church is called to live and work, in the first and essential place, on this basic community level. From the very beginning of her life (cf. the Acts of the Apostles and the Letters of St Paul) the understanding has been that the Church subsists in such basic entities: *the basic local Churches.* We see that the criterion for these communities is not just local or cultural unity, but rather the *grouping of a structured community around the same Eucharistic table,* led and animated by an ordained minister who is in a position to feed the community through the preaching of the Gospel and the celebration of the liturgy, especially the Eucharist, and so to structure it that in its day to day life it can live and work as a conscious entity. It has always been understood that the Church Universal is a fraternal communion of such basic local communities, even if they may be further sub-grouped into ever-wider communities: diocese, province, patriarchate. These wider societies were not meant to be taken as the true basis for every-day life and work, but rather as administrative and supporting devices to help the basic church to live and work harmoniously and efficiently.

Our Church of Lilongwe is a diocese divided into several parishes. But you will all agree that Christian life on the day-to-day level is not lived on a diocesan, nor even on a parish level. It is lived on a narrower level: outstation, sub-parish, or whatever you may wish to call it. It is on this narrower level that the majority of our Christians live and work it is also on this level that they are grouped around the alter, are fed regularly by the Word of God and the celebration of the Liturgy. It is on that same level that they can be structured into a realistic and workable community and be led and animated by the hierarchy.

As you read this, you will realize that our system in the diocese, as practically all the sister dioceses around us, represents a sort of anomaly. We think and work in terms of "parish" and yet nobody is duped. In actual fact, as far as real Christian life is concerned, it is on the sub-parish level that the real thing is going on. Grouped under the rather broad umbrella of parish are several (in most case, quite numerous) basic Churches. These are led really by the resident Church elders, laymen, while the priests do their best to make the presence of the ordained minister felt at longer or shorter intervals. Such a situation is one that cannot be avoided in the state of affairs actually obtaining. What is happening is actually this that several kcal churches, which are entitled to their own resident ordained minister, share a single minister between them. Which makes the presence of this minister in each local Church rather infrequent and transitory. This is the best we can manage in the circumstances. The ideal would of course be that *each real Church has her own minister.* But then what can we do? Would there be any way to make such a situation possible?

30. Again, importance of forming local leaders

The evident thing is to make sure that these local Churches do have the appropriate leadership and organization, capable of adequately structuring them and providing the required leadership and animation. What is needed here is first of all a *good choice of leaders.* The role of the leader (call him *Gurupa* or *Mkulu wa mpingo) is* so decisive that we cannot afford to put just anybody. He has to be a person endowed with basic capacities for leadership, coordination, animation, and service. There surely are many such potential charismatic leaders among our people. We must learn to detect them. The local community, once fully aware of what role is expected from their leader, will often be in a better position to help in such a choice.

But finding capable leaders is not the end of the problem. It would not be fair to appoint a leader and then just leave him to find for himself. He needs to be carefully formed, to be given the know-how, the techniques, the spirituality and the wherewithall needed to fulfill his role properly. We have to *give priority to such a formation of Church leaders.* There is a formal, explicit training given at appropriate institutes. But there is also an on-going, in-service training which can only be given through fraternal collaboration between the clergy and the leaders. In fact, the clergy and the leaders of local Churches in their area form one team of pastoral workers. They must learn to help one another, teach one another, encourage and respect one another. I am confident that this forming of teams of pastoral workers in our parishes will be given all the importance and attention in deserves. On it depends the success of our Churches and consequently the vigour of our diocesan community.

31. Conclusion

Allow me to close this already too long letter. My sincere wish is that the Holy Spirit who animates the Church of Christ will be with us as we humbly examine our work and attitudes. He will supply us with the necessary light to see what Christ wills for his Church today in this part of the world.

May he also give us the courage to submit ourselves faithfully to this will as we implement, with the help of his grace, whatever he will indicated us.

May the grace of Our Lord Jesus Christ be with you all in this year 1973. Be sure that I do not forget you all in my prayers. I am grateful to say that you also do not forget me in yours. God bless you.

Yours ever devotedly in Christ,
+ P.A. Kalilombe

Lilongwe, 1 January 1973

Bibliography

The Documents of Vatican II, especially:

"The Church"; "The Church in the World"; "The Laity"; "The Missions"; "The Religious".
"Parish Council", booklet edited at Lilcuni Press, 1970.
Hastings, A., "Church and Ministry" Gaba pastoral, no. 25.
Hastings, A., *Church and Mission in Modern Africa,* Burns and Oates, 1967.
Hastings, A., *Mission and Ministry,* Sheed and Ward Stagbook, 1971.
Hebblethwaite, P., SJ "Theology of the Church", *Theology Today,* series no. 8, Mercier Press (recommended reading).
Shorter, A. and E. Kataza, "Missionaries to Yourselves", *African Catechists Today,* G. Chapman, 1972.

2 Evangelization and the Holy Spirit

I was a delegate of the Episcopal Conference of Malawi (ECM) to the Synod of Bishops of 1974 in Rome, which had as topic: "Evangelization in the Modern World." On my return from the Synod, I was asked to share my impressions about that meeting and to highlight the ideas that I had found to be particularly important. The following text was part of a talk I gave in Nairobi as a report to fellow bishops from the AMECEA (Association of Member Episcopal Conferences in Eastern Africa) region soon after the Synod. It was later published in AFER (African Ecclesial Review, Eldoret, Kenya). Vol. 18/1, pp. 8-18).

During the 1974 Synod of Bishops in Rome, which had as topic: "Evangelization in the Modern World", one of the most remarkable truths that seem to have been impressed on the Synod members was that Evangelization is first of all God's own work and not a merely human enterprise. This may sound commonplace; but the fact is that those who undertake to preach the Gospel anywhere are prone to pay mere lip service to this truth and then just carry on as if preaching were their own affair.

They often forget that those who go out to meet their brothers and sisters in order to proclaim to them the Good News of Jesus Christ are not treading on virgin soil. They are not going to offer something that is totally novel to their audience. On the contrary, the Spirit of God has preceded them, because God's Spirit has always been in dialogue with and at work among all peoples of the world: individuals and societies, cultures and ages. From the very beginning of humanity God has been present everywhere, and has been at work. For, as the Scriptures say: "The Spirit of the Lord, indeed, fills the whole world, and that which holds all things together knows every word that is said." (Wisdom 1:7)

Indeed, God is present in all humanity: He is at work seconding people's humble efforts in the struggle against sin and death. His rresence, his activity, is very real, even if it is sometimes veiled and anonymous. In every human effort to do good, to avoid evil, to conquer death in all its manifestations, God is mysteriously present and active. He inspires people's minds and strengthens their hearts so that they may be filled with "everything that is true, everything that is noble, everything that is good and pure, everything that we love and honour, and everything that can be thought virtuous or worthy of praise" (Phil. 4:8). This mysterious presence and activity of God in the world is what the Scriptures call God's Holy Spirit. Wherever human beings are to be found, in all cultures and ages, this Holy Spirit is present. He is speaking to them, inviting them to seek the truth and find it, in spite of the darkness of sin and error that overshadows the world.

Evangelization and Contemplation

By insisting on the role of the Holy Spirit in evangelization, the Synod Fathers wanted to recall this mysterious but real presence that slowly leads humanity towards salvation, towards the coming of His Kingdom. They also wanted to say that when the Church goes out to proclaim the Good News to people today, it must realize that it is going to meet this Holy Spirit already mysteriously present in those people whom it intends to evangelize. The Church must, therefore, come with awe and respect for the work that the Spirit has already been accomplishing, and with respect for the ways and methods that the Spirit has been using in this salvation dialogue. For the Church's role in evangelization is not to "abolish the Law or the Prophets, but to complete them" (cf. Mt. 5:17).

Contemplation is vital

Evangelization demands first of all contemplation or a prayerful observation of the presence and activity of the invisible God among the people that have to be evangelized. Whoever would proclaim the Good News must first stop reverently in prayer and open their eyes of faith to discover the presence of the Spirit among the people, and open their ears of faith to capture the mysterious dialogue that is already going on between the Spirit and those to be evangelized, whether individuals, societies or cultures. *Without this contemplation, the evangelizers run the risk of ignoring the presence of God.* And this can be fatal, because they may be tempted to start something not in line with the action of the Spirit. They may want to break what the Spirit had preserved and on which He had been building his saving activity. They may try to build a new structure on a foundation other than the one put by God. Or they may want to keep and preserve what God has been trying to break down and replace. Thus they would run the risk of introducing a totally new "language" of their own, instead of using the idiom that the Spirit has been employing all along. In this way the message they bring will sound inauthentic, hollow, irrelevant, disrespectful. It will be mere human talk and will lack the power of the Spirit. No wonder, then, if the people ignore their preaching. What right have mere mortals to impose their ideas and viewpoints on others with a pretense of sacred authority?

Listening and Observing

In fact only a contemplative can effectively evangelize. Contemplation means the power and ability to "see the Invisible" behind the events and realities of the world, and the capacity to be affected by this Invisible and to enter into a meaningful dialogue with God as revealing himself in these events and realities. *Prayer* is the exercise of this contemplation. *People of prayer are those who move easily in this inner world; who have the habit of God's presence everywhere, and are accustomed, in their ways of thinking, acting, and reacting, in their likes and dislikes, to being guided and influenced by this presence of the Invisible.* Such people have the inner eyes and ears that are capable of "seeing" God at work in the world and discerning his voice in the events and realities of every day. Since through the exercise of prayer they are used to listening to God and to answering Him, when they speak to their brothers and sisters, it is not mere human talk inspired by human motives and methods. But it is a discourse that bears the imprint of this dialogue with God; and so their audience succeeds in hearing God's Word through their poor human words.

Listening to the Spirit

At the Synod, much was said about this need for the evangelizers to first "listen" and "observe" before they venture to preach the Gospel of Christ. They have first to listen to what the Spirit is already trying to say, and observe what he is trying to accomplish, and how. They will thus acquaint themselves with the dialogue of Salvation that is already going on. This dialogue results from God's constant call to salvation made to humankind (individuals and societies), and their response to this call: a response which is always partly "Yes" and partly "No", and never totally "Yes" or totally "No". For there is an on-going struggle in human beings: both societies and cultures, and in the individual; a fight between Good and Evil, Light and Darkness, Life and Death, Grace and Sin.

Sin means human resistance to God's call, and it is expressed in attitudes and actions that are opposed to God's plan of Love, his building of the Kingdom. Such are attitudes and actions of hatred, injustice, oppression, greed, materialism, egoism, etc. Wherever these are found, people are saying "no" to God and to His Kingdom, even if they do not know explicitly that this is so. The hidden Spirit of God is constantly trying to break this opposition by inspiring and promoting good thoughts and intentions, and seconding people's efforts to do good.

For, in spite of sin, human beings are still basically open to God: they can and do say "yes" to grace. And so in every person, in every society and culture, there is to be found an amount of good, the traces of God's success in the dialogue of salvation.

The evangelizers should indeed be deeply aware of human sinful resistance to God. They must take full account of it since their role is to second the Spirit in breaking this resistance and making way for grace. But they must also discover those "seeds of the word" (the "semina Verbi" of the early Fathers), since their role is also to offer themselves humbly to the Spirit as his instruments in promoting and bringing to full maturity these seeds. The Church is called upon to bring the Gospel of Christ and thereby explicate **or** give the Christian name to the often inarticulate and groping efforts of humanity in answering God's call.

And then the Gospel brings to its full expression and destiny the good that the Spirit had already started to accomplish.

Evangelization is First of All "Continuity" with the Spirit's Work

This is what was meant by many Synod Fathers when they insisted that evangelization works "in continuity" with what the Holy Spirit has been doing among people. In this connection a plea was made to the evangelizing Church to develop a sincere respect for all the religious expressions of humankind: the great world non-Christian religions which have moulded the civilizations and cultures of many peoples for ages and continue to do so: Hinduism, Buddhism, Judaism, Islam, etc. The same respect is due also to all those religious expressions of less known cultures and peoples which in the past tended to be globally dismissed as paganism, idolatry, animism, and what have you, - like our own traditional religions of Africa. These too deserve an equal respect, because in them also are to be found authentic traces of the Spirit's salvific action over the ages.

Even the contemporary attitudes which strike us mostly by their negative aspects: materialism, secularization, atheism, negation of what we call the traditional Christian values (e.g. in the attitudes of modern youth and the working class), de-christianization, etc., - even in these, the evangelizer must first listen and observe so as to discover behind the negative expressions the positive and good values that are being sought by contemporary men and women. For no human attitude or action can be totally dark and evil, "there is always the silver lining". This too is the work of the Spirit; and the evangelizers must first take full note of it and give it due respect. This will enable them to work in continuity with the Spirit when they set out to preach the Gospel. They will start from the good that is being expressed and pursued. And that, not just as a clever tactic, but as a sincere respect for God's action, and respect for God's pedagogy in dealing with his children.

Evangelization is Also a "Break" with Human Sin

Many Episcopal Conferences had asked that the Synod explicitly deal with the theme of "Conversion" in evangelization. The preaching of the Gospel represents God's judgment on human sin and resistance. It is true that human beings are open to grace; but it is equally true that sin reigns over them. In each individual as well as in all societies and ages the traces of Original Sin are apparent. In all people there is sin. The preached Word of God comes to unmask this sin, expose it, and deal with it, for in so far and as long as sin reigns in the world, God's Kingdom cannot flourish. In all peoples God's Spirit has been always at war against evil. He has been at work inspiring individuals and groups with a realization of the evil at work in their lives: those attitudes, ways of thinking and acting, institutions and customs, that oppose the flourishing of good. In spite of evil we can discover everywhere, in the conscience (individual and collective) of human beings, real efforts towards "conversion" or the breaking of evil. These efforts may not be very evident or strikingly successful, still they are there: the result of the ever-present and active Spirit.

Penetance ceremony – „Lord have mercy on us"

God Sees Everything

The evangelizers come to put themselves at the disposal of the Spirit in order to further his work of converting people from evil and leading them towards good, to promote a change of heart in them. The Gospel Word, representing the decisive power of Christ in his Paschal Mystery, becomes for them *"something alive and active: it cuts like any double-edged sword but more fmely: it can slip through the place where the soul is divided from the spirit, or joints from the marrow; it can judge the secret thoughts. No created thing can hide from God: everything is uncovered and open to the eyes of the One to whom we must give account of ourselves"* (Heb. 4:13). Evangelization brings to the world: to all societies and cultures, God's judgment which sifts the good from the evil, and condemns the evil and offers ways of destroying it. The evangelizers are not naive optimists who just accept or recommend people's lives wholesale. They know that in all of humanity, all cultures and societies, there is need for conversion. The Synod Fathers insisted on conversion, not only for the non-Christian world but also, and first of all, for the Church itself. "Conversion, or metanoia, is the primary purpose of the preaching of the Gospel, and permanent condition and duty of the pilgrim Church".[1]

The Spirit's Pedagogy of Salvation

If we really believe in the presence of the Spirit in the whole world and take his activity seriously, we are bound to respect also his pedagogy. We must learn to watch the way he is working in the world. His ways may be incomprehensible and rather different from what we human beings may think is ideal. For "the wind blows wherever it pleases; you hear its sound, but you cannot tell where it comes from or where it is going" (Jn. 3:8). But it is we who have to bend to the Spirit's ways and methods: it is worthless to want to do things our own way or follow our wishful thinking. The reality of God's activity is the only valid basis for evangelization.

---

[1] Official list of the Main Questions discussed in the 1974 Synod of Bishops, 2, e.

Non-Christian Religions and People of Good Will

The first reality to consider is the presence in the world of non-Christian religions. We have already seen that through these too the Spirit is at work building God's Kingdom. It is important to realize that the Christian Church, as a historical and tangible reality, is of very recent origin when compared with the whole span of human history. Before the advent of this historical Church many religious systems and practices had been at the disposal of humankind. And even after the coming of the Church, in many parts of the world such non-Christian religious expressions have continued to function. For the vast majority these religions are the only available and practically relevant ways of relations with God.

Even after centuries of Christian evangelization a large section of humankind does not have the Gospel realistically available to them. We know that even in the territories where the Gospel has been or is being preached, many people do not manage to be affected by this preaching up to the point of explicitly accepting Christ - and this, often through no culpable fault of theirs. Often it is simply due to historical, social, cultural or geographical factors that are none of their making.

As regards all these peoples, what does Evangelization mean?

Are they necessarily to be excluded from its scope? In some cases explicit or patently Christian evangelization is out of the question for them, because such a preaching is either impossible or counter-productive (e.g. where prejudice, fanaticism, or ignorance is such that Christianity is invincibly seen as an evil). In those cases, can we still speak of the possibility of real evangelization?

Use the Spirit's Method

Happily, there was at the Synod a group of Fathers who were familiar with such situations, e.g. those living in predominantly Muslim areas or in atheistic totalitarian states. Their reflections were a great help. In the words of one of them (Cardinal Duval of Algiers, North Africa), the evangelizers in such territories should model their action on the Spirit's method. Thus in the work of the evangelizing Church what has to be given priority is charity. This charity means the gratuitous love of the other, a love that is not feigned but sincere; a love that is not conditional or interested, e.g. just in view of winning adherents; but a love that is like that of God "our Father in heaven, who causes his sun to rise on the bad as well as on the good, and his rain to fall on honest and dishonest people alike" (Mt. 5:45). This is how the Spirit works. This charity will inspire the evangelizers with *a sincere and scrupulous respect* for these people, their way of life and their religious convictions. For although these convictions are not fully in line with the Gospel of Christ, still they are the results of the progressive work of the Spirit. The evangelizers must also scrupulously *respect the freedom of conscience* of these people. There must be no vulgar proselytism or pressure, or the using of unfair means and methods to force adherence to the Church, e.g. through education or health services given only in view of attracting "converts". On the contrary, they must respect the Spirit at work in them and the rhythm he is following. This demands a great sense of "discernment of spirits" which helps to discover the good that is already there and also the resistance to the Spirit.

Dialogue

The appropriate method of evangelization here is *dialogue.* By dialogue we mean a *sincere joint searching for the will of God* with the other partner. We do not impose prematurely our ideas (even if they are Gospel ones) before we are sure that the Spirit has led our partners up to the point where they can see these ideas and accept them from a real interior conviction. Dialogue means also being open to learn from the others, remembering that, even if we bear the Gospel of Christ, we do not possess the monopoly of the Spirit. He also speaks in the others, and there can be instances when the Spirit will be talking in and through the others rather than in and through us. On both sides we must be ever open to listen to the Spirit with humility and submission, for the point is not our winning the other over to *our* point of view at all cost, but all of us together finding what the Spirit wants in the circumstances, and then following that with our whole heart. We do not wish to anticipate the work of the Spirit, or try to force him to what we ourselves want, but to respect the rhythm of progress of the Spirit. "In other words, the only thing that counts is not what human beings want to try to do, but the mercy of God" (Rom. 9:16).

The Gospel urges us to go and meet non-Christians

We should not be surprised or scandalized to see that the progress is too slow for our liking. We might find out that God's plan is that these people will not come to the explicit acceptance of the full Gospel, or even that the open preaching of the Gospel will be impossible. This should neither surprise nor discourage us. For it does not mean that God does not want us to evangelize. It only means that he is forcing us to use another method. This method is that of dialogue, whereby we join our non-Christian interlocutors in a sincere search for the good that God is trying to promote and in the work of finding the appropriate means of achieving it. At the same time we jointly discover and acknowledge the obstacles that human sin is putting up against this good, and work together to find ways of destroying these obstacles.

In this work, we who are Christians will be guided and inspired by the Gospel of Christ, but applied to meet the concrete situations. And thus, even if we may not be able to say explicitly that we are preaching the Gospel, our contribution to that dialogue of salvation will be an authentic preaching of the Gospel. The end result will perhaps not be that our interlocutors will become explicit Christians, but they will have been exposed to the evangelical values, and they will be influenced by them. Their life will have been transformed by these values and this will mean that our dialogue has resulted in some progress towards the coming of God's Kingdom. After all, this is what evangelization is for. Pope John XXIII loved to speak about "collaborating with all people of goodwill" to build a better world. This is exactly what such a method of evangelizing does, and it is real evangelization.

In many parts of Africa, where Islam or traditional religions are in power, this method of evangelization is the only possible one. The Church should learn to use it, not as an admission of failure to do the "real thing", but as fidelity to the rhythm and method of the Spirit himself.

Evangelization and Ecumenism

Another reality that has to be faced by the evangelizing Church in Africa is the existence on the scene of our evangelization of many other non-Catholic Christian Churches and communities. They too are sincerely seeking to proclaim Christ's good news of salvation. They do it in a different way from ours since we have different religious beliefs and practices. It is evident that this situation is not the ideal because Christ's will was that all his disciples should be one so that the world would believe that the Father had sent him (Jn. 17:21). It is through the believers' own sin that divisions have arisen and continue to exist. We would all like Christian unity to be re-established, and we must indeed do our utmost to make this come about. And yet, here too, we have to remember that the work is not of us human beings, but God's own.

Human beings are all too capable of creating divisions, but only God can gather again in unity his scattered children. While doing our best to heal these divisions we must nevertheless learn to be humbly patient and leave to God the determination of the exact time and modalities of this healing. We can rest assured that He is at work doing this even if we are not always clear as to how exactly. The important thing is that we become resigned to God's own time and ways and not attempt to create an artificial unity of our own, for this will be to no avail.

Why are there differences?

Meantime we have to accept the fact that in the field of our evangelization fellow Christians are also active. Let us remember that their presence cannot be attributed simply to their bad will, for most of them are people of upright and sincere convictions, just as we ourselves try to be. Moreover the fact that such people have accepted this or that Christian Church is not really the result of their free choice; it is often the result of circumstances of history, culture, or geography which are not of our making. It is therefore correct to admit that this too is a sign of God's will and plan. So, rather than just sit back and pine away in useless regrets, we had better pray to understand better God's intentions and plans in this reality. For it is both a challenge and a programme.

Let us remember first that God's Spirit is really at work in and through our fellow Christian Churches. Just as in our own Church God is at work and we human beings partly collaborate with him and partly resist his will, so also among them. Through them God is trying to build His Kingdom in the world. We must therefore learn to, respect them sincerely. Just as for the non-Christian religions, there must be a true respect of their freedom of conscience. If God is calling them to join us in our Church, He will surely give them the possibility to do so. But let it be through his own ways and not through the sinful methods of us poor human beings. For if God's will is that they will remain where they are, who are we to question His intentions or to ask Him: Why are you doing that? If He wants to do His work through them too, what right have we to feel bad about it? We would do better just to fmd out what He wants us to do about this situation.

Collaboration with sincerity

God's will is surely that if He wants them to join us we do our best to facilitate that. But also, if He does not want this, He surely wants that in our work of evangelization we should collaborate with them in a sincere and fraternal way. The method of collaboration is, as for the non-Christian religions, that of a sincere and respectful dialogue. We should all learn to seek together the will of God for the areas of our joint evangelization. In doing this, we shall find out that there are points of difference among us. Here we must learn to respect one another in those differences even as we frankly work to iron them out.

In this laborious work we should not be impatient and want to make shortcuts in the programme of God, nor should we allow ourselves to resort to sinful methods like hatred, ridicule, heated discussions, slander and calumny, unfair and divisive competition or methods of counter-proselytism that are inspired by mere human motives. Many people think of "Ecumenism" as aimed at drawing members of other

Churches to our own Church at any cost. This is a wrong understanding of ecumenism. Ecumenism is a sincere and fraternal joint effort to find God's full purpose and humbly to try to accomplish it.

We shall also find that there are many points, and basic ones, on which we all agree. True ecumenism means to make sincere efforts to establish fraternal collaboration on such points. Since we are all committed to the building up of God's Kingdom, there are yet possibilities of doing this together in true love and fraternity. In an area where different Christian bodies coexist, there is surely a challenge and a call from God to reflect and pool forces together so that the joint evangelization can result in progress for the Kingdom. We in Africa must learn to base our coexistence on the acceptance of brotherly love. This will inspire us with new and daring insights into methods of joint evangelization while we wait for God's own time of gathering us again in one sheepfold.

Conclusion

The theme of "Evangelization and the Action of the Holy Spirit" which was part of the Synod's deliberations on Evangelization in the Modern World, was a theme that is of basic importance for the Church in Africa. The implications of this theme have a very practical incidence on the work of evangelization in the context of the realities obtaining in most of our territories.

At the Synod itself all these implications could not be given all the importance they deserve, not only because of lack of time, but also because other themes on evangelization had to be dealt with which were of importance for the Church in other continents. But if the Synod will mean anything for the African Church, it is a duty for us in Africa to take time to examine these implications carefully. Our theologians will want to take up the different doctrinal ramifications of the theme and make them the object of solid reflection in the light of Revelation. This study will form the basis for concrete pastoral orientations which will have to be formulated by the leaders of our Churches in Africa.

3 The African Local Churches and the World-wide Roman Catholic Communion:

Modification of Relationships, as Exemplified by Lilongwe Diocese

The following is the text of paper which I presented at a conference in 1975 held at Jos, Nigeria. The theme of the Conference was: "Christianity in Independent Africa". Delegates to that meeting came mostly from various parts of Africa, and others from Europe, to share the results of their research and reflection on significant developments in the Christian presence and ministiy (Protestant, Catholic, as well as African Independent), especially since the 1960s when many nations in Africa became independent. This article was one of the contributions which were later published as a report of the Conference, in Christianity in Independent Africa, E. Fashole-Luke and R. Gray (eds.), London: Rex Collings, 1978, and is found on pp. 79-95.

The *Report on the Experiences of the Church in the Work of Evangelization in Africa,* prepared by Bishop J. Sangu for presentation at the 1974 Synod of Bishops in Rome, had this to say:

> One of the most important developments in Africa in the last 20 years has been the process of de-colonization. Between 1957 and 1969 no less than 42 countries became independent from colonial rule.
> A parallel development has taken place in the Church. Formerly the missions were entrusted to Missionary Institutes which received from the Sacred Congregation for the Evangelization of Peoples the *jus commissionis'*. During the last 20 years most of the missions have become dioceses and the hierarchy has been established bringing to an end the *jus commissionis'*. The mis-

sions have become local Churches, although they still remain 'under' the Sacred Congregation for the Evangelization of Peoples.

This 'coming-of-age' of the Churches signifies a turning point in the history of the Church in Africa. It is the end of the missionary period. This does not mean the end of evangelization, even first evangelization. But it means, in the words of Pope Paul VI during his visit to Uganda: 'You Africans must become missionaries to yourselves'. In other words, the remaining task of evangelization of Africa is primarily the responsibility of the African Church itself.

This fact implies a radically changed relationship between the Church in Africa and the Sacred Congregation of the Evangelization of Peoples, the Missionary Institutes, and the other Churches in Europe and North America.[1]

One cannot but agree with this assessment of the situation concerning relationships between the world-wide communion of the Roman Catholic Church and the local churches now developing in Africa. The statement is seen to be all the more weighty when we realize that the Africa Report was prepared from a fairly large and representative number of national reports from episcopal conferences all over Africa. It is therefore a summing up of a definite feeling which is gaining ground in Africa, and thus deserves careful study.

In this paper I propose to begin by examining the situation of Lilongwe Diocese as it was towards the end of 1972, the year that a first African (Malawian) bishop was ordained for the diocese. This is in the hope that the exposition can serve as a 'case study' of the relationship between a developing local church in Africa and the world Catholic communion.

---

[1] *Report on the Experiences of the Church in the Work of Evangelization in Africa,* The African Continent's report for the 1974 Synod of Bishops on 'The Evangelization of the Modern World', pp. 15-16. A mimeographed text distributed to the Bishops from Africa, delegates to the Bishops' Synod. Henceforth referred to as 'Africa Report'.

Admittedly conditions vary in the different countries and dioceses of Africa.

But it can validly be assumed that the case of Lilongwe is to some extent typical of a large number of 'local churches' on the continent. Secondly, I wish to draw some conclusions from this case study, and situate these conclusions on the wider plane of Pan-African Catholic consciousness as evidenced by what has gone on in meetings of African Catholic church leaders in recent years.

The Diocese of Lilongwe

Lilongwe Diocese, which today comprises most of Malawi's Central Region, is one of the seven ecclesiastical territories of the country. It was raised to the status of a diocese in 1959, and Bishop J. Fady, WF, became its first titular bishop. From the very start this territory was entrusted to the White Fathers, and they have been the majority among the pastoral workers ever since. It was to their society that Rome had granted the *jus com-missionis'* for the territory, a sort of 'charter' putting on the society the exclusive responsibility of building up the church there and administering it. But, when the hierarchy was established in the country, other missionary groups could join the diocese. On 10 December 1963 a group of Carmelite Fathers from Spain arrived in the diocese and have been taking part in the mission work until now. There are also a couple of expatriate secular priests, who together with the local diocesan priests complete the number of clergy in the diocese.

There are several women's religious congregations working in the diocese. The earliest were the White Sisters (Sisters of Our Lady of Africa). They were later joined by the Sisters of Charity of Ottawa (Grey Nuns), and then the Carmelite Sisters of Luxembourg and of Spain. A local congregation, the Teresian Sisters, had been started in the 1930s. They now form the majority of the local religious, although the Grey Nuns and the Luxembourg Carmelites have also local recruits among themselves. In recent years the contemplative Poor Clares started a monastery in Lilongwe. They have been highly successful in finding local vocations who are now by far the majority among them. As for men religious, there are a number of Marist Brothers who are mostly engaged in education work in post-primary institutions. All these religious, except the Poor Clares, are in fact engaged mostly in education, health, and social services. But a certain number among them are full-time pastoral workers in the parishes.

When I was ordained Bishop of Lilongwe in August 1972 and succeeded Bishop Fady, the situation of the diocese was something like this: the total population of the area was 1,400,000 (Malawi's population was estimated at about 5,000,000); the number of baptized Catholics stood at 189,000, while that of catechumens was 50,900.

The diocese consisted of 16 parishes and one quasi-parish which were served by an average of 3 priests per parish. Each parish is normally subdivided into outstations and smaller prayer-churches. These are served by trained and non-trained catechists and a large number of lay church elders. It was estimated that the number of remunerated or full-time catechists was 87, while that of non-remunerated (voluntary and often only part-time) catechists was 268.[2]

The Church was managing three secondary schools, one teacher training college, and one nursing school, plus a number of domestic science centres. In all these a number of brothers and sisters were engaged in the name of the diocese, because, although these schools are state-aided, the Church is responsible for their management. The same is true of the three main hospitals and the other smaller dispensaries and health centres which the religious congregations run in the name of the Church, even if the government offers substantial aid in the way of salaries, equipment and personnel. There was also a large number of primary schools which fall under the management of the diocese. In actual fact, however, the Church's burden for these, both personnel-wise and finance-wise, is very limited in that the government is almost fully responsible for them.

---

[2] Details and statistics taken from the Diocesan Archives and from texts prepared for the Lilongwe Diocesan Mini-Synod (1973-1975). The statistics are valid for the year 1972.

There can be no doubt that the running of the whole diocesan machinery calls for a large number of qualified and full-time church personel. The system is such that the parishes could not function properly without an adequate supply of priests and religious. The schools and health services need a team of highly qualified church personnel working in the name and under the responsibility of the Church if the diocese is to continue its management of these specialized services. In 1972 the total number of priests in the diocese was 76: 51 White Fathers, 13 Carmelite Fathers, 2 expatriate secular priests, and 10 diocesan (Malawian) priests. Not all these were actually or actively involved in parish work. Only 44 priests were in active service in the 16 parishes. Three other priests were professors at the interdiocesan major seminary; two others were teaching at the minor seminary, two were taking care of the language centre, and one priest was full-time chaplain for sisters. Two other priests were engaged in mass media work (printing and journal), one priest was full-time chaplain for secondary schools, and two priests were in administration work for their congregation. Moreover, at that time 16 were on home leave, and two were studying overseas. It may be of interest to note that of these 76 priests, 15 were over 60 years of age, 14 between 50 and 60 years, 17 between 40 and 50, and only 30 were under 40 years of age. It could be said, therefore, that the majority were of an advanced age. This is not an idle remark when it is realized that already at that time the crisis in priestly vocations in the 'feeding' missionary congregations was very acute. It was to be foreseen that when, for any reason, one or the other of these missionary priests were to leave or to retire, they would be very difficult to replace. As for the local priests the prospects were that we had 16 students on the 6-year course at the major seminary. The most we could optimistically hope for, then, was that we might have 16 more priests in the coming 6 years.

Religious Brothers were 20: 9 Marist Brothers engaged in education work, and 9 White Father Brothers and 2 Carmelite Brothers working as auxiliaries especially in 'material' work. Religious Sisters were far more numerous, a total of 132: 45 Teresian Sisters, 30 Sisters of Our Lady of Africa, 24 Sisters of Charity of Ottawa (about 10 of whom were African), 11 Luxembourg Carmelite Sisters (4 of them Malawians), 4 Spanish

Carmelites, and 18 contemplative Poor Clares (12 of them Malawians). Since most of these religious were working in schools and hospitals, as far as strictly parish work is concerned, their number is in itself immaterial, since only a handful are full-time pastoral workers.[3] And yet this large number is cru-cial as far as the diocese itself is concerned. On these religious falls the heavy commitment of the church in the network of schools and health services which are highly complex and expensive.

I was evidently interested in the fmances of the diocese. I thought I should have an idea what was needed to keep such a complicated thing as the diocese going every year. What could possibly be the annual budget? How much money was needed annually, and for what? Where did the money come from? What were the prospects of such money being forthcoming every year? For a new bishop, on whose inexperienced shoulders the burden of the local church was falling, these questions were vital.

A look at the diocesan treasurer's statement for 1971 made me tremble. It was little consolation to learn that the fmancial year ended happily with a credit balance of 1,297 Kwacha (K). The receipts for the year, plus the credit balance left over from 1970, had amounted to K96,650. But the expenses were K95,353.[4] These expenses were analyzed to include: budgets for the parish (priests') communities (to the tune of K23,517!); travel (home leaves for missionaries, and journeys within the country); expenses on seminarists (a total of K6,416), and expenses for studies for priests; salaries for catechists, pensions, taxes, rents, insurances; constructions and repairs of houses and churches; salaries and pocket-money for lay missionaries, some brothers and some priests; administration, etc.

This was an eye-opener as to what the diocese needs money for. I could see that the schools and hospitals did not figure on the diocesan budget. It was explained that this was because these institutions were expected to be self-supporting in the sense that they depended on

---

[3] This was the situation in 1972. In most cases the numbers have subsequently tended to diminish rather than increase.

[4] Details taken from the Diocesan Treasurer's office: statement for 1971 and budget for 1972.

government aid, fees, and gifts which it was the responsibility of those who run the institutions to find on their own initiative. The religious were also largely excluded because each congregation is supposed to take care of its own houses and members with the aid of salaries received, help from motherhouses overseas, or from benefactors. If this was cause for relief, I could not but wonder what the diocesan expenses would amount to if this burden was some day to be thrown on the diocese also.

It was more interesting, and revealing, to examine the analysis of the receipts. As was to be expected, help coming from 'Rome' (Pontifical allocations: Propagation of the Faith, St Peter Apostle, Holy Childhood, etc.) was preponderant: K 35,768 or more than a third of the whole receipts. Another important heading was: 'Gifts from Christians abroad': K 12,209. Other sources of income included gifts from the WF Mother House and grants from government (salaries).

What was of special interest for me, however, was what we may call local resources. One item was listed as 'Local Farming and Industry', things like the printing press, mills, farms, etc. owned by the diocese. That this amounted to some K 7,440 is a proof of serious efforts towards self-support. But here the initiative comes froth the institution itself. What was more revealing was what the local Christians had contributed by way of church tithes.

Apparently tithes for 1970 (4 parishes) and 1971 (10 parishes) plus an extraordinary collection, had given the sum of K14,753. Other church collections (again for 1970: 3 parishes, and 1971: 10 parishes) came to K1,635. This total of K16,388 for the year 1971 and part of 1970 is really not impressive when compared with the whole receipts: K96,650. I was left wondering how 189,000 baptized members and 50,900 catechumens could only manage to contribute this sum over the whole year. The conclusion was obvious: the diocese was not running with local resources but almost exclusively with 'charity' from abroad.

A Dependent Church

This situation of a 'local church' running with the help of other churches was, after all, not such an extraordinary one, nor was Lilongwe an exception in this regard. The church in Malawi and indeed in most 'mission lands' came into being when missionaries from abroad were sent to evangelize the territory. Understandably these missionaries had to start from scratch: to preach the Gospel to people who had not yet heard it, to set up structures for church life and mission in the area, to formulate policies for so doing, and fmd ways and means of realizing those missionary policies.

The only personnel they could initially count on was that coming from other sister churches which had already attained a consistency and vitality strong enough not only to take care of themselves but also to send missionaries abroad to set up the church in other lands. Only later on were they in a position to find and train indigenous church workers and involve them in the task of building up the local church. And indeed it is to the credit of the early missionaries that from the very start they realized that it was their urgent responsibility to train local church workers and thus set the foundations for a truly local church. We see that practically from the start they formed lay teachers and catechists as auxiliaries in their evangelical work, and soon afterwards built seminaries for the training of local priests and houses of formation for local religious.

In the same way the resources needed for the work of the church had initially to be obtained from abroad, precisely through the initiative of those same missionaries who knew how and where to find the needed aid. Thanks to this external help the work of evangelization was made possible and the structures of the local church could slowly take shape. Admittedly the missionaries realized that as the local church emerged, this church should be taught to make more efforts to find its own resources. There is no denying the fact that serious efforts in this respect have been made over the years.

And yet looking at the facts in 1972 one had to admit that the Church of Lilongwe was still basically a dependent church - and this after more than 70 years of missionary work in the area. As the statistics show, out of the 76 priests who kept the diocesan structure running, only 10 were Malawians, and a full 66 expatriates. Of the 20 religious Brothers, only one was Malawian and the rest expatriates. The situation for the Sisters may look much better since of the total number of 132, 71 were local. But we must not forget that the 61 expatriates were among those charged with the most complicated and expensive concerns of the diocese: post-primary schools, major hospitals, and basic administration organizations. And as for resources there is no comparison between the K16,388 contributed by the local people and the K80,262 which had to be obtained from abroad. In both personnel and resources therefore Lilongwe Diocese was running almost completely on external aid.

I was led to ask myself: Suppose tomorrow all the expatriate church personnel were to leave this diocese, would we be able to run the church as it is with only 10 local priests, 1 brother, and the 71 local sisters? And suppose all external aid were stopped, could we make do with only K 16,388 where K 96,650 are actually needed? These are evidently rhetorical questions. You could not possibly hope that in such an eventuality the diocese could. continue in its present state or be able to achieve what it was achieving then - and in the same way. The diocese could carry on only on condition that there was a continuing help from abroad in both personnel and resources. But for how long could we expect to receive such help? Already it was clear that the missionary congregations on which our hopes were founded were suffering from a dramatic drop in priestly and religious vocations, so much so that it was vain to expect reinforcements from that quarter. And as for overseas financial help, it was becoming more and more difficult to get, because in most of the former benefactor churches the attitude towards 'Missions' and 'Missionaries' was definitely becoming cool, not to say downright negative. But even had the prospects been brighter in those respects, that would not have been sufficient reason for unqualified optimism.

In 1972 there were other reasons for second thoughts. In various parts of Africa (e.g. Guinea, Eastern Nigeria, Uganda, parts of Mozambique, the Sudan - just to mention some outstanding instances) events had demonstrated that the continuing presence of expatriate missionaries could not be lightly taken for granted. What was happening in those parts of Africa could very well happen elsewhere. For, after all, those events were symptomatic of a growing sense of dissatisfaction spreading widely in Africa. At this time, when most of the countries that formerly were colonies have achieved their political independence and are hard at work to consolidate this independence in all other aspects of national life, is it not anomalous that the local churches alone should continue to depend for their very existence on the charity of sister churches abroad?

Relationships of Dependence

The quotation from the Africa Report which was given at the beginning of this paper suggests that in the recent developments of African history there is a parallelism between what has taken place in the political field and what has happened in the church. Such a parallelism has often *been* decried as inexact and confusing on the ground that colonialism and the missionary movement are really two very different phenomena. To some extent this is true: it is not legitimate to assimilate purely and simply these two movements because the basic aims and motivations of colonialism were different from those of evangelization. But there is no denying the fact that in the minds of many people mission work has tended to be thought of in similar terms as the colonial enterprise. It has been fashionable to say that the Cross of Evangelization prepared the way for the Sword of Colonialism. But let us be fair. It is perhaps not exact to say that everywhere missionary activity preceded or came in the wake of colonial expansion, or to say that the church was necessarily in collusion with colonial powers. There are many instances where this was certainly not the case. And it is a pity that today, in retrospect, people tend to make unfavourable generalizations about the church being the instrument of colonialism.

Nevertheless, it is to be admitted that missionary activity has been influenced for quite some time by the colonial reality. In any case, in the mind of the people the two movements, coming as they did at about the same time, were bound to be construed as two versions of one and the same type of human encounters, in which a foreign way of life came to invade the local one with the definite intent of modifying the latter.

The assumption was that the local way of life was going to profit by being thus influenced and modified by the foreign one, which comes down to saying that the foreign way of life was superior and better. In the case of colonialism the assumption was that Western civilization was better and should come to improve the more backward and primitive local cultures. As for the church, the superiority came from the fact that she was the bearer of the Gospel of Christ, which was God's fmal answer to man's inazticulate and erring gropings. Since the missionary happened to belong to the same Western civilization, he naturally tended to assume that the Western interpretation of Christ's Gospel was the right and standard one. Western culture and the Christian message could thus be in danger of being identified.

It is perhaps salutary to examine briefly what the exact relationship has been between the developing local churches and the world-wide Catholic communion through the Congregation for the Evangelization of the Peoples (formerly *Propaganda Fide),* the Missionary Institutes and the older churches of Europe and America.

Prior to the 1960s most territories in Africa belonged to what were called 'mission lands'. This means that the work of evangelization there, and the task of setting up and running the church was the responsibility of overseas churches, mostly through the missionary organizations. The Roman Congregation of *Propaganda Fide* was fmally responsible for this missionary activity. It was the department charged, in the name of the Pope and the Universal Church, with the task of organizing these activities all over the world. These mission areas were called Vicariates or Prefectures Apostolic. In other words, they were not dioceses on their own, they were not yet really local churches but dependent churches. In principle it was the Supreme Pontiff himself who was Bishop of these ecclesiastical territories. The bishops or ecclesiastical heads who actually administered them did so in his name and under his direct responsibility through *Propaganda Fide,* which called upon one or other missionary organization to take on the responsibility of evangelizing the territory.

It is important to point out that both the congregation and the missionary institutes working under its supreme authority and direction are the concrete expression of the universal Catholic Church's co-responsibility in the accomplishment of her God-given mission. It is the whole church that is charged by the Divine Missionary with the task of "going out into the whole world to make disciples of all nations" (Mt. 28:19). The Church Catholic subsists in and through the communion of local churches spread all over the world. These local churches render the Universal Church present and operative in the concrete local societies, cultures, and situations in which they are found. The local church is not an isolated or self-contained entity. She is indeed a consistent and concrete presence of the church through her insertion in the local context, but to be really part of the Universal Church she has to remain open to the other local churches with which she is in communion. The tasks, successes, failures, needs, growth or drawbacks of one local church are the concerns of all the other churches in the communion. Therefore wherever and whenever one local church is in need she has the right to be helped by sister churches who are in a position to do something about it. The Roman Congregation, working in the name of the Pope who is the sign and factor of this catholicity, actually facilitates and concretizes the involvement of all the local churches of the world in the creation of new local churches in new territories. And in fact this Roman Congregation was created in the 17th century precisely in order to make sure that the 'expansion' of the church in new territories was the common work of the whole church rather than the project of one national church, or indeed a means of making the church serve the secular or colonial interests of some nations. As a central body in a presumably neutral and non-nationalistic situation - the Roman Congregation is in a better position to serve as an acceptable and impartial recipient of worldwide charities for the missions and a distribution centre with a universal outlook.

To a certain extent the same can be said of the missionary organizations. It is indeed true that most of these organizations or congregations have arisen through the charismatic initiative of individual members of the church, often within the context of a definite local church with inevitable cultural and even national overtones. There are even missionary institutes that are 'national' in the sense that their membership, methods, and support depend mainly on one specific nation or country. Many other institutes however are international. All the same, because of the supreme responsibility of the Roman Congregation over the activities of all these missionary bodies, there is a certain guarantee that through these institutes the whole church is really involved, rather than just one local church or one nation.

Yet we have to admit that the involvement of older churches in the building up and running of mission churches, even if expressed through the agency of the Roman Congregation and the missionary organizations, does involve a danger: that of trying to build the missionary local church in the image of the older 'parent' churches. In other words, there is the danger that the young missionary church might remain for too long a dependent church, a sort of appendage to the overseas churches that have given her birth and continue to support her. We have pointed out, in the case of Lilongwe Diocese, that she was a 'dependent church'. And we tried to show that this was because, in the situation, the type and amount of personnel and resources needed to keep the local church running were such that it will always be necessary to make appeal to overseas or older churches.

In the final analysis such a local church is still just a 'transplanted church'. The shape or form of this local church is still too much a copy of overseas churches. The ways and methods followed in running her are very much those used in the churches abroad where .the missionaries come from. So that in order to keep the church going it will be necessary to use the same 'instruments' as those of the overseas churches, and to employ the same methods and ways with the help of the same type and quality of expertise and experience. If you want to maintain the same system and the same kind of enterprise then you need adapted, 'equipment' and similar 'technicians' as those required for the original 'standard': the overseas church.

In fact, the basic problem in our young churches of Africa is not the need for more priests, more sisters and brothers, and more money to run our churches as they have run up till now. This would be just begging the question. This problem of staffing and resources as expressing itself now is not the basic one: it is just the consequence of a more fundamental problem. If we need more and more of these it is because we are assuming that the actual system has to continue in the same way, just because this is how things are done in other churches elsewhere. Now, as long as such a transplantation of the church continues, it is evident that our churches will be dependent on the churches in Europe and America, our 'prototypes' and the source of our very being. It is illusory to hope for a really 'local' church in Africa unless we are prepared to question even the system itself. The question should be this: If really we want to make the church local in Africa, what has to be done? But this question calls for another preliminary one: What is a really local church?

What is a Really Local Church?

When AMECEA[5] Bishops met in plenary session in Nairobi in December 1974 for a special study session on *'Planning for the Church in Eastern Africa in the 1980s'*,[6] they realized that what was needed was to plan for a really 'local' church in Eastern Africa. They took time to describe what for them would be a really local church. Their way of thinking can be taken as representative of the thinking that is going on in most parts of Africa today. In the Preamble to the 'Guidelines' which emanated from this session we find this description:

> While the Church of Christ is universal, it is a communion of small local Christian Churches, communities of Christians rooted in their own society. From the Bible we learn that such local Churches are born through apostolic and missionary preaching. But they are meant to grow so that with time they become firmly rooted in the life and culture of the people. Thus the Church, like Christ himself, becomes incarnated in the life of the people. She is led by local people, meets and answers local needs and

---

[5] This abbreviation stands for: Association of Member Episcopal Conferences of Eastern Africa. AMECEA comprises the episcopal conferences of Uganda, Kenya, Tanzania, Malawi and Zambia. Every three years the bishops of these five countries meet in plenary session to share taperiences, plan ways of collaborating on a number of points of common interest, or study together one or another point.

[6] A full report on this Session is found in *AFER*, Vol. XVI/1 and 2, 1974.

problems, and fmds within herself the resources needed for her life and mission.

We are convinced that in these countries of Eastern Africa it is time for the Church to become really "local", that *is: Self-ministering, self-propagating and seif-supporting.* Our planning is aimed at building such local Churches for the coming years.[7]

What the bishops meant by these basic characteristics of a really local church had been amply discussed during the session itself.

A self-ministering church

A local church is self-ministering when all the essential services needed for the life and work of the church are actively assumed by members of that local church, and not mainly by helpers from outside. As long as these services are heavily dependent on missionary or external aid, the church is not yet self-ministering. In the context it was insisted upon that when we talk of 'ministry' and 'ministers' we should not think only, or even mainly, of priests or ordained ministers. We should rather consider 'ministry' in its broadest sense.

The ordained ministry is just one (the most basic, I grant) of the indispensable ministries in the Church. There are many other ministries needed for the proper functioning of the Body of Christ. And these ministries are not necessarily 'ordained': they can be exercised by lay people - often better by them! Thus we have ministries of teaching religion, organizing and executing liturgical functions and prayer, leading and ordering Christian communities, sanctifying Christians in all eons of ways, including the celebration of some sacraments, taking care of the material side of Church administration, etc. For these and other ministries, the clergy is admittedly mainly responsible because of their role in the Church. But Christ's will is such that the *clergy alone cannot fulfill them adequately.* And that, not just due to their small number,

---

[7] Ibid., pp. 9-10.

but *because the proper running of these services calls for a variety of charisms and gifts that are not found among the clergy alone.*[8]

In order to build a self-ministering church in the context of our African communities it is necessary to involve the whole church in the active ministry. And evidently the decisive factor will be a more enlightened and involved laity since by far the majority of church members will be the laity.

> Until such time as the laity have been fully involved, and a realistic redistribution of ministries, ordained and non-ordained, has been made, it is impossible to say whether we have too few priests or too many! There is plenty of room for a large number of non-ordained ministries, which could be assumed by the laity. And perhaps, if they were, we would find out that the shortage of priests that is talked about is not of the same type as we tend to assume.[9]

A self-propagating church

A living and effective local Church should possess the outgoing dynamism to attract new members. A self-propagating Church is one that does not rely for this attracting of new members only or mainly on outside missionaries, but on her own members, her own initiatives, her own methods and means.[10]

Where the whole church membership is actively involved in the life and witnessing of the church in an area, this local church not only succeeds in attracting new members, but also exerts its influence on the whole

---

[8] P.A. Kalilombe, *Christ's Church in Lilongwe Today and Tomorrow,* reproduced in this volume, pp. 42-70. It will be seen that the thinking in all this section is tributary to what Adrian Hastings has written about extensively, e.g. in *Mission and Ministry,* Sheed and Ward, 1971; *Church and Ministry,* Gaba Publications, 1972.

[9] *AFER, Vol.* XVI, p. 59.

[10] Kalilombe, *Christ's Church,* pp. 60-61.

society. Being the bearer of Christ's mission to preach the Good News, it is inevitable that an active church will become the leaven in the mass of mankind: helping the Gospel values to permeate the day to day life of the total community. A self-propagating church is one which becomes this salt, light, or leaven through the agency of the members who are actually sharing in the life of the area. In this case the methods used will be those within the range and comprehension of the local people, and the areas of men's life and activity where the message of Christ will be made to bear will be those relevant to the conditions of the people. In other words, when and where those mainly responsible for the spreading of the Gospel are the local people, there is much chance that the church will 'scratch where it itches' rather than give nice answers to problems that are not there or that pose themselves differently from what the answers presuppose.

A self-supporting church

A self-supporting church is one that depends *mainly* on the local members to find money and other material goods to maintain and run her essential services, to support her pastoral workers, and to expand those services that the church needs to develop.

No one can doubt that richer countries have a grave duty to give economic assistance to poor countries, and rich churches to poor churches. The question is how to implement these principles without undermining the real character of a local church and the ecclesiastical reality of subsidiarity and self-reliance. The people of God are an earthly, eating, drinking, buying, selling people. It is not only practically advantageous, it is theologically necessary that a local church be itself an economically viable unit.[11]

A self-supporting church is one which depends more on the local people than on outside help. One important consequence of such a dependence on the local contribution is that the material aspect of church life and work will be determined mainly by the local possibilities and the

---

[11] Hastings, Mission and Ministry, p. 14.

real local needs. In other words it is the 'local pocket' that should dictate what type and size of material realities the church is going to possess and use. A church that intends to become really 'local' must resist the ever-present temptation of becoming a slave to imported needs and standards. This is a point that missionaries will want to remember.[12]

Building Small Christian Communities

The three characteristics of a truly local church are a tall order, and one would wonder whether they are feasible in the circumstances of our African churches. The bishops believe that they are possible, but they pointed cut on what condition. The Preamble to the Guidelines continues with these words:

> We believe that in order to achieve this we have to insist on building Church Life and work on basic Christian communities in both rural and urban areas. Church life must be based on the communities in which everyday life and work takes place: those basic and manageable social groupings whose members can experience real inter-personal relationships and feel a sense of communal belonging, both in living and working. We believe that Christian communities at this level will be best suited to develop real intense vitality and to become effective witnesses in their natural environment.

---

[12] It is perfectly true that missionaries have stressed the importance of paying church tax in season and out of season, even going as far (too far) as refusing the sacraments (including baptism for their children) to those who fail to pay. The question one has to ask is whether this constant endeavour has not been largely vitiated by the context within which it has operated, especially of recent years. A context in which, first, local Christians can see perfectly clearly that missionaries have in fact access to sources of money beyond their wildest dreams; secondly, church institutions have been created and ways of clergy living established which the local church, with the best will in the world, could not support financially. The local Christians draw the obvious conclusion: if you choose to erect institutions totally beyond our means, you can provide the financial support yourselves and not look to our meagre resources." Ibid., pp. 14-15.

> In such authentic communities it will be easier to develop a sense of community whereby the Church can exist as Christ's Body, consisting of 'many parts' (clergy, religious, laity) with many charisms, but making one Body in the one Spirit (1 Corinthians, 12). We want to see collaboration and co-ordination in the life and work of all the different parts of the Christian community.[13]

The forming of such smaller Christian communities has become a major preoccupation and a decisive programme for the church in Africa. The AMECEA territories decided to make it the topic of their plenary meeting in 1976. Already at the 1974 Roman Synod of Bishops the Africa Report was able to state that 'many Bishops' Conferences in Africa strongly recommend that present Church structures and attitudes be modified by establishing basic Christian Communities."[14]

At the root of all this preoccupation with small Christian communities is the conviction that, to be realistic, the formation of a true local church has to start from the bottom, that is by the building up of smaller Christian communities. Because when it comes to real feeling of community and a possibility of on-going community tasks, the community in question must be of such a size, territorial proximity, and sufficient similarity of interests is as to draw its members into a feasible entity. Such a small Christian community is the only level at which 'the Church' can concretely live and work. It is at this level, that the church will be really present in the society at large and will be able to act.

Communities of this type can be built up by grouping people who live in such a geographical proximity that they can meet at regular intervals, can know one another sufficiently to have a feeling of 'family', can pray together, and can experience together joys, sorrows, successes, failures, problems and solutions. They must be able really to work together, plan together, train one another and help one another. They should group a sufficient number of adherents and variety of ecclesial charisms to be able to assure the ordinary non-ordained ministries that keep the local

---

[13] *AFER, Vol.* XVI, p. 10.

[14] 'Africa Report', p. 12.

church alive and active in day-to-day life. It is evident that for such local communities the presence of local, trained and efficient lay leaders is basic. These leaden would support, animate and lead the community in its various needs and services. A local church council, composed of leaders of various aspects of the community's life and work will serve as a co-ordinating, animating and directing organ of the local church.

In most territories of Africa this is not something completely new. Although on paper and in juridical terms we in Africa have adopted the language of older churches with their tradition of dioceses, deaneries, parhes, etc., the reality is quite different. We talk indeed in terms of 'parishl, but in actual fact, as far as real Christian life is concerned, it is on what we may call sub-parish level that the real thing is going on. Grouped under the rather broad umbrella of 'parish' are several basic churches which are the real units of *the* Church. They are usually led by some resident catechist or church elders - laymen - while the priests do their best to make the presence of the ordained ministry felt at longer or shorter intervals.

The African bishops would like everyone to realize that this state of affairs is not a second-best solution, but perhaps the only realistic basis of church existence in our territories. They would like therefore to exploit to the full the potentialities latent in this type of church existence. The conviction is that if the church's life and work is based first and foremost on this level, self-ministering, self-propagation and self-supporting of the church will be possible. At this local and rather restricted level, the needs, problems, structures, and required techniques are of such a simple type that the majority of the faithful can be expected to get involved and feel really part of the church. At the higher levels of parish, diocese, or conference, things get so big and complex that only a minority can be usefully involved, and this minority needs to be specially selected and highly trained. Were we to base the church's life and work on this higher plane, we would need a multitude of such specialized personnel and a lot of complicated instruments and much money to keep things going.

Evidently these higher structures are needed and important. They are necessary as unifying, organizing, directing and animating structures. They serve to insert these smaller churches into the authentic stream of the one and Catholic Church, assure vitality and guarantee authenticity and rectitude. Without them the local churches would disintegrate into sects devoid of real links with the Apostolic Church, and thus unable to represent the Church of Christ. But the point is that once the real thing is going on at the grass-root level, it will be easier to run and maintain the higher structures. It might be that with far less priests and external financial aid we could eventually realize more than we actually are doing. Anyway, this is the hope of the African bishops. They feel that our relations of dependence *vis-à-vis* the older churches would be modified deeply if we succeeded in building thriving smaller or basic Christian communities.

Intercessory ritual

Conclusion

During the first phase of missionary work it was inevitable and quite normal that the young churches growing up in the mission lands were dependent especially in personnel and financial resources on the older churches that had given them birth. This visible dependence has, however, been accompanied by a deeper and more subtle form of dependence: the fact that the older churches have tended to model the young churches on what was going on in the older, overseas, churches. In a way, this might be seen as an attempt to transplant the overseas church on to the African soil.

In the circumstances, there was nothing really wrong in that. But with the growth towards maturity of these young churches, and especially in the recent context of decolonization and political independence, it is being realized more and more that a second phase of development is overdue. The young churches will have to become really 'local' churches, self-reliant, standing on their own feet, and rooted in the life and culture of their country. When this happens, new relations will develop between the older churches and these younger ones. One should see in the current re-thinking of structures by the African bishops and their preoccupation with self-reliance, not a desire to break with the older sister churches of Europe and America, but rather the desire for new and more authentic relationships of collegiality, co-responsibility, and ecclesial communion in the total life of the Church.

4 The Salvific Value of African Religions

This article was originally a paper read at the First Congress of African Biblists in Kinshasa (1978). It first appeared in the June 1979 African Ecclesial Review (AFER), published by the AMECEA Pastoral Institute, P.O. Box 908, Eldoret, Kenya. It was later included in Gerald H. Anderson and Thomas F. Stransky (eds.), Mission Trends No. 5: Faith Meets Faith, New York: Paulist Press, 1981, pp. 50-69.

Are the African traditional religions salvific? Or to be more precise, were these traditional religious systems and practices effective means whereby in the past, before the coming of Christianity, their adherents in Africa were able to "seek the deity and, by feeling their way toward him, succeed in finding him (who) is not far from any of us, since it is in him that we live, and move, and exist" (Acts 17:27-28)? And for those who even today live sincerely by them, are these religions still authentic channels by which the local people live by God's saving activity, so that we could unequivocally assert that the practitioners of these traditional religions are saved through them, and not in spite of them?

Individual Salvation and Salvific Value of Religions: Distinct Questions

We need to distinguish two questions: one is the possibility of salvation for any individual who is not a member of Christ's visible Church. The second concerns the providential role of other religions, as historical, socially structured and outward expression of human communities in their search for God.

As far as the first question is concerned, quite early in Church history the attempted answer took the form of the famous axiom: *Extra Ecclesiam nulla salus*. Such a formulation, however, could never be taken in the absolute form that its wording suggests. As better, more comprehensive knowledge of human history and geography became available, it was necessary to start introducing more and more subtle distinctions, all amounting to the admission that, after all, salvation was possible outside the visible institutional Christian Church.[1] We can consider the question finally settled, at least in its basic elements, now that Vatican II has said in so many words that:

> Those also can attain to everlasting salvation who through no fault of their own do not know the gospel of Christ or His Church, yet sincerely seek God and, moved by grace, strive by their deeds to do His will as it is known to them through the dictates of conscience.[2]

But the problem of religions as such is a more difficult one because it is not possible to bypass here far-reaching implications that touch the very centre of the Church's self-standing and the Ineaning and goal of its missionary outreach. What becomes of Christianity's uniqueness as God's final salvific self-revelation if it is conceded that other religions are also divinely ordained normal channels of God's savific activity? Where is the urgency of the "Great Commission" (Mt. 28:19-20) if non-Christian communities can just as well find salvation in their own traditional religious systems? The Church has had to come to grips with these questions, for they are basic in determining what its own identity is in God's unfolding plan of salvation. They become all the more poignant as the historical Church becomes aware of the existence and dynamism of numerous civilizations, cultures and religious traditions that have developed outside the influence of Christianity. Given the divine command to go and make disciples of all nations, what attitude should the Church have towards these social realities? Opposition or dialogue? Competition or cooperation? Respect or contempt? Fight or peaceful coexistence? Can these religions be seen positively and with respect, or should they be dismissed as of no theological importance? In other words, are these religions in some sort of lineal continuity with Christianity, or are they not?

---

[1] For a summary treatment of the fortunes of this axiom, cf. H. Küng, *The Church*, Garden City: Doubleday Image Book, 1967, pp. 313-319.

[2] *Lumen Gentium*, no. 16.

Karl Rahner[3] asserted in 1961 that unfortunately it could not be said that Catholic theology, as practiced in recent times, had really paid sufficient attention to the question posed in this precise way. Indeed, judging from the normal practice of Christian missionary activity, it has to be admitted that until rather recently it was customary to deaf heavy-handedly with what were called "pagan practices". Although some respect was often paid to elements found in these religions, they were seen essentially as aberrations, and little effort was made to explore the possibility of their providential role in the history of the peoples concerned. The good elements in them which could be respected as positive were accepted as such mainly because they happened to resemble what were taken as authentic Christian values. This did not affect the negative judgment on the religions themselves. Only sporadically, and mainly in recent times, has a serious attempt been made to evaluate the religions themselves and to find out what role they might have in God's plan of salvation for their adherents. But even before Vatican II, theologians[4] finally started discussing the question. Vatican II's *Declaration on Relationship of the Church to Non-Christian Religions (Nostra Aetate)* seems to allude to it in some way. It says:

> The Catholic Church rejects nothing which is true and holy in these religions. She looks with sincere respect upon those ways of conduct and of life, those rules and teachings which, though differing in many particulars from what she holds and sets forth, nevertheless often reflected a ray of that Truth which enlightens all men.

The *Decree on the Church's Missionaly Activity* has more interesting reflections (no. 1, 7, 9, 11) which, though still rather timid and general, furnish avenues for a more hopeful treatment of it by theologians. One

---

[3] Karl Rattner, *Theological Investigations,* London: Darton, Longman and Todd, 1966, Vol. 5, *Later Writings,* p. 117.

[4] Like Danielou, Congar, and others. For a brief evaluation of these essays, cf. Heinz R. Schlette, *Towards a Theology of Religions,* New York: Herder and Herder, 1966, pp. 28-33.

such pregnant reflection, and perhaps the most significant, is Vatican II's favourite portrayal of the Church as "Universal Sacrament of salvation" (A.G. no. 1).

In discussing the question of non-Christian religions all parties and opinions among Christian thinkers were starting from the witness of the Scriptures and basing on it their evaluation and judgment. What questions were being asked? Were all the relevant elements of the evidence carefully taken into account: or was there a tendency to highlight only certain trends of thought appearing in the Scriptures while pushing into the background other important trends which might have modified the nature of the investigation? Were there certain prior working assumptions and attitudes that commanded the selection of the evidence and determined the relative weight given to apparently conflicting lines of thought?

The reading of the Bible is never a totally neutral exercise. The reader who takes up the Bible comes with all sorts of conditionings. Besides the more personal ones resulting from the individual's own psychological and spiritual history, he or she carries along also the effects of his/her belonging to a specific class, family, culture, community or interest group. The individual bears also the imprint of the epoch in history within which the investigation is being made. All this has an influence on how the Bible will be interrogated, what the expectations of the reader will be, what evidence will be readily selected and given importance, but also what "blind spots" will occur in the exercise.

I take as point of departure the fact that, as far as African traditional religions are concerned, the prevailing judgments and attitudes are the result of Bible study conducted *mainly by non-Africans.* These students, however sympathetic and broadminded, were still looking at the problem from the point of view of an outsider who is not really personally involved in the religions at stake. In a way, this was an advantage: it made for a type of objectivity and detachment that would have been impossible for an African. On he other hand, however, they could not claim to be totally impartial since they were in their turn conditioned by other factors of which an African can normally hope to be free.

The main aim of this essay is to show what could happen if the enquiry were initiated from the point of view of an African Christian reader of the Scriptures. The contention is that a fresh vision could ensue in that former problems which used to dominate might be found to take a secondary place, while newer preoccupations might become more important and relevant. A slightly different way of posing the question could also result, demanding a new assessment of the testimony of Scripture. We might even hope to touch on some aspects of the Bible message that have remained "blind spots" until now because they were not really needed from the point of view of former preoccupations.

Examining the Context of Past Attitudes

Within the Christian tradition the problem of the encounter with other religious systems and traditions has not been a purely intellectual one, engaging people's minds on a calm theoretical level. It has always been first and foremost a practical, existential challenge, involving strong sentiments of a sacred duty to be accomplished, calling forth concrete tasks and programs and eliciting a lot of deep-seated emotions. It is necessary to start by examining the main aspects of the context that gave rise to the attitudes that People manifested in discussing this point.

One thing is sure. As far as African traditional religions are concerned, the discussions of professional theologians and biblists are only secondary. The main context within which the decisive attitudes towards these religions were formed is the missionary enterprise, especially in its more recent expressions starting with the mid-nineteenth century. Missionary work was seen as the Church's bonden duty to bring the true faith to pagans, or to save souls that were in darkness. The challenge attracted vigorous and enterprising people, ready for action and for suffering even up to death. It was like a military expedition: it thrived on an ethos of struggle and conquest. Understandably the enemy was Satan. But Satan was disguised and active through his network of false religions. He and his associates had to be encountered, unmasked in their perfidy, and then engaged in mortal battle. The missionary's encounter with the traditional African customs and religious practices was thus not a peaceful one. The missionary may have had sympathy and genuine love for the individual natives, for after all, they were the ones on behalf of whom the war was being waged. But towards their religious systems and practices, and towards those who were guardians and promoters of these practices, there could be no compromise.

And so when missionaries went to the Scriptures for guidance in their encounter with the traditional religions, the texts that struck them most were normally those that had overtones of opposition against the "gentiles" as enemies of God's People and practitioners of idolatry and abominations. It was so simple to see the Christian Church as the People of God, and the non-Christian religious systems as the expression of enmity against Yahweh and his plan of salvation.

The most natural selections were those passages where there are expressions of hostility towards the "pagans", for example, where there is abundant diatribe against the idols of the gentiles. Choice texts would be those in the ridicule style in which Deutero-Isaiah excells (Isa. 44:9-20; 46:1-7), and those portions of the Old Testament which are tributary to this literary form (Ps. 115; Baruch 6; or even Dan. 14). These texts are a reinforcement of the affirmation of strict monotheism (rather than mere henotheism) so characteristic of exilic and post-exilic Judaism (cf. Isa. 45:7-13, 18-25). It was a sort of apologetic style aiming at consoling and strengthening the chastened exiles or at restoring self-confidence to the struggling bands of the "Golah". This helped to develop the theme of the Holy People, separated from all that is impure and profane, a people privileged to have the Law of their God and the only true worship. It was at this time that the great synthesis of the Priestly Tradition was given its lasting form and became the commanding editorial framework of the Scriptures. But there was a dark side to this. From the notion of Holy People and the preoccupation to express this holiness and protect it, the tendency developed towards an exclusivist ghetto mentality. The Law ran the danger of legalism and intransigence as is witnessed by Ezra's fierce treatment of "mixed marriages" (Ezra 9-10). Later persecutions under the Seleucids and the Romans helped only to reinforce these tendencies. The Apocalyptic and allied literatures of these times do have admirable lessons. But they also betray a hardening of attitude towards the "gentiles". There is very little sympathy towards anything outside the "People of God".

These developments are to be seen mostly as prompted by a defensive spirit: the need of a socially and politically disadvantaged group to protect itself from corrosive outside forces and to compensate psychologically for its inferiority by exalting whatever redeeming aspects it believes it possesses. It is to be remembered that the New Testament dawned in the midst of this period. This will help us to put in proper context several texts which reflect attitudes of Christ's contemporaries (and those of the early Church) towards non-Jews. But here we must note that a current opposed to this narrow ghetto spirit and its negative attitude towards the gentiles had developed alongside the more intransigent one. We can only recall such obvious testimonies as the book of Ruth where we sense a subtle criticism of current "purist" ideas about who the "People of God" really are. The satirical novel of the Prophet Jonah is even more explicit in its castigation of Judaism's exclusive claim to God's favour. We have here a rather radical presentation of a theme which was dear to many prophets, as we shall see later on.

In the New Testament times, we have echoes of this more positive tradition. John the Baptist and Jesus himself are examples. The sayings about descent from Abraham are an important evidence. Both the Baptist (cf. Mt. 3:9-10; Lk. 3:8) and Christ went out of their way to stigmatize the misplaced confidence in mere belonging to an ethnic group, albeit a divinely chosen one (cf. Mt. 3:11-12; Jn. 8:37-47). The early Christian community, composed mainly of Jews, had difficulty in ridding themselves of the ghetto mentality, as we can judge by the controversy about the requirements for the conversion of non-Jews (Acts 15). The book of Acts is quite clear in showing how hard it was even for Peter to widen his vision on this point (Acts 10). But the author of Romans feels the need to expound in a new way the theme about descent from Abraham (Rom. 4, cf. also Gal. 3 and 4). These sayings of the Baptist, of Jesus, and of Paul are manifestly part of a tradition of protest against a hard-line attitude towards the "pagans".

There seems to have existed in the New Testament a current of thought which felt that the problem about those outside the visible membership of God's People was not as simple as the standard Jew might have wanted to make it. It was too simplistic to think that God loved his chosen people, but had no time for the others. In interpreting the message of the New Testament, this point is very crucial: it may help to give importance to some forgotten texts. Christian missionaries could have given more thought to this counter current in their assessment of the place of non-Christian religions in divine providence. It would seem strange, in fact, that missionaries would give relatively more importance to the contrary current, for they were interrogating the Scriptures in view of a commitment quite contrary to that of a ghetto community. Jewish religion, in spite of its late efforts at proselytism, remained basically a non-missionary community and tended to see its relation with outsiders mainly in terms of opposition and exclusion. The Christian Church, on the other hand, is institutionally outgoing: sent to go out to the whole world. There does not seem to be any necessary reason for the Christian religion to form a systematically negative viewpoint, and for thinking that the primary normative texts capable of guiding the Church in its missionary enterprise should be those that suggest an easy and blanket dismissal of other religions. The history of Christianity in Europe led to such a close link between the Christian faith and Western culture that it became difficult to distinguish between them, or between the expansion of religion and the expansion of Western civilization. This ambiguity becomes obvious especially starting with the Crusades. It will not have disappeared in the 16th and 17th centuries when the Christian nations of Spain and Portugal will be busy with their conquests in the New World. It certainly had not disappeared when colonial expansion came to its zenith in the second half of the 19th century and well into our own century. However much one hates to say this, it is not by pure coincidence that missionary work flourished most during the colonial period. In the atmosphere of the Western conquest, the meeting of Christianity with other religions was conceived of in the spirit typical of Christendom's crusading tradition. There is a streak of the Crusader in Western Christianity. It tends to identify its own interests and vision with those of God himself. We only have to think of the bitter sectarianism that has pitted Christian denominations against one another over the past generations. And yet they all claim to belong to one and the same Christ. It should not be surprising then that the same spirit of systematic opposition prevails whenever Christianity meets non-Christian traditions.

The source of this type of intransigence seems to be a tendency to simplify realities into an "either/or" pattern, whether it is a question of truths and beliefs or of life-styles and customs. It is as if anything that is different from what I believe to be true or good is a threat to my feeling of security and must be dismissed as bad or inferior. Variations then become oppositions; and it becomes difficult to think of such variations rather as complementary aspects which might create a richer reality by being combined rather than by excluding one another. Seeing variations and differences as complementary aspects first rather than oppositions has an advantage. It helps to discover many things that are valid and good in a position different from my own. And this is salutary when we are dealing with human realities, for such human realities can never claim to have the monopoly of goodness. The tendency to opposition has another side to it, a side we would do well to remember when we are dealing with the encounter of religions. The crusading mentality is usually accompanied by a highly motivated proselytism. When other religions and systems have been proven wrong their adherents are not simply left in peace: they must be persuaded to abandon those false religions and to adopt the true religion as presented by the crusader. This persuasion may be peaceful, relying on respectful dialogue and the power of moral attraction. Often, however, the crusader becomes impatient when conversions are not being realized fast enough for his liking. He may then resort to other methods of persuasion. It may not be outright physical force (although both Islam and Christianity have not always abstained from such methods), but it can be other ways that to a greater or lesser extent do not fully respect the religious freedom of the people. There have been instances where, for example, works of charity were used as mere instruments of proselytism. But in any case such a compulsive desire for converts can affect the modality of the encounter between the religions. It can push the crusader to falsify the picture in view of more immediate successes: the Christian religion will be presented only in its idealized form, while only the weaker and repulsive aspects of the other religions are highlighted.

What I am trying to say is that in the encounter of Christianity with other religions, the spirit that motivated the missionary was not always of a type to facilitate a more positive assessment of these religions. This may have impeded a fruitful study of the salvific nature of those religions. It also explains in part the choice of scriptural evidence adduced to account for Christianity's attitude towards them. As we have seen, the texts by which most store was laid were those which form part of a definite trend in the Old Testament: Israel's and Judaism's opposition to the gentiles, and the exclusive claims of God's Chosen People to divine favour.

Christianity claims to be the new People of God. It inherits that feeling of being a privileged people which Israel has had because of the Covenant (Ex. 19:4-6). By the same token, Christianity has inherited also the danger that stalked Israel throughout its history: the danger of misunderstanding the real nature and aim of this choice by God, and of drawing false conclusions from it concerning God's relations with other peoples and nations. The Covenant then, as a fulfillment of the promises made to Abraham and the ancestors, ran the risk of losing its *raison d'être as* a nationalistic privilege, independent from, or even cancelling, God's world-wide salvific interests. Israel's prophets were often obliged to rectify such misunderstandings. Amos (9:7-8) reminds the Israelites that the distant peoples are just as much objects of God's solicitude as they themselves. Yahweh is as concerned with what these foreign nations do to one another as with the way Israel and Judah are acting (Amos 1-2). The first chapters of Genesis (1-11) serve as the setting of the whole scene within which God's plan of salvation is to unfold: the whole of creation, the universe where the history of mankind takes place. Abraham's calling and the election of Israel would have no meaning except as part of this encompassing plan. So while he is dealing with the Chosen People, God's eyes are on the whole of mankind. The authentic traditions of Israel saw the Covenant at Sinai as a covenant within a wider Covenant; for creation itself was the primordial Covenant; and God does not break his word. To him belong heaven and the heaven of heavens, the earth and all it contains. Even when he makes special choice of Abraham's descendants, he is never partial or to be bribed (Deut. 10:1518). It is significant that the Wisdom literature which flourished especially among the Jews of the Diaspora shows a broader view of God's active presence in the world. The reflections of the book of Wisdom on God's dealings with Israel's enemies are astounding in their insistence on divine forbearance. For indeed God "is merciful to all, because he can do all things and He overlooks men's sins so that they can repent ... he loves all that exists and holds nothing of what he has made in abhorrence, for had he hated anything, he would not have formed it" (cf. Wisdom 11:26). We can feel here the same spirit as the one that prompted the author of the book of Jonah, and which refused to imagine God as partial or narrow (Wisdom 6:8).

The Historical Visible Church and the Non-Christian Religions

There is, as we mentioned earlier, a current in the New Testament which carried on this open vision of God's dealings with the universe. The early Church was conscious of its task of proclaiming the Good News of Jesus up to the ends of the earth, because the Christ was the final revelation of the true God. The Apostles and the early Christians were convinced that only through faith in Christ could the world be saved, "for if all the names in the world given to men, this is the only one by which we can be saved" (Acts 4:12). But this conviction does not seem to have become an easy explanation of God's dealings with those who as yet did not know Christ. These were not only the ones called "gentiles" by the Jews, but also the Jews themselves in so far as they had rejected the Messiah. The pressing question then was to determine where this Chosen People stands since God's election is now through Christ. The state of the gentiles was only a subsequent problem. Were the Jews at any real advantage as compared with the non-Jews as far as faith in Christ was concerned? As we saw, this is basically the point at issue in the controversy about the conditions for conversion to Christ (Acts 15; Romans and Galatians). Although the resolution of the question at Jerusalem was rather a compromise as far as practical tactics were concerned, on the theoretical level a great step had been taken. It was now accepted that "in Christ Jesus, whether you are circum-cized or not makes no difference - what matters is faith that makes its power felt through love" (Gal. 5:6). Or as the letter to the Romans would say: "A man is justified by faith and not by doing something the Law tells him to do. Is God the god of the Jews alone and not of the pagans too? Of the pagans too, most certainly, since there is only one God" (Rom. 3:2830). This was a radical statement: it says clearly that through Christ God has shown that he has no favourites: "Pain and suffering will come to every human being who employs himself in evil - Jews first, but Greeks as well; renown, honour and peace will come to everyone who does good - Jews first, but Greeks as well. God has no favourites" (Rom. 2:9-11). In this context Paul is able to turn to the "gentiles" and state that "pagans who never heard of the Law but are led by reason to do what the Law commands, may not actually 'possess' the Law, but they can be said to 'be' the Law. They can point to the substance of the Law engraved on their hearts - they can call a witness, that is, their own conscience - they have accusation and defense, that is, their own inner mental dialogue" (Rom. 2:14-16).

This statement of humanity's basic equality before God is where the study of the salvific nature of non-Christian religions should start. It shows God present within the whole of mankind, in different ways perhaps, but really present nevertheless, whether through the agency of the Law among the Jews or through the working of conscience for the others. All peoples are subjected to sin and God's wrath; but just so are they all open to the saving faith in Christ. Another way of putting it is to affirm that "God wants everyone to be saved and reach full knowledge of the truth. For there is only one God, and there is only one mediator between God and mankind, himself a man, Christ Jesus who sacrificed himself as a ransom for them all" (1 Tim. 2:4-6). It is possible to situate within proper context Paul's statement during his speech at Athens (Acts 17:26-28). It is a validation of the insights found in the first chapters of Genesis: there is a cosmic Covenant of love between God and mankind by the very fact of creation. Mankind may break this Covenant through sin and infidelity. But again and again God renews it and reaffirms his salvific intention. His special choices (that of Israel and that of the Church) are not an abolition of the cosmic Covenant. If anything, they are a hopeful sign or proof of what in less evident ways he is doing all along with the whole of mankind, and they are meant to serve this wider Covenant.

This does not answer all the questions. But if we start with it, then the answers to those other problems will follow a particular line where we do not have to come back on this important basis. For example, it will be necessary to find out what is meant by the affirmation that only faith in Christ brings salvation. The easy way out would be to say that those who do not know Christ explicitly cannot have faith in him: and cannot be saved. But our starting point will oblige us to return to the Scriptures and ask whether and how Christ can be really present even if his face is not explicitly revealed. This might help us to give fuller consideration, for example, to John's statement: "The Word was the true light that lightens all men ... He was in the world that had its being through him, and the world did not know him" (Jn. 1:9). We would return to the Wisdom literature in the Old Testament and meditate on the fuller meaning of the theme of God's Wisdom. And then we might take up the Captivity Letters. We would see that the Christ of God's plan of salvation (cf. Eph. 1 and Col. 1) is a cosmic presence that is not contained within the limits of the historical visible Church only.

Another problem would be to assess the role of this visible Church. Is God's intention to introduce every human being into this historical Church under pain of not being saved? The history of Israel would furnish us with food for thought. God did not call every person and nation in that special way by which he had called Israel. But as we have seen, this special election did not mean that God was neglecting the other nations in favour of Israel alone. On the contrary, although Israel often forgot this, the special election of the Chosen People was a call for service. Deutero- (and Trito-) Isaiah makes this quite plain, especially in the Songs of the Suffering Servant of Yahweh (Isa. 42:1-9; 49:1-6; 50:4-9; and esp. 52:13-53:12). In these texts the meaning of Israel's calling, history, suffering and fmal triumph is of world-wide validity. She lives, suffers, dies and rises again as an instrument of Yahweh's salvific designs for the whole world. Although the other nations are not racially or physically integrated into the Jewish nation, in a sense they are all brought into real association with her. In a way that is hard to explain in terms of experimental evidence, these nations can look up to Zion as to their "mother, since each one of them was born in her, and all have their place in her" (Ps. 86:5-7). Not only are the explicit proselytes accepted (cf. Isa. 56:1-8), but all the nations walk in her light (Isa. 60) bringing in their riches into the world-wide commonwealth of the redeemed. Israel therefore is a sort of prototype, a light to enlighten the nations and make them realize their God-given destiny. The New Testament echoes this by comparing the New People of God to "Light," "Salt," "Leaven" of the earth, to a "City" up on the mountain whose presence assures the world that God is in the midst of his people (Mt. 5:13-16; also Phil. 2:14-16). This is the, meaning of Vatican II's favourite description of the Church as "light of the nations" (L.G. no. 1) and universal sacrament of salvation (A.G. no. 1).

It would seem therefore that the Church's destiny is to be inserted into the heart of the world as a sacrament, i.e. visible and effective sign, of the coming Kingdom of God, pointing towards this Kingdom, and proving its efficacious working by acting as a privileged champion of the tenets of the Kingdom. By looking at the Church and by hearing its prophetic utterances, the rest of the world is challenged by the judgment of God on them, a judgment that, like light, reveals the dross and the good metal, and like fire burns the dross and refmes the precious metal. If this is so, the Church's preoccupation should be less with mere recruitment of numbers, and more with the authenticity and effioacy of its witness in the world. The other religions should be seen, not so much as an adversary or a threat, but as the field within which her witness makes the good grain grow and bear fruit a hundred fold, while the tares are being pulled out and burnt.

The Salvific Value of African Traditional Religions

What could happen if the problem of non-Christian religions were examined by people who are part of the societies among whom these religions have a validity? What would happen if African traditional religions were to be assessed by African Christians themselves? Perhaps the main lines of the enquiry would shift.

There would be a first basic change: it would be an enquiry from the insider rather than from the outside. I would have to return in spirit to where my people were. So we would not be talking anymore about the customs and beliefs of those "pagans" in the bush of Africa: I could not have the heart to speak of my own ancestors and religion in this contemptuous way. We are dealing with concrete people now: my father and mother, my uncles and aunts, my brothers and sisters, my relatives, friends and neighbours, a lot of people who mean a lot to me and whom I cannot handle as if they were mere objects of curiosity and detached study. And especially, I would remember that I am looking at a venerable and sacred tradition handed over by generations of ancestors. These beliefs and customs will command my respect and careful consideration, even when I may not share them. I cannot act as if these are childish superstitions or mere primitive mumbo-jumbo, for I feel with my whole person the seriousness of the problems, questionings, preoccupations, hopes, fears, desires and joys from which these religious attitudes spring. I have no right to look down on my father's culture or to offer simplistic solutions to questions I know to be very complex.

We can think here of Paul's case, when in the letter to the Romans (9-11) he had to meditate on the fact that the majority of his fellow Jews did not believe in Christ and were thus hostile to what was most precious in his own religious experience. His sorrow was so great, his mental anguish so endless, for these were his own flesh and blood. With them he shared a rich history of relations with God and the ancestors. So his questions take on a dramatic and deeply personal character. He sees difficulties and problems where perhaps a fellow Christian, but of a non-Jewish origin, might not have seen them. He finds himself unable to accept several easy answers that suggest themselves to his questioning mind. The problem of Jewish incredulity is not as simple to him as it might look to an outsider. It is not just a question of bad faith or blindness on the part of the Jews. The complicating factor is that God himself and his promises are all part of the question. And so Paul is forced to go back to the Scriptures and start a thorough-going *midrash* in order to find out the theological implications of the problem. In so doing he comes up with scriptural texts which take on a new meaning as approaches to the solution. We have an example of con-textualized Bible investigation where the reading and interpretation are shaped by the personal involvement of the inquirer.

It is some such process that an African would have to initiate if he wanted to re-examine the problem of his ancestors' religious traditions. He would not start from a position of assumed righteousness and superiority as a member of an already Christianized culture might be tempted to do. He would therefore avoid selecting as guidance those texts of the Bible that represented doubtful tendencies of a superiority complex *vis-à-vis* the other cultures, or of an exclusivist mentality which would want to restrict God's favour and interest to one's own group as if God can be partisan and a respector of persons.

But, above all, he would start from the conviction that God has been ever present among his own people, just as he has been in all peoples, cultures and religious tendencies of the world, not just as a condescension. We must therefore assume that in all serious efforts of mankind to make sense of its own life and destiny, God has been in and with his peoples. The Spirit of God has indeed filled the whole world. There are enough serious trends of thought in the Scriptures to show that this feeling is not just sentimental, but is based on revelation. The African Bible reader will thus not fear to state that the religious systems of his ancestors were not just tolerated by God. They were the results of the efforts of our cultures wherein the Spirit of God was an active agent. And therefore, there would be no fear in me to assert that, as long as these religions were the serious searchings of our cultures for the deity, they are to be respected as the normal divinely-given means for salvation, put by God in his will for the salvation of all the peoples.

This will not mean that everything in those religions is good or to be retained. Scripture will remind us strongly that human nature and its strivings are under the shadow of sin, and therefore constantly subjected to God's judgment whereby the evil is always condemned by him and by mankind's deepest level of conscience. But because God's Spirit is nevertheless actively present, it will be necessary to assume that there are also a lot of good and valid elements in this "groping"; and these positive elements must be worthy of respect and survival since they are the results of God's activity which is never ultimately defeated by sin and death.

But I shall remember that, according to Scripture, this judgment is not reserved only to those nations that have been favoured with a special election by God. For according to the Bible, the whole world lies under the wrath of God: "Jews and Gentile alike, because all have sinned and have fallen short of God's glory. God's wrath and condemnation tend to begin with his own household." And so I shall not be bothered by tendentious readings of the Bible which give easy superiority to any special historical group.

Let us admit that this caution in assessing African non-Christian religions, and the systematic favourable prejudice in their regard, will come easy to me because I feel personally involved in these religions. But that does not need an apology: it simply shows that it is not fair to give a final judgment in such important matters only from a partial stand-point, be it Jewish or Christian, primitive or civilized, black or white. The problem of the salvific value of non-Christian religions should be tackled from a holistic standpoint in which full

Fr Edele calls blessings over a fellow White Father

account is taken of the special choices or elections of God, but also of all the elements in God's relations with the whole of mankind. Only thus can full justice be given to the witness of the Scriptures. For, indeed, "God has no favourites" (Rom. 2:11).

5 Lessons from African Traditional Religion: Unity from Below

This article was originally published and printed as Selly Oak Colleges Occasional Paper No. 11 (Selly Oak, Birmingham, 1993 pp. 1-15), with the title: "Unity from Below: Lessons from African Traditional Religion". It came from a paper which had been presented at a Selly Oak College Conference on "Mission and Ecumenism" in 1992.

The reflections offered here are in the nature of explorations rather than firm conclusions resulting from a completed study. They are meant to invite responses and dialogue - in other words, an honest critical exchange which it is hoped can enrich us all in our reflections on mission and ecumenism.

I would like to look at this theme from the standpoint of someone coming from a traditionally and historically non-Christian religious context. My contention is that in a culture and religion different from the Western cultures within which Christianity has developed, there is likely to be found a different way of handling interaction between groups that practise religion differently. It is quite possible that what traditionally Christian communities see as issues of mission and ecumenism are not seen in the same way in those other cultures. Is it possible to articulate some of those differences? And could these suggest some new ways of addressing those issues?

Christianity and the African Context in Central Africa

But let me make clear the concrete point of reference on which my reflections are being made. The African traditional religion that I shall be referring to is the version known and practised by my Chewa/Ngoni people of Malawi, Zambia and Mozambique. I do not wish to give the impression that everywhere in Africa religious ideas and practices are exactly the same as in my part of the continent. There surely are differences and diversities in the many African cultures and religious systems.

Nevertheless, as D. Zahan points out, these diversities do not mean total differences. There is in the cultural and religious field an astonishing convergence in the underlying outlook, values, and attitudes of most sub-Sahara religious systems:

> The variation in religion has less to do with the ideas themselves than with their expression by means of dissimilar elements linked to the occupations and the flora and fauna of the area.[1]

When I refer to Christian missionary activity, I am thinking mainly of the work that missionaries from Europe and America have been doing in our countries between the middle of the last century and say, the middle of the present one. As for the ecumenical efforts by Christian churches, my context is what was studied in the years 1976-1981 and is reported in the book: *Ecumenical Initiatives in Eastern Africa*.[2]

Lastly, it must be noted that my point of departure is the story of my own extended family. This story, so I think, draws together elements of Christian mission in its impact on traditional religion; but it also draws in elements of denominational interaction, since members of my family belong to different Christian churches. Thus, from an actual case study we shall be able to proceed towards a discussion of wider issues. I hasten to add that, in taking my personal story as a case study, I do not mean that it necessarily presents a typical or normative African situation in the matters of mission and ecumenism. Other Africans may indeed fmd my case very different from theirs, or even conclude that it is aberrant and a-typical. All I am saying is that, nevertheless, it is a significant instance and, as such, deserves the kind of reflections that I shall make on it.

---

[1] Dominique Zahan, *The Religion, Spirituality, and Thought of Traditional Africa*, Chicago and London: University of Chicago Press, 1979, p. 2.

[2] Mugambi, J., J. Mutiso-Mbinda and J. Vollbrecht, *Ecumenical Initiatives in Eastern Africa*, Nairobi: AACC/AMECEA, 1982.

One family, but different religions and churches

I was born in a family that had already been converted to Catholic Christianity. My father had, as a young man, been received into the Church while he was employed by the missionaries at Mua Mission, some 10 miles from his home village in Mtakataka. He married a girl from a neighbouring village back home who later followed [him into the Catholic church. They naturally brought up their children in this same church, the more so as the family was resident at the Mua Mission compound where my father was working as a carpenter. He was also involved in the work of the church as an elder.

But we, the children, were told that, before the arrival of the Roman Catholic missionaries at Mtakataka in 1908, both families (that of my father and that of my mother) had been in contact with the Dutch Reformed Church which had built an outstation near the two villages. It even seems that members of both families had either been baptized or were at least 'hearers' (followers and catechumens) in the DRC. My mother's father had a second wife some 30 miles away near Dedza, in a village where the DRC were also active. Most of the members of that other family ended up as Protestant Christians. When the Roman Catholic missionaries came to establish themselves at Mtakataka, not far from the DRC outstation, parts of my parents' families moved over and became followers of that new church. But another section remained with the DRC. Later on, a cousin of mine from the DRC section in Dedza joined the Seventh-Day Adventist Church while he was a student at their school. And so a few members of our family are SDA Christians.

In the meantime quite a large number of relatives in all these families have remained uncommitted to any of these Christian churches. They continue to follow the traditional religion of our ancestors. This was clearly the case with both my father's and mother's fathers whom I knew as non-Christians for a long time, and only saw them come into the RC Church on their death-bed. I seem also to remember that one of the women that my paternal grandfather married came from a Muslim village near the lake and never, to my knowledge, became a Christian. So our extended family, the group of relatives and kinspeople with whom our Catholic nuclear family kept constant and intimate relations, were members of different religions, and the Christians, of different denominations.

Mission or ecumenism in the family

My recollections are that in our extended families each religious or denominational group seemed to be quite attached and faithful to their kind of religious belonging. And yet, in the course of everyday living, and especially in moments of family significance: marriages, births, sickness, death, and other family celebrations, there was cooperation and unity which the divergent religious affiliations did not seem to impede. I can still remember how my father, a staunch Catholic if there ever was, would contribute money and other articles for the performance of ceremonies and rituals which were clearly non-Christian, though he himself would scrupulously abstain from taking an active part in those rites which his church forbade as 'pagan'. The other members of the family would respect this as a matter of course. In the same way members of the extended family would be present at the functions concerning their relatives even when these functions took place in a religion or church different from their own. I used to wonder why my father did not act more forcefully in trying to bring into our church the relatives who did not yet belong to it, since he seemed to accept what the church preached, namely, that 'outside the RC Church there is no salvation'. Where was his sense of mission?

On reflection, it struck me that all of us, in our different religions and churches, did not seem to feel our divergences were tragic. There was no compulsion on anybody's part to pressure the others into converting to their own kind of religion: we seemed quite satisfied that they were happy where they belonged. And yet it. was understood that each one would be faithful in following the requirements, customs and practices of their church or religion, while respecting those of the others. The kinship and family oneness did not seem to be jeopardized by this diversity of church and religious belonging. My conclusion was that this family oneness and its functioning were the real foundation of our lives, and that the variations in religious belonging did not need to threaten this unity. How can this be explained? My tentative suggestion is that we were all following the kind of conception of religion which is that of African tradition: a non-denominational' kind of religion.

'Non-denominationalism' in African traditional religion

h is difficult to put into words that peculiar characteristic of African religion that I call 'non-denominational'. But it stems in the first place from the fact that religion is not conceived of as a separate aspect of individual or corporate life. Religion, life, and culture are all one. This is in line with what has been said about 'community religions':

> It is practised by all the members of a society and by no one outside it. These religions are, therefore, co-extensive with single societies. They are the religions of societies as communities. They are the religions into which one is born, not to which one is converted. The missionary impulse and the belief that there might be only one true religion are foreign to them. Rituals are central. The belief notions guiding them are inarticulate, varied and vague. Other marks are constant revelation and tangible salvation. Their believers hold that spiritual beings often are in touch with human beings through dreams, visions, oracles, spirit possession, prophetic inspiration and shamanistic trance. The salvation they expect is material: health, wealth, children, and other tangible blessings.[3]

The assumption, in our case, would be that, in spite of 'conversion' to new religions and churches, the members of my extended family still retained some of these basic characteristics of traditional religion. They most probably are not the only ones to do so; and the point here is not to make a value judgment on the sincerity of their 'conversion', but simply to take into account the practical significance of such a retention of basic attitudes of traditional religion.

---

[3] G. ter Haar, A. Moyo, and S.J. Hondo, African Traditional Religions in Religious Education: A Resource Book with Special Reference to Zimbabwe, Utrecht: Utrecht University, 1992, p. 12.

It has also been realized that in most African languages there is no special word for what we call 'religion' in European languages. As J. Mbiti remarks:

> Religion has been for Africans the normal way of looking at the world and life experience itself. For that reason it is found wherever people are. It is integrated so much into different areas of life that in fact most of the African languages do not have a word for religion as such. They only have words for religious ideas, practices and objects or places.[4]

This means that the religious or worshipping community is determined by the concrete living circumstances, especially in so far as life is first and foremost structured by the communion within a kinship and affinity group. Where your living context is, there also is your religious group:

> Religion is not preached from one people to another. Therefore a person must be born in a particular African people in order to be able to follow African Religion in that group. It would be meaningless and useless to try and transplant it to an entirely different society outside of Africa, unless African peoples themselves go with it there ... For that reason, a person from one setting cannot automatically and immediately adjust himself to or adopt the religious life of other African peoples in a different setting.[5]

And Mbiti continues:

> Even if they are converted to another religion like Christianity or Islam, they do not completely abandon their traditional religion

---

[4] John S. Mbiti, Introduction to African Religion (1st ed.), London et al.: Heinemann, 1975, p. 12. Ibid.

[5] Ibid.

immediately: it remains with them for several generations and sometimes centuries.⁶

How can we explain this? Religion and life are one because they are both based on a world-view which is the explanation of the leading ideas and values, rituals and practices, activities and attitudes of individuals and communities. This understanding of realities, or world-view, is very similar among most African peoples, which explains why their cultures and religious practices are also so analogous. A description of it, such as is given by Mbiti, would be largely accepted as valid by most African peoples.⁷

The main elements of it are the following. The universe of realities consists of God as encompassing everything (above and below) since he is the creator and sustainer of all. But there are also invisible powers and forces which, under him, influence what happens among the living. These are deities or minor gods (in some areas of Africa) who are in charge of different aspects of the universe in so far as it relates to the living humans; but also (and in some parts of Africa, especially) the spirits of the dead, benevolent or malevolent (ghosts). Then there is the whole complex of the 'bush' or other parts of the world: flora, fauna, land, mountains, rivers, sky, etc. which is also in interaction with the living.

At the centre of consideration are the living humans in relation to whom the whole universe is seen. The universe is conceived of primarily as a complex system of powers and forces which are in constant interaction, influencing one another for good or for ill.

The basic assumption governing life is that the community of humans who are living on this side of death is involved in a dramatic struggle between life and death; and that the outcome depends on how successfully the human community can relate with the different participants in the universe so that life is assured and death is defeated. The key to success is the solidarity and cooperation among the commu-

---

⁶ Ibid., p. 13.

⁷ *Ibid.*, pp. 32-39.

nity itself, which includes both the living and the dead. For God's supreme presence is mediated by this solidarity among the visible and invisible forces. Human living, culture, and religion are the way this struggle takes place.

It is possible now to understand why and how such a conception of religion is 'non-denominational'. Religion is co-terminous with the project of successful living. And this living is based upon the values of community soli-clarity and cooperation in the common struggle for survival and well-being. The 'religious group' is the group that by force of circumstances - kinship, affinity, neighbourliness or history – constitutes the living unit. Among such groups the struggle for life on the religious sphere is basically the same for all members because they are all committed to the same world-view. The point therefore will not be whether or not they believe different things about God, the spirits, or the world, for they share basic assumptions in regard to all this. What may differentiate various groups is that they live in different living contexts and have different interests, or that the spirits or deities they have to deal with are different because each group deals with those linked up with their life. But these spirits or powers are not in 'theological' competition or struggle, since each one has to deal with their own environment. By the same token, It is meaningless to proselytize: the one God is common to all, while the differentiating spirits and powers are particular to each group. African traditional religion is thus not preoccupied with religious competition between different groups, or with trying to force beliefs and practices on others. That is why I call it non-denominational.

I would submit that, in my case of different family members belonging to different religions or denominations, the fact of having been 'converted', for various historical reasons, to one or the other system of new religious beliefs and practices was taken simply as an additional factor for restructuring the 'map' of concrete living groups on religious grounds. The new configuration did not, or was not expected to, disrupt the basic human solidarity at the service of which all religious practice exists. This means that there is an in-built attitude of tolerance and mutual acceptance in spite of the variety in religious expression, provided the basic human solidarity is not thereby endangered.

Christian Mission and Ecumenism: 'Denominationalism'

The Christian faith that was preached to our people by missionaries was different from this attitude of African traditional religion on several important points. First of all, Christianity was presented as a new or rival religion, totally different form the 'paganism' which it found. Missionary evangelization demanded that prospective converts relinquish their traditional religion and take on the new one as a package. Such a demand assumes that religion is separable from human life, so that you could change religion even if you continued to live as an African. Religion was something added onto ordinary life: a sacred or supernatural reality over against the secular or profane foundation of human existence This presupposes that it is imaginable to have different, even competing, versions of this added reality, religion, while the profane substratum of human living remains intact and valid.

We an already see here the problem that many African communities have had to face on accepting Christianity. The request to squeeze out (pagan) religion and leave only the profane aspect of African life, which then is subsequently filled in with Christianity, was evidently based on an inadequate understanding of traditional culture. As long as the people remained African, such an exercise was impossible since religion and the rest of human life are not thus separable. You would have first to wipe off the whole of the culture in order to take out the 'religion' from the people! African converts have tried this feat. But even with the best of intentions, most of them simply ended up only adding elements of the new religions system to their traditional world-view. The result has been a painful experience of split-personality. As long as things are peaceful, the converts happily follow the demands of their new religion. But when real life crises occur, Christianity has no valid answers: people simply resort (secretly of course) to the proven responses of traditional religion.

There was another difference. According to the Western conception, religion, conceived as separate from the profane part of human life, assumes a distinctive shape. Classical scholars of religion speak of 'religious experience and its expression'. Thus Joachim Wach discusses *the three constituents* of this theoretical 'expression': *doctrine;* practical expression or *cult;* and sociological expression or communion or collective and individual religion.[8]

Max Weber adds another important factor, namely the *prophet* or *founder* of the particular religious expression. Religions (and 'denominations' in the case of Christianity) derive their differences from variations in the components of these expressions.[9] As a consequence, the exact formulation of doctrine, specific regulations for the cult, and the organizational requirements of the communion are of major importance, for it is in these differences between one religion and another, or one denomination and another, that the distinctive nature of each religion clearly comes out. Similarly the personality and teaching of the founder are major differentiating factors.

African traditional religion does not attach a similar differentiating role to these expressions. What may be seen as 'doctrine' is not captured through the kind of shape and configuration that are customary in religions of a written tradition. African religious tradition is essentially oral. What is specially characteristic about oral tradition is that it has indeed some basic root insights, but these manifest themselves and operate not in standardized expressions that attempt to 'comprehend' the truth content in word formulas, but through media that 'evoke' the insight and seek to communicate its power through such things as symbols, song, dance, ritual, visions, and human interaction. Such media are eminently symbolical; their reference to meaning remains always open and not closed.

In the written tradition the verbal formula constitutes a medium which seeks to 'enclose' truth, that is: to reduce it to an objectified form suggesting that the religious insight has been successfully 'captured' and can now be handled and manipulated (symbols of faith, etc.). Once it is thus molded into an almost tangible form, religion can use it as a norm or standard (canon). It is then liable to become the possession of the

---

[8] Joachim Wach, *Sociology of Religion,* Chicago and London: University of Chicago Press, 1944, pp. 17-34.

[9] Max Weber, *The Sociology of Religion,* Boston: Beacon Press, 1922, pp. 46-59, ET 1963/1964.

religious group, and is available to be used as an identifying shibboleth in opposition to other groups. In order to function in this capacity the doctrinal formulation is usually invested with an aura of 'absoluteness': as if the truth could not be expressed validly and meaningfully in any other form. It is this absolutizing of particular forms that seems to me to be characteristic of denominationalism. By it the transcendence of the supernatural is reduced to a particularized formula in the very act of being appropriated by contingent human groups.

What happens in the area of doctrine is usually repeated in the two other areas of ritual and community organization. The same absolutizing tendency appears there too. Specific ritual forms are easily elevated to the state of norms of fidelity; and the same is true of rules and regulations of the religious community. And so religious groups become enclosed and enclosing structures. They relate to one another, not in terms of mere variations or alternatives, but in terms of mutually exclusive opposites.

This way of conceiving religion and its practice seems to be just an instance, especially in the Western world, of a more pervasive cultural imperative: what one might call 'ritualized absolutization'. I mean by this the tendency to organize interaction between diverse elements in terms of mutually excluding competition, where the exclusion of the different is motivated by a claim to absolute validity. I call it 'ritualized' because this claim to absolute validity is not usually taken as based on fact, but simply as an accepted tactic of the game.

Instances of this tactic are observable in the standard competition of political parties. In the struggle for authorization to take power and run the body politic, each party tends to present its programme as the only comprehensibly valid one; and yet the electorate knows very well that such a claim to absolutism is only a game. Another instance is advertisement or the promotion of salable goods. Here too, each promoter lays extravagant claims for the goods it offers, as if these goods had all the desirable qualities while other variants had little or none. Prospective buyers are of course aware that this is just a ritual game: the claims are not necessarily as absolute as they are made out to be.

Relations between diverse religious systems, and certainly between different Christian denominations, have tended to be modelled on this kind of ritual absolutism. There is abroad an in-built compulsion co aggressiveness and competition in relations among different realities: nationalities, cultures, races, interest groups, and beliefs systems. The other possible model, that of complementarity and cooperation, seems to be less in vogue, perhaps because it is seen as a sign of weakness, let alone of compromise or capitulation.

In the religious field, mission and ecumenism are seen in light of this ritually absolutizing model. This may be one reason why in history the Christian missionary movement has often taken the shape of an aggressive crusade, thriving on the destruction, or at least exclusion, of whatever appeared to be different versions of the religious search of humankind. The alternative model, that of dialogue and mutual exchange, has not been generally promoted. By the same token, attempts at ecumenism among Christian bodies are notoriously difficult, almost hopeless - as long as the game is in line with this exclusive and absolutizing tendency.

The Model of African Traditional Religion

After contact with the Christian missionary movement from the West, African believers seem to have adapted quite well to this denominational type of religion. Sometimes it even looks as if some of them surpass their mentors at it!

The point here is not whether this adoption of denominationalism is a bad thing or a good thing. I just wish to insist that this attitude towards differences in religious beliefs and practice is not really in line with the tradition of African religion. As we said above, African society groups and solidarities of religious living are not distinguished primarily by how they express religious beliefs or truths, but by how actual living conditions bring them together or force them apart. For it is the concrete life circumstances that group people into communities in which they have to seek together workable ways of making life successful or worth living. Often what we might call religious beliefs, and even ritual systems or specific rules of communal living, are very similar across the board. And yet in real life people will be living in their separate groups for practical reasons, and not because they claim that their convictions are better than those of the other groups, or that their customs are necessarily more authentic. In fact, it often happens that for some practical reason individuals or whole communities will change allegiance from one group to another, and then naturally begin to follow the religious practices of the new allegiance.

Bishops calling blessings over a fellow bishop

Thus when a person moves into a new family because of marriage, or when a family moves into a new neighbourhood, the newcomers usually participate in the religious life of their new community as much as is required for meaningful living together. They may retain some customs or ritual proper to them, but this will only be so if such customs do not constitute an obstacle to the main communal living of the new group. Their neighbours will therefore be quite prepared to accept those diversities. Similarly a community may break up on such grounds as irreconcilable disputes around leadership, succession, inheritance, witchcraft accusations, or because of family feuds, or simply because of a change in the available resources for living. A group will then hive off and go to start life elsewhere. This group automatically becomes a new religious entity; but the distinguishing factor will not be some basic differences in religious conviction or practice.

What makes this rather strange 'indifference' to religious variations possible? We have already suggested several reasons. One is because life is seen as a totality, and therefore the crucial criterion whether people are one or not is whether the group can live together meaningfully, rather than whether one artificially distinguished aspect of their living (the 'religious' one) is shared by all members in exactly the same way. Another reason is that the basic religious insights, which they all share, are deemed to be a sufficient foundation for a human oneness which varieties in concrete expression do not invalidate. And so, religion as such does not necessarily create separation or barriers among groups. In this sense African religion is not denominational.

It is remarkable that Africans have demonstrated the capacity to apply this attitude even to Christianity. I am thinking of the way African Independent Churches usually function. Typically they are not denominations in the usual sense, but rather groupings of Christian believers distinguishable from one another not so much by their formulas of belief or shape of ritual practice and community organization (even if they often like to make it look that way), but rather by the mere fact of being self-consciously different socio-religious entities. Many of them love to parade under sonorous names which might suggest they believe differently from other (actually very similar) bodies or that their 'doctrines' or practices are really distinct. They even lay much store by the personality of their 'founder' and the marking experience which was at the origin of the specific church.

In reality, however, whole collections of such churches usually have so much in common that you wonder why the groups belonging to the same tradition do not simply form one church. On the other hand the differentiating lines of demarcation are quite fluid and porous. Adherents easily move from one group to the other, for reasons that have very little to do with denominational convictions - which is why membership in these churches is rarely consistent. The churches themselves keep breaking up and regrouping into ever new entities. Such changes are not seen as involving principles of denominational fidelity, as would be the case in the 'mainline' churches. Nor are they taken as a negative reflection on the seriousness of the believer's faith. It is simply a question of where a believer feels most at home in the circumstances and at any particular moment.

Lessons for Christian Mission and Ecumenism: Are there any?

This might sound like a strange question. But why should we not explore it? Is there something to be learnt from this 'non-denominational' way of dealing with religious differenes? Can Christian churches, especially the mainline ones, fmd here some new avenues in their attempt to push forward their search for a positive way of doing mission and evangelism, and a more hopeful way forward in ecumenism? I think so.

This necessarily involves making some sort of comparison between the situation in the African traditional setting and the situation of the churches in Europe or America. However the two contexts are so different from each other that it would not be very helpful to suggest any lessons from one to the other before analyzing carefully some significant cultural and historical differences.

African traditional religion developed and became what it is because of specific cultural and historical circumstances. The African society I have been reflecting upon was mainly composed of small-scale communities, elagaged in subsistence agricultural activities. Life was judged as successful in the measure in which living together offered security, support, and the satisfaction of basic needs. Communities consisted of extended families in which members regarded themselves as belonging together because of real or putative kinship or affinity through marriage. The important point in this kinship is the fact that it binds the members together into an interdependent group within which rights and duties are exchanged unconditionally in the search for life. Participation in the community is a crucial source of the individual's feeling of identity and security. It was indeed a basic asset in a technologically undeveloped society in which survival and meaningful living depended on cooperation and mutual support. That is why living together and being related is a fundamental value. As has been often remarked, where Descartes said: 'I think, therefore I am', Africans would rather say: 'I am related, therefore we are'.

Religion was simply a dimension of this living together. Its 'significance' was not primarily for the individual, but for the community. Good religion was one that helped people to live together in a mutually supporting community and equipped them to solve the basic problems of human living.

Maybe where the African religious tradition might offer lessons to Christian churches in the area of ecumenism is in this understanding of religion as being primarily aimed at building a successful community life among people. Let me unpack this by lining up several suggestions:

1. In the area of faith or belief, the central core of convictions or insights which constitute the common bond should be those that are really fundamental and explain sufficiently the already existing oneness shared by all. In the case of Christians, there is already such a common and basic core, if only people are prepared to find it.

2. The first preoccupation should be how, starting from this common basis, different groups can collaborate and share so as to enrich one ano-ther's life as believers. The key is always and in everything to maximize the scope of working together rather than to be stuck on what is different.

3. Where there are differences, the preoccupation should be to strive to see in what ways those differences constitute variations or alternatives rather than mutually exclusive contradicttions. This is best done by taking account as much as possible of the factors of history, culture, circumstances, preoccupations, priorities, etc. In other words: try to avoid absolutising the differences.

4. If, however, the differences are found to run deep, the preoccupation should be not to let that fact become a pretext for renouncing the basic unity which already exists. While striving to discuss and struggle with one another in the search

for the truth, the practice of mutual love and respect, good will and co-operation in what is still possible must continue, or even be intensified, precisely in order to facilitate the process of fmding solutions.

5. The objective should not be uniformity, but oneness in diversity, provided these diversities are not made into absolutes. Diversities of identity should not be seen as inevitable obstacles to oneness.

Bibliography

Kalilombe, P.A., 'An Outline of Chewa Traditional Religion', *Africa Theological Journal,* Vol. IX/2 (July 1980), pp. 39-51.

Mbiti, IS., *Introduction to African Religion* (1st ed.), London et al.: Heinemann, 1975.

Mugambi, J., J. Mutiso-Mbinda and J. Vollbrecht, *Ecumenical Initiatives in Eastern Africa,* Nairobi:"AACC/AMECEA, 1982.

Mveng, E., *L 'art d'Afrique Noire: liturgie cosmique et langage religieux,* Yaounde: Editions CLE, 1974.

ter Haar, G., A, Moyo and S.J. Nondo, *African Traditional Religions in Religious Education: A Resource Book with Special Reference to Zimbabwe,* Utrecht: Utrecht University, 1992.

Wach, J., *Sociology of Religion,* Chicago and London: University of Chicago Press, 1944.

6 Black Theology

Reproduced from The Modern Theologians, Vol. II (ed. David F. Ford, Oxford: Blackwell, 1989, pp. 193-216). The article had been specially prepared for inclusion in this two-volume introduction to modern trends in theological thinking, and was aimed at introducing the various versions of Third World thinking as developed among Black Theologians in the USA and in Africa: in both South Africa and the independent nations north of the Limpopo. The article was written before the end of the Cold War, the 'far of the Berlin Wall, and the end of Apartheid in South Africa and the establishing of Black majority rule there. How these events will affect 'Black Theology" is not quite clear even today. But it is interesting to see how Theology among the Blacks was being done at a time when these dramatic events were just "hopes" and "dreams."

Introduction: The 'Black Theology' Type of Third World Theologies

In this essay the term 'Black Theology' is being used in a rather general and comprehensive way. It is just as well, therefore, that we should begin by describing what exactly we mean by this term here. The term 'black theology' usually refers to theologies deriving from either the South African or the North American black contexts. Theologizing in these two contexts is concerned mainly with present day situations of oppression and discrimination, and addresses questions of liberation and political freedom and justice. A distinction is often made between this black theology and what are called 'African theologies' in the independent countries farther north, which are considered to be more concerned with questions of culture and to focus more on the past than on the present.[1]

---

[1] Justin S. Ukpong, *African Theologies Now: A Profile,* Eldoret: AMECEA, 1984.

However, despite their differences, these three theologies: the South African and the North American black theologies and the 'African theologies', have recently been discovering a common root that binds them together, namely, the experience of being black. In MI of history, Christian and otherwise, being black has never been a neutral, merely racial characteristic. It has usually been a predicament carrying with it concrete and painful consequences in human interactions. In varying degrees, this experience is shared by all black people: Africans in South Africa as well as in the rest of the continent, and also blacks in North America and in other parts of the world. And therefore any meaningful theology from these situations must necessarily be influenced by this common experience. There is, thus, a point in accepting a wider sense of 'black theology' which would include the South African and North America varieties, as well as the 'African theology' trends. It is this wider meaning that we adopt here.

The significance of this common blackness as a basis for a specific type of Third World theologies has become clearer since the formation, in 1976, of the Ecumenical Association of Third World Theologians (EATWOT). The theological methodology of EATWOT stresses the importance of contextuality: the need to take into account specific human situations. The Third World theologizing communities of Latin America, Africa, and Asia share common conditions of poverty, exploitation, and powerlessness. They are, as a group, representative of the 'losers': those on the 'underside of history'.[2] On this common experience of oppression, poverty, and exploitation is based the liberation thrust of all Third World theologies.

And yet, in spite of the commonalities between them, 'black theologies' are different from Latin American liberation theologies, as discussions within EATWOT have been demonstrating. The nature of these differences may be explained in this way. Although like African and North American types of liberation theology, Latin American theologies are strongly rooted in socio-economic and political questions, still,

---

[2] Cf. Sergio Torres and Virginia Fabella (eds.), *The Emergent Gospel: Theology from the Developing World,* Maryknoll: Orbis, 1978; original subtitle: 'Theology from the Underside of History'.

differently from the others, the Latin American brands tend to be more influenced by Marxist analysis, and are mainly concerned with the class struggles in their countries. That is why Black Theologians have often insisted that Latin American Liberation Theology should not be taken as the unique model for all Third World theologies. The realities of Latin America are not exactly like those of Africa or North America. Africans, for example, have become more and more aware that 'anthropological poverty' (the denial of their culture and very humanity) is more significant for them, while Black Americans are particularly conscious of the history of slavery and their experience of being uprooted. The class struggle that concerns Latin Americans is not important to the same extent or in the same way for these Blacks. For them race relations are of greater importance, whether these are a result of slavery, of colonialism or of neocolonialism.

Therefore the three types: African theology, black theology in South Africa and black theology in North America, have as a common additional Third World element the fact that throughout history the plight of blacks has been related to their blackness. The issue of race cannot be ignored, for their suffering and powerlessness are intrinsically bound up with their race and colour.

North American Black Theology

Historical development

The roots of black theology in North America are to be found in the experience of slavery. Blacks had been brought across the Atlantic as slaves. They were commodities that could be bought and sold, always dependant, vulnerable to exploitation and abuse, and hardly to be considered human beings. Slavery both created and reinforced the myth of black inferiority; and so widespread and so pervasive was this myth that blacks themselves were constantly in danger of developing a low self-esteem.

When the slaves first arrived, they were forbidden to practise their African religion, but were exposed to the religion of their white masters

– Christianity, mostly in its Protestant form. Special missionaries and preachers were employed to teach them Christianity, for the religion they learned was designed to legitimize their state of slavery and to provide a taming influence by promising an escape from their misery into the 'green pastures' of life hereafter. And yet, contrary to their masters' intentions, the Christian message offered the slaves something quite different: the encounter with a God of liberation and equality, with a Christ who understood and sympathized with their plight. Away from their master's watchful eye, in their cabins or in the secret meetings of the woods, they re-interpreted the Scriptures in stories, songs, and dances, giving their own exegesis to the venerable texts. The 'Negro Spirituals' represent an early stage of black theology.[3]

Such an independent appropriation of Christianity was obviously seen as dangerous and subversive by the masters, who then tried to restrict and control the slaves' exposure to the Bible. But this only served to drive the movement underground where an independent type of Christianity, penetrated by African beliefs and customs, developed among the Blacks. When, after emancipation, they were able to come into the open, we discover two types of church belonging among the Blacks. Some were members of the white-led denominations, often contributing to them a distinctive black flavour. But many others belonged to independent churches, in many cases breakaway groups from the white-led denominations where they had experienced discrimination or had been grudgingly given a second-class membership. In both cases, however, religion has been crucial for black survival: the main source of that astonishing resilience in hope and dignity which has kept the community going on as human beings in the face of tremendous odds. In the Church Blacks found a haven where they could recapture and affirm the humanity denied them in everyday life. There they could freely exercise their gifts, could take initiatives, assume positions of leadership, and create a sacred space where the vision of the Kingdom of God on earth becomes credible.

---

[3] Cf. James H. Cone, The Spirituals and the Blues: An Interpretation, Maryknoll: Orbis, 1991.

Even after emancipation in 1863, black experience in America has remained difficult. For many Blacks freedom hardly meant a change in their situation. They were indeed emancipated, but as a group they have remained poor and powerless. They feel they are treated as second-class citizens by the white-dominated establishment. Although in theory they are considered as part of the American 'melting pot' and called to the same 'American Dream' of progress, affluence and world power, the actual working of socio-economic and political structures is loaded against them. Through practice, and often through unfair legislation, they are kept apart and debarred from free and equal cohabitation with the Whites. There were the black belts of the south where Blacks were mostly dependent sharecroppers and work-hands, and in the north there developed the black ghettos in the decaying inner cores of the industrial centres. Segregation in education keeps Blacks confined to poor schools; segregation in jobs and professions reserves for them less significant occupations in which they have little chance of competing with the Whites. To this state of relative poverty and powerlessness two types of response have developed within the black community, which continue the contrasting responses of slavery times: resignation. and revolt. One trend, represented in the nineteenth century by Booker T. Washington, avoids confrontation between the races. It continues the traditional response of many blacks: a more or less conscious acceptance of the negative image given them by the white establishment. It promotes harmony and accommodation, seeking to improve the black people's lot through patient and realistic programmes of self-help, development, thrift, and industry. The other trend, following in the footsteps of Bishop Henry M. Turner and W.E.B. Dubois, is more combative and suspects accommodation or assimilation as being an acceptance of the black people's submission to white supremacy. It sees social and political equality, and the winning of civil rights, as a prerequisite for black progress. Confrontation with the institutionalized white power structure is unavoidable, and premature accommodation can only weaken the chances of success. This trend continues the tradition of black resistance which has erupted in revolts throughout American history.[4]

Survey

The conscious development of a distinct black theology is a relatively recent phenomenon. Its origin is usually placed in July 1966 with the declaration: 'A Statement by the National Committee of Negro Churchmen'.[5]

Three main stimulants have been identified as having led to the need for black theological reflection.[6] The first is the Civil Rights movement of the 1950s and 1960s. The involvement of many black church leaders in the struggle for freedom, alongside Martin Luther King, demanded a fresh confrontation with the message of the gospel. The second was the reaction provoked by a book published in 1964 by the black scholar Joseph R. Washington, Jr entitled *Black Religion: The Negro and Christianity in the United States*.[7] Washington had said that black religion and the black churches did not have a real Christian theological content because they were separated from the white churches, and only if they became integrated into the mainline Christian tradition would they develop a real theology. Such ideas provoked lively discussions about the true nature of black religion. The third and more immediate stimulant was the rise of the Black Power movement. At this time Martin Luther King's non-violent struggle began to be seen as inadequate, and a more militant, separatist movement began, especially among the youth. Its slogan, 'Black Identity and Black Power', summarizes well its objectives. Confronted with this movement black church leaders were obliged to examine the issue of the relationship

---

[4] Lerone Bennett, *Before the Mayflower*, Baltimore: Penguin, 1966.

[5] G.S. Wilmore and James H. Cone (eds.), *Black Theology: A Documentary History, 1966-1979*, Maryknoll: Orbis, 1979, pp.23-30.

[6] J.H. Cone, *For my People: Black Theology and the Black Church*, Maryknoll: Orbis, 1984, pp. 611.

[7] Boston: Beacon, 1964.

between black religion and the quest for identity and power among their people.

Gayraud S. Wilmore distinguishes three stages of development from the 1960s to the present time.[8] Between 1966 and 1970 it developed mainly within the churches, as it was largely black church leaders who responded to the different questions in various meetings and pronouncements. The second stage came in the early 1970s when the discussion of black theology moved from the churches into the universities and seminaries. Black studies became an academic discipline. The influence of the churches decreased, with the result that, as those doing the theology were less accountable to the black community and its current experiences, the theologizing itself became less radical. The third stage, which began in the mid-1970s, saw links being made in various directions. In 1975 the 'Theology in the Americas' project brought black theologians into dialogue with Latin American liberation theology, while at the same time involving other minorities of the United States (Indians, Hispanics, Catholics, women) in the thinking process. Since the inauguration of EATWOT in 1976, American Blacks have been participating in its conferences: in Africa, in Asia, in Latin America, and elsewhere. Thus in this phase black theology is opening up into global concerns, sharing in ecumenical discussions, contributing its own insights as well as receiving challenges and stimulus from other quarters: black feminism and African theology in particular.

Naturally racism is a central theme in black theology, examined not only as a practice of secular society motivated by interests of a political, economic, and societal nature, but also in theological terms. It starts off as a critique of traditional theology of both the white churches and the black community. White church theology has at best tended to ignore the uncomfortable topic of racism, and at worst provided a justification for it. Black traditional religious attitudes have let racism off the hook because of an almost exclusive concentration on 'spiritual matters' and on life after death.

---

[8] Wilmore and Cone, *Black Theology,* pp. 4-11.

In the face of black suffering, the 'theological' and 'christological' issues take on a radical urgency. Who is God? On whose side is He? Black theology re-reads the Bible, and there discovers a liberating God, the champion of the oppressed (Exodus, the Prophets). Christ is 'black',[9] not in a facile racist sense, but theologically, since "in a situation where the colour of a person's skin determines his or her opportunities in life, the gospel is not colour blind".[10] What, then, does such a God want us to do? Here comes the theme of liberation as a process towards the building up of the 'beloved community' (Martin Luther King's favourite expression). But liberation conjures up a whole series of ethical questions. Being freed from oppression demands struggle, and struggle can be violent or nonviolent. Which is the gospel way, and on what conditions? Liberation is a process for change. Is it to be gradual evolutionary change, or a radical revolution? If racism is a sin, then conversion is called for, and only after such a renunciation of racism and after a change in attitudes can harmony and reconciliation take place in society. Such and many more are black theology's issues, as can be seen from a rapid examination of one of its representative proponents.

James H. Cone

Ever since James Cone wrote his *Black Theology and Black Power* (1969) his personality and thinking have been central to black theology. He was among the first to thrust this new type of theology on to the attention of academic scholarship, and has been its most representative exponent in the dialogue with other Third World theologians, especially within EATWOT. Among his major works and numerous articles, *For My People* (1984) is, to date, the most comprehensive survey of his thinking. But *God of the Oppressed* (1975)[11] marks the decisive turning-point, not only of his personal development, but of black theology itself. It is here that one sees the link between theology, the personality of the

---

[9] Cf. Albert B. Cleage, *The Black Messiah*, Kansas City: Sbeed Andrews and McKeel, 1968.

[10] Theo Winehet, *A Place in the Sun: An Introduction to Liberation Theology in the Third World*, London: SCM, 1985, p. 73.

[11] New York: Seabury, 1975.

theologian, and the community from within which that theology is being done.

The book starts with a personal witness: how he was born and grew up in Arkansas, that typical arena of black experience. This early involvement in the black church and community in the American South was followed by academic training in the more liberal North. Subsequently Cone has taught in the South before taking up his present post at Union Theological Seminary in New York. All this was an appropriate background for the theological reflection in the book: The main contention is that "one's social and historical context decides not only the questions we address to God but also the mode or form of the answers given to the questions".[12] In the first chapters (2-4) the significance of this social context is examined: theology is indeed based on biblical revelation, but even in the Bible social existence gives the concrete shape to divine revelation. The study of Scripture is itself further determined by that same social context, which explains why 'white' theology in America interprets the divine Word differently from 'black' religious thought.

It is important therefore to address seriously the problem of ideology, as H. Richard Niebuhr did in *Christ and Culture* when he explored how human speech about divine revelation is conditioned by cultural and historical relativity. Black Theology results from the interface between God's Word and black experience. Chapters 6-10 take up the main questions. Who is Jesus Christ for us today? What is liberation? How does divine liberation relate to black suffering? In the area of Christian ethics, what relation is there between liberation and violence, between liberation and the reconciliation between Blacks and Whites?

God of the Oppressed is primarily an essay in theological methodology; but at that stage in the development of black theology it was a decisive contribution. Before black theology could begirt to be taken seriously, the legitimacy of applying the principle of contextuality to black experience had to be established. In this, as in many other areas, James Cone's contribution has been programmatic. A weakness in Cone's early

---

[12] Cone, God of the Oppressed, p. 15.

works was his almost exclusive basing of his reflection on the issue of black power, and a relative ignoring of the black church experience at the grass-roots.[13] Although a balance has been established in this respect, it still remains that Cone's works are more for the consumption of fellow intellectuals than a means of dialogue with the common black folk. There is also a combative strain which makes the vision of an eventual reconciled black and white community difficult to imagine.

Debate, achievement, and agenda

One area or questioning that North American black theology had to deal with in the early years was that of its relations with African theology.[14] Some African theologians (e.g. J.S. Mbiti and E. Fashole-Luke) refused to recognize that there were real links of kinship between the two theologies. North American theology, because of its roots in slavery, tends to promote separation between black and white, even among Christians. It insists on struggle, seems to condone violence, and is preoccupied with social and political issues. African theology on the other hand is based on culture and religion. It has a distinctively joyful and open spirit, where black theology is negative and narrow. But North Americans criticized African Theology for being too much oriented towards the past while ignoring the burning issues of today. Since the foundation of EATWOT this controversy has lost its virulence. Instead, the two theologies now see each other as complementary and mutually challenging prongs of the same struggle.

Within black theology itself there have always been issues and trends confronting one another. Some theologians, for example, are more prone towards reconciliation (e.g. J. Deotis Roberts) while others underline the need for confrontation (e.g. James H. Cone). Should black theology develop primarily as a reaction to white theology with nothing really original from its own resources? Black theology is by no means a

---

[13] Cf. his brother Cecil Wayne Cone's criticism *in The Identity Crisis in Black Theology,* Nashville, Abingdon, 1975.

[14] Josiah U. Young, *Black and African Theologies: Siblings or Distant Cousins?,* Maryknoll: Orbis, 1986.

monolithic entity. To capture all its richness one should study its various protagonists. Besides G. S. Wilmore and James Cone, there are others like Cecil Cone, G. Eric Lincoln, Cornel West, Charles Long, Vincent Harding, and feminist representatives like Jacquelyn Grant, Delores Williams, or Kelly Brown.

Black theology started as a theological reaction to racism in both church and society, a prophetic voice against the typical 'internal colonization' in the United States. It has extended its arena, through contact with other Third World contexts, to include other manifestations of discrimination, poverty, and oppression. Its main contribution remains its experience in confronting racism at close range and on the home ground of the powerful American establishment whose influence all over the world is a marked feature of our times. The way forward seems to be along the line of mutual enrichment and challenge with the other Third World theologies. As black theology listens to Asia, to South Africa, to the Caribbean, the Pacific, the women, the disabled, etc., its own methodology will be enriched while its agenda is widened and its views challenged or confirmed. Multi-racial Britain could very well become its next partner in dialogue.

African Theology

Historical development

It is difficult to pinpoint exactly when and by whom the expression 'African Theology' *(theologia Africana)* was first used, but the movement itself has a long history. Its roots lie in the ideas sown by Caribbean and North American blacks of the nineteenth century, e.g. E.W. Blyden (1893) and W.E.B. Dubois (1890). These early pan-Africanists, reflecting on slavery and colonialism, were concerned mainly with political questions, but they saw that the promotion of black peoples was dependent upon a reaffirmation of African culture and religion.

Moving into Africa, at the turn of the century, such ideas were translated into various forms of ideological resistance, not only to European colonial incursions, but also to the imposition of the white man's Christianity, as is evident in the early rise of independent churches in South Africa and elsewhere.[15]

Thus, as African nationalism took shape between and after the two world wars, there was in the churches also a latent corresponding trend of critique against the way evangelization had taken place. Becoming Christian was often presented as a rejection of the past in favour of adopting Western Christian ways of thinking and behaving. Implicit in this was the conviction that Christianity could not be based on traditional culture and that there was no real continuity between African traditional religions and the Christian message. Thus Christian evangelization was based on the same assumptions as colonialism: a rejection of the African personality and the need to impose Western civilization on Africans. It was against such racist attitudes that African thinkers began to rebel.

There is evidence that already in the years between the wars this movement of cultural and political vindication was growing, especially among young black students in the schools of Europe. In the 1930s a group of Caribbean and African students in Paris, led by such figures as Aimè Césaire (Martinique) and Leopold Senghor (Senegal), launched the famous Nègritude movement with its review *Presence Africaine,* an affirmation and rehabilitation of black cultural identity in history, literature, and art. Fr Placide Tempels's *La Philosophie Bantoue*[16] was a seminal work by a European missionary in Africa. There he affirmed that there exists among the Bantu peoples of Africa a coherent thought system, "a complete positive philosophy of existence, of life, of death and life after death".[17] He claimed that this philosophy was centred on one value, "vital force" *(la force vitale),* and then proceeded to show how a whole system of ontology, criteriology, psychology, and ethics derived from this centre.

---

[15] Cf. Bengt Sundkler, *Bantu Prophets in South Africa,* 2nd ed., London: Lutterworth, 1961.

[16] Paris: Editions Africaines, 1949.

[17] *La Philosophie Bantoue,* p. 14, translated from French as *Bantu Philosophy.*

Later critics have rejected Tempels's concordism which artificially forces African thought into scholastic European categories. But the main contention, that the African way of life had a valid philosophy, was not lost on thinking Africans. In 1956 a team of black ecclesiastics studying in European universities published a collection of essays under the title: *Les pre-tres noirs s'interrogent.*[18] Following the idea of adaptation in vogue at the time, the writers proclaimed the need to Africanize Christian doctrine, cult, pastoral practice and art, basing them on African culture and religious traditions. These ideas, in line with authoritative Roman Catholic pronouncements, find later support in the Second Vatican Council (19621965). They represent the standard thinking among Catholic progressive thinkers in the 1960s and 1970s.

In 1960, at the newly founded Catholic Institute of Lovanium in Kinshasa (Zaire), a young student (later to become auxiliary Bishop T. Tshibangu) affirmed the possibility of a "Theology with an African colour" based on the specific thought patterns of African culture. For, although divine revelation is one, and the principles of human reasoning are shared universally, there are special African characteristics which make it possible to do theology in an African way. Tshibangu's professor, Canon A. Vanneste, disagreed. For him Christianity and its theology are of universal validity since they are based on divine revelation which is one. It does not make sense, therefore, to speak of an African theology. The most one can concede is that doing theology *in Africa* should take the African experience into consideration, especially in catechesis and pastoral work. But this is not the same as accepting the possibility of an African theology.

Tshibangu's view has clearly won the day, for since the 1960s more and more Africans have joined in the effort to do their own theology. If among Catholics the Second Vatican Council gave impulse to this development, among Protestants the main stimulus has been the All African Council of Churches (AACC), founded in 1963.[19] The conferences

---

[18] Black Priests are Asking Themselves, Paris, 1956.

[19] Gwinyai Muzorewa, The Origins and Development of African Theology, Maryknoll: Orbis, 1985.

and consultations which it has been sponsoring have helped many scholars in the churches as well as in the universities and colleges to become acquainted with the movement for African theologizing. In 1977 the Ecumenical Association of African Theologians (EAAT) was started in Accra. It has now become the main forum for the development of African theology.

Survey

The earlier phase of African theology was mainly apologetic in character. It sought to affirm the validity of African traditional cultures and religions as bases for Christian theology.[20] But even in those years, definite themes and topics had already begun to emerge. Besides rather general works such as Kwesi Dickson's *Theology in Africa*,[21] or John S. Pobee's *Toward an African Theology*,[22] there are now more specific themes, e.g. F. Kabasele et al., *Chemins de la christologie africaine*.[23] In these last years a liberation type of theology has been developing, the most impressive example of which is possibly Jean-Marc Ela's *The African Cry*.[24]

The main themes in African theology are those aspects of Christian faith and practice which Western culture has either neglected or played down, but which Africans seem to value specially. Such is the importance of community and communion (as against individualism). The value of solidarity and human relationships is affirmed not only among the living (family, clan, tribe), but also with the deceased, especially the ancestors. It goes farther in that life is seen as a constant interaction with the invisible (God, minor deities, and spirits). The whole creation is in fact dealt with as a partner in total existence rather than as an object out there (nature) which humans can exploit at will. There

---

[20] Cf. Idowu, African Traditional Religion.

[21] Maryknoll: Orbis, 1984.

[22] Nashville, Abingdon, 1979.

[23] Paris: Desclée, 1986.

[24] Maryknoll: Orbis, 1981.

are in this attitude practical implications of an ecological nature. Similarly life is considered holistically as is apparent in traditional conceptions about health and sickness, good and evil. No wonder African theologians find the Old Testament very much alive and near to their way of life, including the propensity to symbolism and ritual.

By its very nature African Theology pursues two tasks: a negative and a positive one. Negatively, African theology exposes and refutes several ways of thinking, both cultural and religious, which have underpinned the tendency to despise and do away with traditional cultures and religions. Of these the crudest is the one that claims Africans are sub-human, inferior, or underdeveloped simply because they have not followed the same path of progress as the 'civilized' peoples of the industrialized West. This powerful and deep-rooted myth made slavery and colonialism acceptable, and even conferred on them an aura of benefaction. To this end African theology examines Scripture and takes up the theme of humanity's oneness in spite of its diversity; the theme also of the 'image of God' present in every human being, and the fundamental equality and right to respect that this demands.

It also examines the theme of God's presence and salvific activity among peoples who are not visibly confronted with the historical manifestation of Jesus the Christ. By implication the project of African Theology raises the question of what unity of Christian faith means as opposed to uniformity, and how the universality of the one Christian faith is to manifest itself in concrete forms. Many people who reject the whole idea of African or Black theology do so on the ground that there can be only one universal Christian theology which admits of no distinctions of colour or race.

But Africa is, in the final analysis, a continent of oral tradition rather than of the written word. Perhaps the most exciting elaboration of African theology is being done in obscure corners where writing plays only a minimal role. Thus what is being lived in the independent churches in celebration, sermon, song, dance, prophecy, dreams, visions, and healing rituals constitutes authentic and original material for African theology. In the same way a new ecclesiology, new interpretations of the gospel message, and new modalities of liberation are being elaborated within the popular circles of the small Christian communities or the revival groups within main-line churches as well as beyond them.[25]

Offertory – „Fruits of the earth and work of human hands"

An example of such a theology, so elusive to traditional academic formulation, is Archbishop E. Milingo's ministry of healing and exorcism. What one can read in his writings[26] is but an inadequate expression of a truly theological praxis which has not yet found the kind of verbal form to give it the place it deserves in scientific circles. Among the skills most needed in African academic theologians is that of being sensitive to these theological productions of ordinary people at the grass-roots and being able to locate them, and then translate them into inter-cultural communicable form without betraying their original native quality. How African theologizing is actually done can best be seen through an essay of one of its practitioners.

---

[25] Cf. P.A. Kalilombe, "Doing Theology at the Grassroots: A Challenge for Professional Theologians", reproduced in this volume, pp. 166-194.

[26] Emmanuel Milingo, *The World in Between: Christian Healing and the Struggle for Spiritual Survival*, London: C. Hurst and Co., 1984.

John S. Pobee

Reverend John S. Pobee was born in 1937 in Ghana. A member of the Anglican Church, he studied at Oxford and subsequently taught in his home university of Ghana, Legon. But his acquaintance with different trends of Third World theology has deepened through involvement in Christian ecumenical work, culminating in his post at the World Council of Churches headquarters in Geneva in the department for theological education. He writes extensively on theological topics and has been a fervent promoter of conferences and consultations. His book *Toward an African Theology*,[27] although written in 1979, is the most appropriate place for capturing both his thought and methodology.

The first half of the book, consisting of four chapters, describes the concern of African theology thus: "to interpret essential Christian faith in authentic African language in the flux and turmoil of our time so that there may be genuine dialogue between the Christian faith and African culture".[28] For Pobee, his native Akan culture is an example of Africa's other cultures. Thus several elements are involved: faith, revelation, reflection. Contrary to some past missionary attitudes, according to which 'non-Christian' cultures are to be destroyed and wiped out *(tabula rasa)* so that 'Christianity' (i.e. in its Western form) can be put in their place, the right attitude is adaptation, localization or indigenization of Christianity to local cultures. For although Christianity is based on God's special, complete, and definitive revelation in Christ, nevertheless Scripture itself "affirms that there are revelations of the deity other than the revelation in Jesus Christ".[29] Even if this natural revelation through human cultures is a groping, and is subject to misunderstandings and corruption, there are valid elements in it which Christianity can assume and use in order to bring Christian revelation to the people. With right Christian faith and appropriate reflection, an African theology is therefore not only possible but highly desirable.

---

[27] Nashville, Abingdon, 1979.

[28] Pobee, Toward an African Theology, p. 22.

[29] Ibid., p. 74.

The rest of the book gives a series of examples in the application of these principles: Christology (Christ as the Akan chief *okyeame*, mouthpiece of the paramount), sin and evil, Christian marriage, and the ethics of power. Typical of African Protestant/Anglican theologians, the method is invariably first to describe the Akan viewpoint, with abundant relevant proverbs, and then to bring in the Scriptures as congruent or critical of the culture. The last example, ethics of power, is evidence against those who accuse the cultural trend of shying away from confrontation with present-day socio-political issues or of simply looking back to a dead past. It is a lucid analysis and condemnation of the misuse of power in modern Africa, using not simply biblical evidence but also what is positive in African traditional culture.

Nevertheless, the limits of African theology are apparent in that even the best lnculturated' examples make appeal to aspects of Akan culture which, in present-day culture change, might soon lose their power of appeal and usefulness.

Debate, achievement and agenda

The objection still being made against certain ways of doing cultural African theology is that this theology tends to deal with an artificially reconstructed past culture when it is not sure such a culture has much practical relevance in modern life. Clearly the question here is how one defines culture: as an idealized static collection of items from the past, or as the dynamic ever-evolving way of life of people which is the result of various influences, from the past and from the present, from within and from without? It is a pity that in many writings of African theologians this central notion of culture is not carefully defined or discussed.

African theologians do not speak the same language concerning the question of God's presence and salvific activity in non-Christizn religions. While some find no difficulty in accepting the possibility of salvation outside the visible Christian church,[30] others are more

---

[30] Cf. P.A. Kalilombe, 'The Salvific Value of African Religions', reproduced in this volume, pp. 105121.

cautious. They are sensitive to the dangers of 'syncretism' and what they call 'false universalism of salvation'.[31] In most cases, it seems to depend on what type of Western theological tradition the theologian has inherited. For similar reasons the distinction between 'African theology' and 'African Christian theology' is more meaningful for some than for others. 'African theology' would mean the thinking about God in traditional religion outside Christianity, whether it is considered positively or negatively; while 'African Christian theology' is the confrontation of the Christian faith with the way Africans think, assuming usually that they have been exposed to Christian faith. Here too, unhappily, many African theologians do not discuss fully and explicitly the basic issues implied.

The former type of African theology has probably seen its heyday. As life becomes more and more affected by contact with the wider world, the cultural specifics on which it based most of its reflection will slowly lose their relevance. Nevertheless, the significance of it lay in the values of African culture which it has identified, values which are potential elements of revitalization for world-wide Christianity. The lasting importance of the project of African theology itself lies in its protest against the cultural mutilation of other people's self-consciousness and self-respect, which produces 'anthropological poverty'. It is an achievement of the African theology project to have exposed and refuted any racial superiority complex attempting to justify itself through the Christian Scriptures.

Judging from what the Ecumenical Association of African Theologians has been working on in its recent conferences and consultations, it is permitted to foretell several future trends. There will be less naivity in portraying African traditional cultures and religions: we are more aware today of the wide varieties, contrasts, and complexities. The process of cultural change will be taken more seriously through a more careful analysis of the impact of outside influences, and a more sophisticated use of tools for historical reconstruction. Although the interest in inculturation will continue, more theological work will go into questions

---

[31] For example, Byang H. Kato, Theological Pieälls in Africa, Kisumu, 1975.

of development and liberation. It would seem indeed that the role of women and other marginalized sections of society in setting the theological agenda has been increasing. Africa is becoming more and more patently the scene of endless wars, famine, despotism, refugees, and militarism. The themes of justice, human rights, social and community restructuring will be dominant in theological reflection and praxis.

South African Black Theology

Historical development

Black Theology in South Africa has its roots in a long tradition of protest against racial discrimination, appropriation of land, and economic exploitation to which the non-white groups have been subjected in the long history of European settlement in this part of the continent. This is because the Dutch immigrants (forebears of the modern Afrikaners) interpreted their occupation of South Africa and their confrontation with its inhabitants in the light of their Calvinistic faith.

> 'In obedience to Almighty God and to His Holy Word', so ran the 1942 draft constitution, 'the Afrikaner people recognizes its national calling, manifested in the history of the voortrekkers, as being that of developing South Africa in accordance with the Christian faith'.[32]

Such an exegesis of history is based on a peculiar application of the doctrine of predestination. On the South African scene it means that God chose the white people as his own possession and ordained them to subject the heathens (in this case the blacks, the 'kaffirs' - unbelievers) making them into hewers of wood and drawers of water. Colour and race became powerful symbols of distinction and apportioning of power and privilege.

---

[32] *Vivante Univers*, 1987, p. 8, no. 369, (translation).

In South Africa this blending of religious faith, colour symbolism, and down-to-earth socio-economic and political objectives has been directing the trend of history. The white minority, relying on Christian faith, progressively captured for itself positions of material and cultural superiority over the original black population and, later, other communities of non-European origin. In the name of the same faith a system of relationship; emerged which serves to keep the racial groups separate and unequal. This practice of racial segregation became an officially entrenched juridical system (apartheid) when the Afrikaner Nationalist Party came to power in 1948.

The response of the oppressed black population has been expressed on both the secular and the religious levels. In 1912 the African National Congress (ANC) was formed with the intention of protecting the rights of black people and promoting their development. When its non-violent methods were judged ineffective, the more revolutionary Pan Africanist Congress (PAC) arose in 1958 as a rival branch, with 'Africa for Africans' as its slogan. In recent years the ANC itself has felt pushed to opt for more forceful methods in response to repressions from the state.

Over the years it has become more and more evident that this apartheid system is not the sole responsibility of South Africa. It has links with the world-wide economic system, and is an extreme manifestation of the unjust relationships between the North and the South: between the Centre, consisting of the affluent and powerful nations of the East and the West, and the Periphery, consisting of the poor nations in the Third World. In spite of pious words of condemnation directed towards South Africa, most nations are at heart reluctant to dismantle the system because they gain from it.

But since the apartheid system is based primarily on religious belief, black opposition has had to express itself on that level too. Even in the churches, the principle of separate but unequal existence was at work. In many cases Christian denominations have existed in separate congregations according to racial and colour differences: white, 'coloured', and black. Obviously such distinctions, when justified by God's Word, provoked a re-examination of Christianity itself. Was the God of white people the same as the God Africans acknowledged? Was it the Christ of the gospels that sanctioned discrimination between white and black?

The most impressive of the different reactions against the white people's Christianity has been the well-established and fast-growing movement towards African Church independency. Even if very little elaborate thinking has been produced within these churches, their very existence must be seen as an inchoate black theology.

Survey

A consistent project for a black theology began to take shape in South Africa during the 1970s. Popular resistance was being met with naked repression, as was the case in the Sharpeville murders of 1960 and the Soweto incidents in 1976. Although the inter-racial Christian Institute, founded in 1963, had drawn the wrath of the regime and was forced to close in 1977,[33] theological reflection could not be stopped. The multi-racial University Christian Movement (UCM), established in 1967, became a forum for social and political reflection. The series of seminars on black theology which it organized in the course of 1971 gave birth to the first important publication of the movement.[34]

In 1969 the all-black South African Student Organization (SASO) was started by Steve Biko as a breakaway from the UCM, initiating the Black Consciousness Movement. SASO's 1970 Manifesto on black consciousness stresses the need for South African blacks to reject all value systems seeking to make them foreigners in their own country, to define themselves and not to be defined by others, to become aware of the power they wield as a group, and to involve all oppressed sections in a joint commitment.[35] Predictably this sudden burst of black consciousness and black theology was included in the general

---

[33] Peter Walshe, *Church and State in South Africa*, Marylmoll: Orbis, 1983.

[34] Cf. Basil Moore (ed.), Essays in Black Theology, Johannesburg, 1972. English editions: Black Theology: The South African Voice, London: Hurst, 1973; The Challenge of Black Theology in South Africa, London: Hurst, 1974.

[35] Moore (ed.), Black Theology.

proscription of 'subversive movements'. Steve Biko himself died in police custody in 1977.

But black theology itself could not be banished or silenced. It has carried on, especially through such prominent church leaders as Archbishop Desmond Tutu,[36] Bishop Manas Buthelezi and Reverend Allan Boesak.[37] The power of this theology is in its constant fink with the leaders' pastoral involvement in the suffering of their people. They speak from personal experience as they too share the lot of their brothers and sisters: vexations, arrests, loss of passport, denigration, even threats of death.

In academic circles, too, there is a growing number of thinkers who brave the dangers involved in creative critical thinking and continue to produce work of theological scholarship: veterans like Gabriel Setiloane, or G.M. Motlhabi, and younger people like Thakatso Mofokeng, Bonganjalo Goba, Simon Maimela, Buti Tlhagale. Since 1976 and 1977 when EATWOT and EAAT were founded, these voices have been joining other Third World theologians in conferences and consultations, offering the challenge of a South African contribution.

Significantly, even the African Independent Churches and the evangelical denominations, which up to now could be considered as eschewing political involvement, have got down to a more realistic theology, much in line with what black theology has been saying all along.[38] Black theology is thus becoming a type of Christian consensus in the face of the South African crisis.

Black Theology hinges on the fundamental theme of colour, because the condition of being black or white has become a factor determining relationships between communities and individuals. To be black, or to belong to a given race, straight away determines the whole of life, social, economic, political, as well as religious. Colour separates: to

---

[36] Desmond Tutu, Hope and Steering, Grand Rapids: Eerdmans, 1984.

[37] Allan Boesak, Black and Reformed, Maryknoll: Orbis, 1984.

[38] Evangelical Alliance, Evangelical Witness in South Africa: A Critique of Evangelical Theology and Practice by South African Evangelicals Themselves, Oxford: Regnum, 1986.

some it gives privileged rights and to others it denies even the most elementary ones. But above all, one colour (white) grants power and superiority over the other (black).

All this raises fundamental theological questions. Against a long established system of oppression and injustice, is it realistic to put hope in reforms or should people contemplate radical revolution and the elimination of the system itself? But then that implies conflict. In the Christian vision, is there place for creative conflict? Is there such a thing as liberating violence? Christ came to bring reconciliation and love. But what are the requirements for an authentic reconciliation? Since the church is a community of love, what role should it play in a situation of racial discrimination and division?

In the *Kairos Document*[39] most of these questions have been taken up in a short but profound discussion. Theological reflection in South Africa bases itself on the Bible. But in addition to the usual Exodus theme, the more fundamental question of Creation widens the reflection. What does it mean to be made "in the image of God"? Where do dignity and the rights of the human person come from? Colour or ethnic belonging? Then come themes of power, its nature and the reason for its existence, its use and its abuse. What should one do if the very humanity is denied or ridiculed? Has one the duty to struggle to safeguard it? Are God and his Christ on the side of an oppressive group or are they with the poor and oppressed?

South African theology gives great importance to questions of reconciliation, of redemptive suffering, of nonviolence. It insists on the fact that the liberation hoped for is for both blacks and whites. It is a theology deeply rooted in the life of the church and could not be accused of secularism, still less of Marxism. A look at one of the best known South African theologians should help us to see the kind of questions that are usually dealt with.

---

[39] Kairos Document: A Theological Comment on the Political Crisis in South Africa.

Allan Aubrey Boesak

The choice of Dr Boesak as representative of black theology in South African is appropriate for two main reasons. He is a 'coloured', that is, of mixed blood: in his very person are manifested the tragedy and the contradictions of the apartheid system. At the same time he is a prominent leader in the Calvinist Dutch Reformed Church, and thus knows from the inside the tradition in which apartheid fmds its theological basis.

A South African by birth, he studied in Holland and has intimate knowledge of black theology in the United States. At the assembly of Ottawa in 1982, when the white wing of the Dutch Reformed Church (the NGK) was expelled from the World Reformed Alliance and apartheid was declared a heresy, Boesak was elected President of the World Alliance of Reformed Churches. A fitting symbol of creative protest.

In *Black Theology, Black Power,*[40] he exposes the 'innocence' of both white and black churches, which "hides painful truths behind a facade of myths and real or imagined anxieties".[41] Among whites the myth is that apartheid is based on Christian love: separation and alienation can be tolerated provided the white can do something for the blacks. The blacks innocently accept and internalize the negative image made about them. To demythologize both myths, a biblical analysis of liberation (chapter 1) and power (chapter 2) is necessary.

Liberation starts when the blacks discover that in the specific context of South Africa, Christ cannot be white but black; the Black Messiah; the presence of Yahweh the liberator of the oppressed. His gospel is for the poor; his love for them is in view of eliminating their 'nonhumanity' so that they can begin to love the image of God that is in them. Loving themselves in this way does not mean hating the oppressor, but it means refusing to accept a 'brotherhood' where the one brother is master of the other.

---

[40] Allan Aubrey Boesak, *Black Theology, Black Power,* London: Mowbrays, 1978.

[41] *Farewell to Innocence is* the original, Maryknoll: Orbis, title of the book.

Liberation is not possible without an adequate consideration about power. Oppression and exploitation come form a misuse of power, a usurpation of power-over-others reducing them to dependency. Blacks must protest against such oppression, first by rejecting negative self-images, and then by affirming their God-given power: the Holy Spirit.

In chapter 3, 'Where the Spirit Moves', Boesak examines the meaning and implications of God's Spirit as empowerment. Liberal and nationalistic theologies, as well as black nationalism, are here subjected to criticism. The book ends with a 'Quest for a Black Ethic'. The ethic of black liberation is necessarily situational, in the good sense. Values like hope, reconciliation, love of justice should not be discussed in the air: the total context of South African realities should be taken into account in the search for a truly Christian ethic.

Black Theology, Black Power is not an exhaustive or definitive statement of black theology. It can even be accused of being rather one-sided since it offers little in the way of positive and workable suggestions for conversion and change on the side of the white community. But it does offer a helpful model and methodology for confronting theologically the tragic situation in apartheid South Africa. Its great virtue is in not being a recipe for despair. Basically it is a declaration of courageous faith in the possibility of a new South Africa striving towards God's kingdom.

Debate, achievements, and agenda

There was a time when people contrasted South African theology with its insistence on struggle for liberation, and the culture- and tradition-orientated theologies in the North. It is important to understand exactly why South Africans like Manas Buthelezi have expressed suspicion about the zeal to revalorize traditional customs of the past or to insist on maintaining Bantu cultural identity. The danger is not simply that of distracting attention from the real issues of modern life. In the context of South Africa, the apartheid ideology has made so much of national characteristics and has used the idea to keep different ethnic groups separate and divided (cf. the Bantustans). It is dangerous to play into the hands of such divisive and weakening tactics. At the same time, however, scholars like G. Setiloane have pointed out the need for the blacks to discover the basis of their own humanity, for future generations will want to have the assurance of a valuable past on which to build a new, post-apartheid, South Africa.

The two preoccupations need not exclude each other. The present trend is towards a harmonious integration: more and more South Africans are realizing that the blacks will not be able to liberate themselves unless they first regain their cultural and human identity. At the same time theologians of inculturation have learned to give more attention to the present-day problems of post-colonial Africa. The particular significance of South African black theology lies in that it forces the victims of the worst type of human oppression to fall back on the Word of God as the most promising and creative reaction to their plight. Black theology in South Africa is, on the whole, a truly Christian reflection. It goes beyond mere condemnation of white oppression by stressing that both the oppressed and the oppressor are victims of their fears. It also proposes reconciliation as the final objective, adding, nevertheless, that true reconciliation can only come after genuine conversion from egoistic preoccupation with sectional security and privilege. The basic Christian imperative of 'love chasing away fear' is at its centre.

South African black theology is a developing reality: its future shape cannot now be determined in advance. But the main orientations it has taken are a timely challenge to Christian theology generally. Politics and economics can no longer be considered peripheral issues in a world where Christian nations are directly involved in creating wholesale poverty and inhuman suffering through systems of exploitation that attempt to hide safely behind God's Word. This South African theology might become the crucial ingredient in tackling theologically the global issue of North-South relationships.

Bibliography

General

Chenu, B., Theologie chretiennes des tiers mondes, Paris, 1987.

Ferm, D.W., *Third World Theologies: 1. An Introduction; 2. A Reader*, Maryknoll:Orbis, 1986. '

Witvliet, T., *A Place in the Sun: An Introduction to Liberation Theology in the Third World*, London: SCM, 1985.

Young, J.U., *Black and African Theologies: Siblings or Distant Cousins?*, Maryknoll: Orbis, 1986.

North American Black Theology

Cone, J.H., *Black Theology and Black Power,* Maryknoll: Orbis, 1969.

Cone, J.H., *A Black Theology of Liberation,* Philadelphia, 1970.

Cone, J.H., *The Spirituals and the Blues: An Interpretation,* Maryknoll: Orbis, 1972.

Cone, J.H., *For My People: Black Theology and the Black Church,* Maryknoll: Orbis, 1984.

Gardiner, J. and D. Roberts Snr (eds.), *Quest for a Black Theology,* Philadelphia, 1971.

Jones, M., *Christian Ethics for Black Theology,* Nashville: Abingdon, 1974.

Lincoln, C.E. (ed.), *The Black Experience in Religion,* Garden City: Doubleday and Co., 1974.

Malcolm X, *Malcolm X Speaks,* New York, 1965.

Roberts, J.D., *Liberation and Reconciliation,* Philadelphia, 1971.

Wilmore, G.S., *Black Religion and Black Radicalism,* Garden City: Doubleday and Co., 1972.

Wilmore, G.S. and J.H. Cone (eds.), *Black Theology: A Documental} History 1966-1979,* Marylmoll: Orbis, 1979.

African Theology

Appiah-Kubi, K. and S. Torres (eds.), *African Theology en Route,* Maryknoll: Orbis, 1979.

Imasogie, O., *Guidelines for Theology in Africa,* Achimota, 1983.

Magesa, L., *The Church and Liberation in Africa,* Eldoret: AMECEA, 1976.
Mbiti, J.S., *African Religions and Philosophy,* Garden City: Doubleday and Co., 1970.
Mbiti, J.S., *New Testament Eschatology in an African Background,* London: SPCK, 1971.
Nyamiti, C., *Christ as our Ancestor,* Gweru: Mambo, 1984.
Parrett, J., *A Reader in African Christian Theology,* London, 1987.
Sawyerr, H., *Creative Evangelism: Towards a New Christian Encounter with Africa,* London: Lutterworth, 1968.
Tshibangu, T., *Le propos d'une thgologie africaine,* Kinshasa, 1974.

South African Theology

Becken, H.J., Relevant Theology for Africa, Durban, 1973.
Biko, S., Black Consciousness and the Quest for a True Humanity, Durban, 1972.
Boesak, A.A., Black Theology, Black Power, London: Mowbrays, 1978.
Boesak, A.A., Black and Reformed, Maryknoll: Orbis, 1984.
Buthelezi, M., An African Theology or a Black Theology, Durban, 1972.
de Gruchy, J.W., The Church Struggle in South Africa, Grand Rapids: Eerdmans, 1979.
Kairos Document, A Theological Comment on the Political Crisis in South Africa, 2nd ed., London, 1986.
Kretzschmar, L., The Voice of Black Theology in South Africa, Johannesburg, 1986.
Mabona, A., White Worship and Black People, Durban, 1972.
Mabuza, W.M., Christianity and the Black Man in South Africa Today, Durban, 1972.
Setiloane, G.M., The Image of God among the Sotho-Tswana, Rotterdam: Baldema, 1976.
Setiloane, G.M., African Theology: An Introduction, Johannesburg: Skotaville, 1986.

7 Doing Theology at the Grassroots: A Challenge for Professional Theologians

This article appeared in two parts in AFER (Part I: in Vol. 27/3, June, 1985, pp. 148-161, and Part II: in no. 4, August, 1985, pp. 225-237). It was the text of a paper read at an EATWOT Conference. The article contains many ideas and reflections that have been dear to me and appear in various forms in many of the chapters in this book. That is why its title has been adopted as the overall title of the whole book.

Introduction

As the title of this chapter indicates, its aim is to reflect on a basic claim of Third World theologians, namely that the theology they are doing is not a monopoly of a select few, but a joint enterprise that includes even those ordinary men and women who have had no formal training in the scientific handling of God's Word. When theology is understood in this broad sense, its practice becomes a challenge for those of us who have been trained to do theology at a rather sophisticated level. Is it possible for us to join the rest of God's people in this task without feeling awkward or being hampered by attitudes of superiority or paternalism? On what conditions can this best be done?

In the first part of this essay the conception of a grassroots theology is examined. Then the second part attempts to show that such a theologizing is not easy for the ordinary people since, in the prevailing circumstances of modern society, they have not been involved in the formulation of policies and projects of public importance even when these determine their everyday lives. And yet, the vision of a grassroots theology is not necessarily *a utopia*. It *can* be realized. Already here and there examples are appearing which demonstrate that this new way of doing theology is quite possible. In the final section of this paper I shall be suggesting a number of points which might be of interest in the development of a grassroots theology.

These suggestions are intended simply as an invitation to colleagues to search for practical ways of translating our visions into reality.

Grassroots Theology

Characteristics of Third World theologizing

Among other things, today's theologizing in the Third World distinguishes itself from what may be called the customary or traditional theology because of its claim to be a *communitarian* enterprise. The Statement of the Sixth Ecumenical Association of Third World Theologians (EATWOT) Conference expresses this by saying:

> Because commitment is the first act, theology is inseparably connected with the Christian community out of which it emerges and to which it is accountable. Theology partakes of the rhythm of action, contemplation, worship, and analysis that marks the life of the people of God.[1]

This is an allusion to what, perhaps, is the most significant tenet of Third World theologizing which is starting from a deliberate departure from the usual description of what theology is all about. In the words of Gustavo Gutierrez, theology is "a critical reflection on Christian praxis in the light of the Word of God".[2] Implicit in this description is the understanding that "theology *follows;* it is the second step"[3] - it presupposes and is based on the life and commitment of the Christian community. This has been called an "epistemological break", and has

---

[1] Statement of the Sixth Ecumenical Association of Third World Theologians (EATWOT) Conference: "Doing Theology in a Divided World: A Dialogue Between First and Third World Theologians", Geneva, 5-13 January 1983, no. 38. Cf. *Voices from the Third World,* Vol. 6/1 (June 1983), pp. 12-13.

[2] Gustavo Gutierrez, *A Theology of Liberation,* Marylmoll: Orbis, 1973, p. 13.

[3] *Ibid.,* p. 11.

been repeated time and again in EATWOT circles, beginning with its inaugural meeting in Dar es Salaam:

> We reject as irrelevant an academic type of theology that is divorced from action. We are prepared for a radical break in epistemology which makes commitment the first act of theology and engages in critical reflection on the reality of,the Third World.[4]

How radical this break is can be gathered from this elaboration by the Asian theologians:

> To be truly liberating, this theology must arise from the Asian poor with a liberated consciousness. It is articulated and expressed by the oppressed community using the technical skills of biblical scholars, social scientists, psychologists, anthropologists, and others. It can be expressed in many ways, in art-forms, drama, literature, folk stories and native wisdom, as well as in doctrinal-pastoral-statements.[5]

Contextuality

It becomes evident from all this that the communitarian character of Third World theologizing ties in with several other hallmarks which are usually mentioned. The first is *contextuality*. The matter which should spark off theologizing is the life experience of the persons and communities involved: their total life, with its many facets, aspects and dimensions. Doing theology demands encouraging and giving room for the constant look at and careful study of the situation within which the theologizing communities are immersed. Such a study entails the

---

[4] Torres and Fabella (eds.), *The Emergent Gospel,* p. 269. See also Virginia Fabella (ed.), *Asia's Struggle for Full Humanity: "Christianity in the Context of other Faiths",* Maryknoll: Orbis, 1980; "The Final Statement: Towards a Relevant Theology", p. 156.

[5] Fabella (ed.), *Asia's Struggle,* pp. 156-157.

courage to engage in a serious analysis of society. The real life experience on which reflection and praxis are to be based must involve the whole community, and not only a few people. Tissa Balasuriya says:

> Not only professional, scientifically trained theologians but also others more directly engaged in the effort to transform their lives and society motivated by the Christian faith can make valuable contributions to the elaboration of a theology relevant to our situation. In this, both groups need to listen to, learn from, and creatively challenge each other to an ever more faithful response to the demands of Jesus Christ.[6] The aims and objectives of authentic theolcgizing are too important for everybody to be left to only a select elite. No one section of the Christian community can think and decide unilaterally for the whole body. Wherever only one section of the community monopolizes the theologizing enterprise, the result is a theology that is parochial, tendentious and incomplete, and in many respects, irrelevant to the majority.

Inter-disciplinary

By the same token this grassroots theology has to be *inter-disciplinary.* Adequate reflection on human life in the light of God's Word, in view of transforming people's living, calls for contributions from first-hand experience and expertise in the various facets of the human predicament. Theology needs input from any quarter that can explain what is really going on, and can help in formulating and implementing orientations of human life, both individual and collective. Third world theology refuses to accept the facile and artificial separation between the spiritual and the material, the religious and the profane, or the eternal and temporal spheres of human life. If it is legitimate to

---

[6] Tissa Balasuriya, "Towards the Liberation of Theology in Asia", in Fabella (ed.), *Asia's Struggle*, p. 21.

distinguish these spheres, however, separating them as if they did not coexist and influence each other in real life, is irresponsible and self-defeating.

It is easy to misunderstand the often-recommended separation of church and state, and of religion and socio-economic and political tasks. When this separation results in excluding the challenge of God's Word from "worldly affairs", then theology is reduced to a marginal role. It is withdrawn from those areas of people's lives which in day to day activities are the principal pre-occupations. These are, for instance, social links and relationships, economic pursuits, political choices and arrangements, and in general, the actual structure and process of human living in this life. Theology is restricted to the hereafter, or to the private sphere, to interior sentiments, to "spiritual matters" conceived as only a partial aspect of people's lives.

Thus life is split. The "religious" areas are accepted as being under God's influence and judgment, while the rest of human life, the profane, is, for all practical 'purposes, outside God's Kingdom. Lesslie Newbigin has warned that when such a dichotomy is accepted, what is said to lie outside the spiritual sphere is really not a neutral zone; it falls inevitably under the demonic power of human sinfulness.[7] By insisting that theology be interdisciplinary, Third World theologians seek to avoid this fateful dichotomy.

Ecumenism

When theology is done in and by the community it is bound to be *ecumenical*. Here "ecumenism" is far wider and more radical than the customary intra and inter-Christian dialogue among denominations. It extends indeed, as the word suggests, to the whole of the inhabited human world, including persons and communities of different faiths or non-believers (if such do exist!).

This does not mean an illusory all-embracing and indiscriminate theology. We are still talking of a genuinely *Christian* theology. But that

---

[7] Lesslie Newbigin, *The Other Side of '84,* London: BBC, 1983, p. 40.

theology is produced by a Christian community which does not live in isolation from the rest of society, but is part and parcel of the total human community wherever it is found. Its members usually move and function among other fellow human beings who are not necessarily of the same denominational or even faith commitment as themselves. And yet the "praxis" on which the Christian community is to reflect critically in the light of the Word of God is within the real world where Christian members of one denomination live and work with Christians of other denominations, and *where* Christians live and work with people of other faiths and ideologies. The realities on which the reflection of the Christians is made to bear are the product of all these different people together, and not of the Christian members alone.

This is true anywhere in the world but more conspicuously so in most of the Third World areas. There, it is common to find Christian believers living as members of families, communities, enterprises, and localities in which people of other faith commitments are full participants and make their own faith orientation to bear on the common life. And so, even when Christians meet alone to do theology, their 'reflection is in constant contact with other faiths. Indeed, often it is not meaningful (or possible) for Christians to reflect all by themselves. The other members of their communities will quite naturally accompany them.

This is dialogue - a sincere joint searching for the will of God together with other members of God's people. It is based on a solid theological conviction that the project of God's Kingdom embraces the whole of humanity and is by no means restricted to believers in Jesus Christ. The presence and working of the Spirit outside the visible community of Christ's followers is thus recognized and respected even (and especially) by Christian believers. They take it into account when reflecting on life and its commitments.[8] The Word of God is understood not just as the

---

[8] Cf. Balasuriya, "Towards the Liberation of Theology in Asia". The late Bishop Lakshman Wickremesinghe struggled with the same question in Fabella (ed.), *Asia's Struggle*. See also my attempt to address these questions in G.H. Anderson and T.F. Stransky (eds.), "The Salvific Value of African Religions", *Mission Trends No.5: Faith Meets Faith,* pp. 50-68; see also pp. 105-121 in this book.

Christian revelation but also as the wider encounter of humanity with the hidden Logos.

An irruption

The claim that Third World theologizing is communitarian has, therefore, very serious implications. Basic questions about theology itself are here being posed anew - What is theology? Who does theology? For whose "consumption" is theology produced? And how is theology to be done? The definition of theology as "a critical reflection on Christian praxis of liberation in the light of the Word of God" is not a benign assertion; it is a programmatic and revolutionary pronouncement. Through it, an "irruption" is made by hitherto unauthorized people into a carefully guarded enclosure, an exclusive "club': where only duly qualified elites once had right of admission.[9]

For a long time only trained academicians, equipped with an agreed baggage of specialized scientific skills and knowledge, and at ease with a certain in-group jargon, could lay claim to this prestigious title of *theologian*. But in the grassroots theology these credentials are brushed aside so that even the simple people can join in the task. Is such a theology realistically possible?

Problems of a Communitarian Theology

Neither neutral nor theoretical

The project of theologizing in the way described above involves problems which need to be lucidly analyzed. These problems arise, first, because that type of theology is neither neutral nor merely theoretical. It is a theology that aims at transforming society by constantly question-

---

[9] This is exactly what was meant by the title of EATWOT's Fifth International Conference of Delhi: *Irruption of the Third World: Challenge to Theology,* which became the title of the book reporting on this meeting (Marylaioll: Orbis, 1978); cf. Torres and Fabella (eds.), *Irruption of the Third World.* See especially Fabella's "Preface", pp. ix-xix.

ning the status quo and working to change it. It uses the See-Judge-Act methodology.[10] Since society tends to maintain equilibrium and stability for its institutions, norms, values and ways of acting, such constant revision of life is bound to disturb the guardians of social order, especially when the interests of privileged groups in society are threatened.

The collaborative nature of this theology is another potential source of problems. The enterprise brings together members from different social groups - those who hold power and influence and those who do not; the rich and the poor; the more successfully modernized and those who are less so, theoreticians as well as activists, etc. All these people expect to work together in a joint analysis of realities, to strive towards common decisions, and then to share in their implementation. And yet, it is to be expected that, coming from different backgrounds, these participants will bring with them contrasting viewpoints and potentially conflicting group interests.

It is a question, therefore, not of just any simple collaboration, but of a dialogue in which there needs to be a lot of give-and-take and much mutual listening. In the final analysis we are talking of power-sharing in society, and that is where the real problem lies.

Power problem

It is clear that currently in most African countries power-sharing is the big question. Young nations are becoming more and more openly polarized between those who can acquire and wield power and influence in society and the disadvantaged. Admittedly, the difference between the powerful and the less powerful has always existed, even in our tribal past. But the present widening socio-economic and political

---

[10] In the Roman Catholic lay apostolate movement this method has been associated with the kind of spe-cialized Catholic Action of the milieu of which the Abbe (later on Cardinal) Cardjin was a marking animator. It is used by cells of Young Christian Workers (YCW), Young Christian Students (YCS), rural and urban groups, factory workers' groups, family movements, etc. In it the reflection on the Scriptures is accompanied by an analysis of the realities of society and appropriate projects of action.

differences is of another kind and brings with it grave and ominous consequences.

Traditional community life

Although in the past individuals and groups did differ in status and power, they shared, nevertheless, a common basic outlook on life. In traditional communities the values of mutuality and interdependence regulated relations between potentially competing sections of the community. Even between rulers and their subjects the system provided a range of checks and balances, and institutions of participation and dialogue, for example the frequent palavers,[11] and the councils of clan and family elders. Moreover, since society was structured mainly along lines of kinship, affmity and alliances among neighbouring family groups, the overarching mode of interaction was more of cooperation than competition.

Weaknesses

We should be careful, of course, not to idealize too much the traditional community life. It had its fair share of frictions, divisive rivalries, and feuds. Moreover the ideals of interdependence and reciprocity tended to be practised only within a well-defmed circle of relatives and acquaintances. Strangers from outside risked to be treated as enemies until they proved friendly. Only then would the community goodwill and protection be extended to them too. And indeed the greater possibility for achieving reasonable integration and self-sufficiency was due to the fact that these communities were usually small-scale or microcosms. They did not need to struggle with diversities and pluralism in the same dramatic way that modem society is obliged to. Relative homogeneity and size were the sources of their strength, but also of their weaknesses.

---

[11] See the interesting collection of essays entitled *Socio-political Aspects of the Prayer in Some African Countries,* UNESCO, 1979.

Invasion

When these traditional communities were invaded by the Western industrialized cultures through European colonialism and Christian evangelization, the structures and institutions which used to give society its coherence lost their autonomy. The communities became mere parts of a widened macrocosm and were forced to struggle for survival in the adverse context of unfamiliar values and norms. For example, the imposition of colonial administration changed the modality and context of traditional leadership. Not only was the autonomy of the tribal authority abolished, new classes of power-holders emerged, e.g. soldiers, policemen, clerks, traders, progressive farmers, employees of European concerns. These people drew the legitimation of their power and influence not from the traditional norms but from their insertion within the new system.

In the same way, the coming of Christian churches created a new class of religious leaders who could effectively compete with the custodians of traditional religion. Some of the most successful among the new power-holders were of the type which in the old system would not have been entitled to positions of authority, e.g. ex-convicts, members of commoner lineages, etc. Similarly, the introduction of a money economy, cash employment, commercialized agriculture and private land ownership undermined the old economic arrangements and gave power and influence to a new class of citizens - the products of Western education.

Western education

We need to stress the role of Western education in creating these new types of elite and making them different from their fellow citizens. These differences created and facilitated domination, exploitation, and other injustices. Modern education and the exposure to skills and techniques of the industrialized West have not been equally available to all. By force of circumstances, and in some cases by design, only a relatively few individuals have had the chance to go to school or to acquire the knowledge and skills for a successful handling of the sources of power and influence in the modern world. It was hoped that these privileged minorities would accept to share the benefits with their less fortunate brothers and sisters. On one hand, this hope has been fulfilled in quite a number of cases. But on the other hand, there is always the tendency for the advantaged to protect and maintain their privileges against the rest. When they share, it is within restricted circles of relatives and friends or with individuals whom they hope to turn into "stepping stones" for furthering their interests. It is a natural temptation for those in power to use it to dominate and exploit others. The modern set-up with its institutions and norms predominates over the traditional system in that it has the capacity to determine and control the overall direction of the whole of society. The power to organize society one way or the other, to determine objectives and enforce their implementation is held, in the first place, by the modem state. Quite naturally those who hold power and exercise authority are tempted to run things according to their point of view and in a way that promotes and protects their interests.

Disappointment

That is why equitable participation in national life is such a problem in many countries of Africa today. The masses realize that the benefits which were promised them before, independence are actually being enjoyed only by a small minority. The institutions which were meant to guarantee their participation in decision-making and in influencing policies, e.g. elections, parliaments, political parties, trade unions, etc., have lost their meaning. They are being manipulated for the benefit of the powerful. Happily there are countries in Africa where these problems have been recognized, and where serious attempts are being made to ensure meaningful participation of all sections of the population in national life.[12] But in many other countries the problem is worsening.

---

[12] Tanzania with its philosophy of Ujamaa was an instance. In the newly independent countries of bkrzambique and Zimbabwe the question of popular participation was still being taken seriously (at least iireoretically). The typical questions can be seen, e.g. in Frances Moore Lappe and Adele Beccar-Varela, *Mozambique and Tanzania Asking the Big Questions*, San Fransisco: Institute for Food and Development Policy, 1980, and J.H. Proctor (ed.), *The*

During the colonial times in Africa real power and authority lay with the metropolises in Europe. In the colonies, authority was exercised by the colonial administration which consisted of expatriate officers assisted by subordinate local executives recruited from the local elite. But the local assistants exercised only delegated authority, they were simply instruments of the colonial powers. The struggle against colonialism was aimed at changing this situation. But as serious studies attest, in most countries this struggle was in two very distinct stages.[13]

Aim of nationalist movements

The early nationalist movements and organizations simply sought to make sure that Africans participated in the running of their country and that their voice was heard and taken into account by the colonial administration. It was understood, however, that those who would participate in the administration would be from among the elite, since they alone had been prepared for the job. These, it was thought, would represent their fellow Africans and serve as their voice. This is why most of the pioneer nationalist movements or parties were really elite associations which claimed to work cm the people's behalf.

A radical change

The second phase of the struggle came when these elite movements proved ibeffective. The objective then changed. Instead of merely claiming participation in the colonial administration 'system, the Africans now turned their attention to a radical change of the whole system. They wanted independence. The elite could not achieve this alone, they needed to mobilize the whole population into an organized mass movement for independence. At this stage, in many countries

---

Cell Systems of the Tanganyika African National Claion, Dar es Salaam: Tanzania Publishing House, 1971.

[13] In the case of Malawi, for example, there is a big difference between the early native welfare associations along with the Nyasaland African Congress, and the restructured Malawi Congress Party ird by Dr H. Kamuzu Banda which alone succeeded in bringing independence. Cf. Bridglal Pachai, *Malawi: The History of the Nation,* London: Longman, 1973, pp. 225-235.

nationalist movements were radically transformed. They became popular fronts. Their structures and methods of operation were revamped to facilitate an active participation of the masses in the struggle for independence by enlightening them politically.

The success of the struggle was due to this conscious and enlightened participation of the educated as well as the non-educated urban dwellers, as well as the rural masses: men, women and youth. Each category, in its own way and with the resources at its disposal, contributed towards the common goal. The structure and the operation of the nationalist parties were characterized by a ready participation of all and a sharing of responsibility. This was made possible because of everybody's expectation of freedom - something good which would benefit all.

Colonial remnants

After the colonial period in many new nations the most visible aspects of colonialism were abolished. Leadership was transferred from foreigners to local citizens. Those who inherited the positions of leadership sought to assure the general public that the participation which had characterized the period of nationalist struggles would continue into the new phase of nation-building and development. But in most African countries the instruments for such popular participation were the remnants of colonial "democratic institutions". These were, for example, parliamentary systems through general elections conducted within the structures and operation of the party system. The same pre-independence "parties", and/or perhaps new ones modelled on the latter, were involved for the quite different purposes of post-independence politics. They have not succeeded much in enlisting sufficient participation by the masses in the running of the complicated affairs of a modern state.

The objectives and the functioning of the pre-independence political movements were quite specific and restricted. They were intended to help in the transfer of visible leadership from the foreign colonial powers. They did not have to include actual sharing by the general membership in the formulation of strategies and policies or in influencing or critiquing the basic decisions or orientations of the movement. Because the main objectives of the nationalist struggle were relatively straightforward and uncomplicated and there was a general consensus about them, an extensive sharing by the ordinary people in specific decisions would not have made much difference.

The post-independence situation

After independence the situation has changed. Here the new tasks are more complicated. There is a wider variety of options and alternatives in decision-making and in the implementation of the decisions for the formulation of policies that will assure a just and meaningful future for all. At the same time a variety of interest groups becomes more visible and consequential. Any decision that is adopted is likely to benefit more one part of the citizenry than others.

In most cases the decision makers, in implementing different decisions, do so without forgetting to safeguard their own interests regardless of other groups' interests. That is why, after independence, there is more need for democratic institutions and effective participation by all sectors of the citizenry than before. There must be guarantees for safeguarding the interests of all groups in the new state and enabling them to share in the task of shaping meaningfully the overall programme of nation-building.

But there is a fundamental difficulty in the elaboration and functioning of such generalized participation. The tasks of the new states attempting to bring development and well-being to all are dependent on a world-wide, international network of relationships. Decolonization or independence has not brought real autonomy to our nations. Today, even more than before, the so-called independent countries of Africa are involved in a complicated relationship with the political and economic international arrangements and processes.

A growing gap

In working out their political processes, organizing their economies, or planning their internal and external security, the young states are involved in dealings and procedures of international dimensions. These require competence and skills which are acquired only through Western education. Only those who have had the fortune of this education, exposure and skills are in a position to take a meaningful part in these modern state affairs and to assume influential positions and decision-making roles. One needs this modern education to be able to find well-paying jobs and openings to lucrative undertakings in business, industry, professions, or other advantageous positions.

In most African countries only a small percentage of the population has got this basic advantage. There is a growing gap between the modernized few and the large majority who, because they are still caught up in the old ideas and ways of small-scale traditional life, find it difficult in coming to terms with present-day realities.

Empty rituals

In this situation, the educated class, who have the resources for dealing with modern life, are tempted to presume that they alone are entitled to take responsibilities and make decisions about public interests. The common people are thought not to understand the complications of modern statecraft, and so there is very little they can contribute in the elaboration of policies and the choice of options. The need to consult the masses or to keep the leadership answerable to the public is weakening. The external apparatus of participatory democracy, like parliament, party machinery, elections, public rallies, etc., quickly lose their meaning. They are often retained, but they remain empty rituals of populism, giving the false impression that the people are effectively sharing in the running of national affairs, when in fact they are not. Real power is held by just a few people.

False assumption

Again, the elite justify this situation by saying that where the masses are unable to understand the mechanisms of modern politics, it is only right and proper that their enlightened leaders should think and plan for them. The assumption is, of course, that these leaders will act responsibly in the public interest, and that they understand the needs of their people and have a genuine sensitivity for them.

But in the past few decades of national independencies, in most African countries experience has shown time and again that this assumption has remained just an ideal. The general rule seems to be that, whenever a small group assumes power without an adequate system of public participation and accountability, the interests of the general public are largely neglected. The result is an increasing enslavement of the people through the application of the double-principle of "cut-throat struggle for the survival of the fittest" and "might is right". There is a growing polarization between the few who, through different means, accumulate power and wealth, and the majority who fmd themselves gradually powerless and poorer and poorer.

A sinful humanity

This development is not difficult to understand. We are dealing with sinful humanity in which natural egoism and selfishness are at work. When individuals or groups have advantages over others, they tend to protect jealously such advantages and to use them for their own interests even to the detriment of other people. Only adequate checks and balances in societal structures, including mechanisms for public accountability, can stem such disastrous tendencies.

It is in this concrete situation of contemporary Africa that we are asking ourselves about the possibilities for the powerless and impoverished masses to participate in the kind of theologizing we described earlier. But before attempting to give an adequate answer, it is useful to push on the analysis by examining how exactly the people at the grassroots react in face of their growing powerlessness and exploitation.

Grassroots People's Problems

People at the grassroots, everywhere, are likely to go through bad experiences of such degree and frequency that they become disillusioned and disappointed. They may end up accepting the image of themselves as powerless, ignorant, or outdated. They develop reflexes and attitudes of inferiority which render them even more vulnerable *vis-à-vis* the powerful ones. Sociologists have analyzed, for example, the processes whereby in the context of sudden and unevenly induced socio-economic changes, the peasants find it difficult to adjust to the new situation. They are turned into victims of forces that they vaguely perceive but cannot deal with effectively.[14] The main features of the peasantry are operative among present-day African masses whose integration into the modern state is not yet stabilized.[15] We can recall quickly some of them here, though bearing in mind the differences that exist among parts of the African continent.

Isolation

In face of the dominant group considered as an outside power imposing itself on them, the peasants tend to see their life in terms of a project of self-defence. One manifestation of this is the attempt to cut themselves off as much as possible from unnecessary contact with the powerful groups. They try to insulate themselves in little worlds of their own where they can continue to live and relate among themselves according to the values, norms, and processes familiar to them, and which they can handle confidently. Thus the traditional Way of life with its systems of kinship and neighbourhood communality, subsistence economy, traditional authorities, statuses and roles will still continue. They will also continue the customary power struggles and negotiations, mutual exploitations, intimidations, and alliances that are typical of life among peasants.

---

[14] Eric R. Wolf, *Peasants*, Eaglewood Cliffs: Prentice Hall, 1966. Also some of the articles in J.M. Potter, M.N. Diaz, and George M. Foster (eds.), *Peasant Society: A Reader*, Boston: Little, Brown and Co., 1967 and Teodor Shanin (ed.), *Peasants and Peasant Societies*, Harmondsworth: Penguin, 1971.

[15] L.A. Fallers' remarks in "Are African Cultivators to be Called 'Peasants'?" (Potter, Diaz, and Foster (eds.), *Peasant Society: A Reader*, pp. 35,40), have limited utility as far as the contemporary scene is concerned since they refer mainly to dynamics and relationships of past traditional societies.

But such attempts at isolating themselves are largely futile. The working of the modern state's wider and more comprehensive system reaches down to them and makes demands on their life. They have to obey new laws and regulations, pay taxes, contribute goods and services for projects and concerns which often do not concern them directly and about which they may not have been consulted. If they choose to disobey, they know that they will be punished and they cannot escape. So in the fmal analysis these people cannot afford to ignore the wider world, but must learn to cope with it.

Defeatism

Such frustrating experiences build among the masses a numbing feeling of helplessness. They get used to believing that there is very little they can do to change their situation. So a sense of defeatism invades them. They accept and interiorize the image of an ignorant, backward and incapable lot which is usually made for them by the dominant groups. Hence the attitude of fatalism which is characteristic of many marginalized communities. Oppressed people tend to lose self-confidence, and often, even self-respect.

Dream world

Feeling helpless before the oppressive forces, the masses are likely to attempt strategies of survival that in the long run prove self-defeating. They might try to take refuge in occupations that provide an illusory escape from troubles and frustrations - amusements, dances, intoxication, some types of religious cults, or other distracting hobbies. The most attractive distractions are those which somehow give them the illusion of being like the rich, the powerful, or those more fortunate than themselves. We need only to think of sports, films, advertisements, parades, ceremonies, and similar things which oppressors and exploiters like to use in order to distract and put the masses to sleep (the famous Roman *panem et circenses*). The danger here is that the people get used to living in a dream world. They lose the sense of reality and proportion, and dissipate their limited energies and resources on things which reinforce their weaknesses and drain their chances of self-defense and autonomy. It becomes difficult for them to analyze realities and events soberly, to understand what is going on, how and why, or to discover what they could do in order to improve their lot.

Dependence and parasitism

A more fatal strategy for survival is that of dependence and parasitism. The disadvantaged are tempted to seek the favour and support of the rich and the powerful in the hope of a better life. They accept to serve the big people in some small ways, to give them support (in elections and group rivalries) and to follow them or become their henchmen for their dirty jobs. Of course, the favours of the rich and powerful are never gratuitous. They have to be paid for with loyalty, submission, obedience, and indeed servility, failing which there are corresponding sanctions. And so, the strategy of alliance does not solve the problems of the marginalized; it only makes them worse.

In Africa this relation between the powerful elites and the masses tends to take a special dimension. The two groups are not radically opposed. The powerful or rich minority comes from, and is still intimately linked with the grassroots base because of the persisting traditions of kinship and regional solidarity. The alliances usually run along these old lines, so that a successful and prominent citizen will seek to retain the loyalty of his indigent relatives or fellow "countryfolk". The latter will identify with him and bathe in the glow of his success. They will do this because they consider his power and riches as a community achievement to which they should continue to contribute since they are entitled to share in its benefits.

Typical evils

The outcome are the typical evils: nepotism, favouritism, regionalism, and corruption in most African societies caught up in present-day socio-economic and political changes. Rather than classes of the dominant being pitted against classes of the poor and the oppressed, what we usually see is an interest group consisting of elites and their clientele struggling against other similar coalitions. And yet, in the long run, it is the dependent clientele that finally loses out. The reason for such an outcome is that such dependence reinforces the alienation of the clients. They surrender their autonomy and become mere tools of their masters. This is especially dangerous in situations of injustice, oppression, or exploitation. The hangers-on end up accepting and interiorizing the distorted values, the inequitable system, and the evil practices on which these social ills thrive. Once this is done, the whole of society is infected; even at the grassroots level the system of exploitation, injustice and oppression is reproduced.

Selfishness, greed, and lust for power which divide the wider society into the haves and the have-nots, the powerful and the powerless, the great and the small, become operative also at the more restricted level of village and neighbourhood interaction, even in the kinship and clan relationships. Individual and clique interests split the communities into smaller competitive groups. Petty jealousies erupt, competitions of an overt or covert nature pit groups against each other in an ever-shifting pattern of coalitions. People suspect one another, and it becomes difficult to trust even one's nearest relative or next-door neighbour.

Fragility

One major weakness among peasants is indeed the fragility of their coalitions. It prevents them from developing strong, coherent and lasting projects for collaboration even when they have to face a common enemy.[16] One is often struck by the mutually crippling squabbles among the masses, their small vicious intimidations, blackmail, gossiping and petty mutual exploitations. Often the resentment from their collective victimization by the powerful, against whom they feel impotent, is vented on their weaker and more helpless neighbours.

When pushed too far by oppression from above, the masses are capable of revolting, and do indeed resort to violent mob reactions. But this is usually a mere outburst of revolt, uncoordinated, confused and short-lived. Because these reactions are unplanned and lack conscious

---

[16] Wolf, "Peasant Coalitions", *Peasants,* pp. 81-95.

unity of purpose, they are easy to break up and neutralize. The worst enemy of the marginalized is their division.

Potential for change

And yet, when the situation is examined globally, in the special circumstances of contemporary Africa, it is the people at the grassroots that have the potential for meaningful change. In our type of underdeveloped, unindustrialized nations (especially where agriculture and animal husbandry is the backbone of the economy), the strength of the total society is derived from what comes out of the common people; that is: what they produce and the abundant (often ridiculously cheap) labour they offer. The few wealthy individuals and those able to accumulate power and influence draw their resources first and foremost from the contributions of the less fortunate citizens. The poor people contribute to these elites either because they are forced (exploitation) or because they believe, rightly or wrongly, that this contribution will come back to them by way of favours. Even when governments secure outside help, it is usually in the name of the people. Furthermore, no such aid can bear lasting fruits except in so far as it is combined judiciously with the people's participation at the grassroots. Therefore, if the ordinary people withdrew their collaboration no national development programme and welfare would succeed.[17]

People's participation

Most of the failures in the development programmes of African countries come from the fact that the people's potential is either neglected, misused, or misdirected. Either because of the leaders' own mistaken scale of priorities or due to constraints induced by the dictation of outside dominant powers, the young nations fail to mobilize

---

[17] This has been the overriding lesson learnt from the failure of the period of developmentalism everywhere in the Third World between the 1950s and 1970s. It was not enough to pump financial aid, industrial equipment, and scientific expertise into the less developed countries. The key to success was the people themselves. See for the case of Latin America the articles in James D. Cockcroft, Andre Gunder Frank and Dale L. Johnson (eds.), *Dependence and Underdevelopment*, Garden City: Doubleday and Co., Anchor Books, 1972.

their material and human resources first and foremost to satisfy the basic needs of all their citizens. Instead, the national effort is reduced to a little more than a peripheral and subsidiary contribution to foreign interests and objectives, which benefits only a small percentage of the population. To improve the situation, the first condition is that the people themselves become conscious and active agents of their own progress. They must be enabled to shake off the enslaving myths of their own ignorance and incapacity. They must learn to identify their real needs, to assess the resources at their disposal, and to accustom themselves to getting organized for purposive action. In short, the key to real development lies in an intelligent and organized participation of all the people in the affairs of their nation.

Need for facilitators

History has demonstrated time and again that the peasants' potential for bringing about meaningful and lasting change is rarely activated from "within" themselves alone. By themselves the masses usually fail to initiate and carry through projects of socio-economic and political change. As a rule the decisive factor comes from outside. A group of well-organized and consciously motivated activists, who know both the strengths of the masses and the weaknesses of the dominant or oppressive elements, become an ally of the masses and gets them organized, and then leads them into successful projects of transformation.[18] Often this revolutionary group is animated by leaders who themselves belong to the powerful classes (aristocrats or middle class) but have opted out of their groups to defend the underprivileged. Thus, change is effected through the alliance between the disunited peasants and a group of revolutionaries, willing to join their particular resources with those of the disadvantaged. As we said earlier, African independencies came about only when the enlightened Westernized elites associated themselves with the silent masses. In the present situation, when the people are again victims of domination from their

---

[18] Wolf, *Peasants*, pp. 89-95, 106-109, deals with this question, recalling the dynamics of revolutions - the Russian and Chinese - in which the masses could achieve changes when they were organized by earismatic revolutionary leaders helped by trained activists.

former allies, there can be no real hope of change unless a new group from among the power holders throws its lot with the oppressed in a commitment for a new revolution.

Prayer over the gifts

A condition

There is, of course, a high element of risk in such an alliance. The fmal outcome depends on the intentions of the revolutionary leaders. If they simply want to use the masses to further their own selfish aims, then the ensuing change will not be a genuine revolution but merely a change from one oppression to another. This has often happened and has led the people to become suspicious of any revolutionary firebrands claiming to join them for liberation. But if the liberation leaders are people of integrity and work for the common good, they can contribute towards that type of breakthrough into a promising future which many exasperated nations in Africa are after.

Promoting Grassroots Theology: A Challenge for Theologians

What is the point in all this discussion of socio-economic and political matters? What relation does it have with the *project of theologizing at the grassroots as a challenge for professional theologians* that we introduced at the beginning of this essay? There is a connection indeed. It can be expressed in two ways. First, since we are talking about Third World theologizing, the questions we have been dealing with show the context within and upon which the reflection of the Christian community is to be made. But secondly, the relationships among individuals and human groups which we have described in socio-economic and political terms as regards the general society are mirrored also in the churches where theological reflection is to be made. In the churches too, there is a distinction between those few who have power and influence and the large majority, especially the laity, who have a relatively small part or none at all in the process of decision-making.

Dependence: an obstacle

Similarly, the dependence of many local churches in Africa on their central authorities in Europe and America is very much like that of the young nations on the world powers. Just as the local secular leaders, in running their own nations, are often obliged to follow the directions coming from abroad, so also in many ways must local church leaders conform their actions to the norms and directives from overseas headquarters. This may not necessarily be a bad thing. It may in fact be, in some respects, one source of the security enjoyed by the young churches. Nevertheless, when we are talking of doing theology at the grassroots, this dependence is likely to form a serious obstacle. The dominating powers from outside do not usually allow people at the grassroots to be genuinely co-responsible partners in the life and work of the church.

If the doing of theology by people at the grassroots is so difficult, that is because it is potentially a revolutionary and explosive enterprise. It is capable of unleashing a power among those who hitherto have been powerless, so that they can begin to change the *status quo*. And so those in whose interest it is to maintain this *status quo* will do everything to prevent the emergence of a genuine and effective theology of the powerless.

The Word of God

When people who are expected simply to obey orders begin to think for themselves in a critical way, the *status quo* runs a great risk of being questioned. Since this critique is not merely academic or theoretical, but bears on reality, it will soon lay bare the sordid realities of domination and oppression which are usually covered up with legitimizing myths and ideology. And because the reflection is meant for concrete projects of liberating activity, it equips the little people with power to change and transform society. This change is likely to be revolutionary. This is so because the reflection is done in the light of God's Word (the Scriptures) which is a mighty double-edged sword that judges the desires and thoughts of people's hearts and lays them bare to the God to whom we all must give an account of ourselves (Heb. 4:12-13).[19]

Grassroots theologizing is a project of empowerment. So it does not just happen. It requires certain conditions in order to come about and succeed.

I would like to suggest some of these conditions, taking into account especially the situation in those parts of Africa with which I am more familiar.

Option for the poor

The first condition is that a large enough number of those who, by force of circumstances, belong to the category of the powerful, should consciously and deliberately opt out of that category and join the

---

[19] We use the version of the *Good News Bible* throughout.

powerless and the oppressed. They are not expected to throw away their knowledge and power but to convert them from being tools for domination into tools for facilitating the liberation of the oppressed through sharing and identification.[20] This is what has come to be called the "Option for the Poor".[21]

Sterile power

Let us make no mistake about this. Whenever and wherever the masses are excluded from meaningful participation the reserves of power which nevertheless still remain among them are, as it were, sterile and unusable. The structures and institutions imposed upon society by the powerful keep the masses hemmed in. The result is that in their feeble efforts to break free they turn precisely to those powerful ones, their oppressors, who cannot be expected to free them. Following the only valid paradigm of salvation and liberation that we know - the incarnation of the Son of God, the breakthrough can only come from outside,

> Rich as he was, he made himself poor for your sake, in order to make you rich by means of his poverty (2 Cor. 8:9).
> Of his own free will he gave up all he had, and took the nature of a servant (Phil. 2:7).

Leaders and specialists

In the churches, power wielders are the leaders and administrators (ministers, priests, church workers). Their position in the community or congregation puts at their disposal instruments of authority and

---

[20] *I have tried to describe this alliance between the specialists and the common people when I dealt with "The Role of the African Biblist in the Church in Africa Today", Biblical-Pastoral Bulletin*, no. 2 (1981), reprinted by Gaba Publications, Reprints no. 232, June 1981.

[21] The documents of the Second General Conference of Latin American Bishops, Medellin, *The Church in the Present-day Transformation of Latin America in the Light of the Council*, 2 Vols., Division for Latin America - USCC: Washington, 1973. Also J. Eagleson and P. Sharper (eds.), *Puebla and Beyond*, Marylmoll: Orbis, 1979.

legislative, executive and coercive institutions by which the community is held together. And in the course of exercising their duties they acquire skills for controlling individuals and groups, skills the rest of the faithful do not have to the same degree.

But another power group is that of trained specialists like professional, scientifically trained theologians and qualified church lawyers. Their expertise puts them in a position of influencing and directing the thinking on which public policies are based. When these two groups are in alliance they are able to concentrate real power in their hands, leaving the rest of the faithful in a position of total dependence.

1. Sharing and conversion

The breakthrough proposed above takes place when a good number of Church leaders and specialists make the deliberate decision to put their authority, expertise and skills at the service of the disenfranchised members of the Church. What happens then is that the two groups initiate a process of collaboration and sharing. Here, the leaders and the specialists need a "conversion" in attitudes and relationships. They need to learn to respect the other members of the Church as fellow servants of the Lord, and not to treat them as "subjects" or mere clients. For the common members, a conversion is also necessary. They must regain confidence in themselves as full citizens of Christ's Church:

> a chosen race, the King's priests, the hol) nation, God's own people, chosen to proclaim the wonderful acts of God who called them out of darkness into his own marvelous light(1 Pet. 2:9).

At the same time the simple faithful should learn to value and use the special contribution that the leaders and experts bring with them for the common task. As Balasuriya says:

> There is thus a need to build mutual confidence and respect among persons of these two levels of orientation in theology or Christian reflection and to learn to benefit from each other's expertise in their common endeavor towards a relevant

theology. Committed persons from action groups can bring the sensitivity of lived experience and struggle, while professional or technical theologians can contribute a more scientific understanding, especially of the Scriptures, in the light of advances in modern knowledge.[22]

2. Concientization

A second condition for success in building a grassroots theology is "conscientization" of the common members of the Church. This is that special process through which oppressed and powerless masses are liberated from the obstacles that keep them tied down to their state of powerlessness and dependence.[23] As Paulo Freire has explained, conscientization or *consciousness-raising* is a process whereby people are helped to see the reality as it is and to begin to discern the forces at work in their life, especially the forces of domination, oppression and exploitation. Instead of looking at events in a superficial way or through the distorted rationalizations and myths entertained by the dominating groups, they begin to make a realistic analysis of the causes of their poverty and dependence. They see that things are the way they are not simply because that is the ineluctable destiny prescribed by God, but because of a whole network of human decisions and planning which can be influenced and changed. They discover that they themselves, in God's plan are entitled to be co-responsible agents of their own history, and that for this they possess resources for participating meaningfully. Progressively, then, they rid themselves of the inhibiting attitudes of fatalism and passivity which are the result of internalized ideas about themselves induced by their dominators. Only then can they begin to struggle for their liberation and embark on projects of self-reliance and genuine development.

---

[22] Tissa Balasuriya, "Towards the Liberation of Theology in Asia", *Logos,* Vol. 20/1 (March 1981), p.2.

[23] The classical literature on "conscientization" is Paulo Freire's *Pedagogy of the Oppressed,* New York: Herder and Herder, 1972. Also his *Education for Critical Consciousness,* New York: Seabury, 1973.

This phase of *consciousness-raising is* a condition for doing theology. Unless they are conscientized, the Christian masses tend to doubt whether they can do their own reflection on their faith, and work out how to share with their leaders and specialists the responsibility of organizing their Christian life. They have been conditioned to imagine that their faith is authentic only when it is given to them ready-made from above through catechisms, sermons and instructions.

It is necessary for them to realize that the guidance and teaching they rightly expect from their ministers and religious specialists does not become a working power until they themselves have struggled with it in the concrete circumstances of their life. They alone can find out how the faith measures up with their life experience. The leaders and specialists cannot do this work for them. After all, the ministers, priests, or trained theologians are usually not around in the villages, the locations, or places of work when the faithful are confronted with the task of applying their faith to daily realities. Conscientizing the ordinary Christians consists, first of all, in helping them to see that there is a large area of their Christian life in which nobody can take their place. It consists, too, in making them realize that they already have adequate resources for assuming their part of responsibility in running their Christian life. The most important service that liberated leaders and specialists can render to their fellow believers at the grassroots is first, to initiate this process of *consciousness-raising.* Secondly, they need to accompany and encourage them as they experiment with confronting God's Word in their daily life and commitments.

We have a concrete example of how this can be done in the experience of the little community of Solentiname in Nicaragua.[24] A group of simple people, some educated individuals, and one or two professional theologians used to meet for prayer and reflection on the Scriptures. It was a dialogue in which each member was able to contribute according to each one's capacities and experience. This is the kind of "grassroots theology" that animated and directed the Nicaraguan revolution.

---

[24] Ernesto Cardenal, *Love in Practice: The Gospel in Solentiname,* London: Search Press, 1977 - A translation from the Spanish original by Donald D. Walsh.

3. Community set-up

This example alerts us to another condition for the success of theology by the ordinary people: the community set-up. The theologizing we are talking about is a critical reflection on the Christian praxis in the light of God's Word. Although faith has individual and personal dimensions, the believers do not live it in isolation from each other or in isolation from the wider communities of which they are integral parts, at least not in the African villages or urban areas. In spite of the tendencies towards individualism which have been trying to influence African societies in the wake of Westernization, communalism is still the overriding characteristic of people's life, especially of those who have been less radically acculturated to modern lifestyles. Now as in the past, people conceive life as a project of cooperation and reciprocity. They see it as a continual exchange of rights and duties based on unity. In the past, this unity was based mainly on natural kinship, affinity, and neighbourliness. Today it is expected to result from the common faith in Christ and the one Baptism (Gal. 2:26-29). The project, common today in many.parts of Africa, which bases Church life and commitment on small Christian communities is the best promise for the development of theology at the grassroots.

4. People's methods

There is a last condition. Theologizing with and by the ordinary people asks that the ways or methods for reflection include those the common people are familiar with and which they can employ effectively. Academic and technical terminology can only be useful when dealing with academicians. Most of the people do their reflection and communicate in other ways too. They communicate in songs, stories, proverbs, artistic and symbolic expressions, drama, celebrations, etc. Professional theologians may not be very familiar with these ways of human expression and communication. But if they want to accompany their fellow Christians in a common reflection they will have to learn these other ways for which their professional training may not have prepared them sufficiently.[25]

Conclusion

Indeed the main challenge that confronts professional theologians when they attempt to do theology with ordinary people comes from the fact that their training has cut them off from the community. The seminary, theological college or university programmes are geared towards the production of professionals who may theologize *about* or *for* the people, but really not *with* them. If the project of grassroots theology is to become a reality, there will have to be a serious overhauling of the whole system of theological training.

---

[25] In recent years African theologians have been giving much thought to this question. There is also a growing concern in the world-wide theological community. This is witnessed by recent developments of theology through stories, or narrative theology. One example is George W. Stroup's *The Promise of Narrative Theology*, London: SCM, 1984.

8 A Malawian Example The Bible and Non-literate Communities: A Malawian Example

The following article is part of a collection of essays which addressed the topic of "Interpreting the Bible in the Third World" (cf. R.S. Sugirtharajah (ed.), Voices from the Margin: Interpreting the Bible in the Third World, London: SPCK, 1991, pp. 397-411). It deals with the predicament of those who are non-literate or semi-literate, when it comes to taking part in reflecting on the Bible as God's Word in written form. If such people are to be included among those who "do theology", what should be done about their inability to read the Scriptures directly?

African theology, as the Ecumenical Association for African Theologians (EAAT) would want to practise it, must be a tool for human liberation in obedience to the Word of God as revealed in the Scriptures. This is why EAAT's inaugural declaration indicated as the first source of theology the Bible and Christian Heritage, saying:

> The Bible is the basic source of African theology, because it is the primary witness of God's revelation in Jesus Christ. No theology can retain its Christian identity apart from Scripture ... Through a rereading of this Scripture in the social context of our struggle for our humanity, God speaks to us in the midst of our troublesome situation.[1]

But it is not just any use of the Bible that serves the purpose of liberation. As Mesters has reminded us: "The Bible is ambiguous. It can be a force for liberation or a force for oppression. If it is treated like a finished monument that cannot be touched, that must be taken literally

---

[1] "Final Communiqué: Pan-African Conference of Third World Theologians: 17-23 December 1977", in K. Appiah-Kubi and Sergio Torres (eds.), *African Theology en Route*, Maryknoll: Orbis, 1979, pp. 192-193.

as it is, then it will be an oppressive force."² In the past the Bible has often been invoked in such a way as to legitimize the most obvious social, economic or political injustices, to discourage stirrings of revolt against oppressive or discriminatory practices, and to promote attitudes of resignation and compliance in the face of exploitative manipulations of power-holders.

Even today there seems to be an intensified invasion of certain types of biblical interpretation which can only be characterized as simplistic and distracting. They centre so much on the spiritual and interior needs of the people that the connection between the Word of God and the realities of every day becomes secondary, almost irrelevant. Ominously this kind of biblical faith is being promoted with particular effect in countries of the Third World, that is, precisely among those peoples for whom the facts of material deprivation, violations of human rights and sheer exploitation are the most pressing concerns. In such circumstances the Bible is hardly a credible liberating power, and can even become a tool for continued enslavement.

It is, however, in these same areas of the Third World that special efforts are currently being made to discover and employ the power of the Bible for people's full liberation. There are conditions for this liberating force to come out. Advocates of liberation theology have been studying, as a matter of urgency, this question of the use and misuse of the Scriptures, acknowledging that what might be called a "political" reading of the Bible is not only legitimate, but highly desirable.³ These investigations are useful and enlightening. And yet they are at such a level of scholarly sophistication that it is not immediately evident how useful they can be when we consider the problems of biblical usage by ordinary people engaged in the project of liberation at the grassroots.

---

² C. Mesters, "The Use of the Bible in Christian Communities of the Common People", in N.K. Gottwald (ed.), *The Bible and Liberation*, Maryknoll: Orbis, 1983, pp. 124.

³ The collective work, N.K. Gottwald (ed.), *The Bible and Liberation* (cf. note 2), is a good example of such studies. J. Severino Croatto's penetrating study, "Biblical Hermeneutics in the Theologies of Liberation" (Torres and Fabella (eds.), *Irruption of the Third World*, pp. 140-168), will be familiar to EATWOT members.

Liberation theology is of practical use only in the measure in which it is practised by these ordinary people; otherwise it remains a merely intellectual activity indulged in by comfortable academics. By the same token a liberative handling of the Bible becomes effective only when the people themselves are practising it in their own struggle. It is necessary, therefore, to examine carefully how the people at the grassroots actually use the Scriptures and how this use can relate to their liberation.

The Special Predicament of the Non-literate

When Mesters warns against the possible oppressive use of the Bible, it is clear that the central issue is that of interpretation: what meaning do we give to the text of the Scriptures? This assumes that the biblical text is itself available to the people and can therefore become the object of interpretation.

My interest is with a more radical situation. What happens when the text of the Bible is not available, or when its availability to one section of the community is controlled and regulated by another section? This is the case when part of the community is illiterate and cannot therefore have direct contact with the written Word of God. Such people are at the mercy of their literate neighbours if they wish to know what the Bible has to say.

Those who can read and write are in a position to share with their less fortunate brothers and sisters the contents of the Holy Book. But they have also the possibility of withholding parts of the contents and distorting what they report from the Bible. They may choose to share only some selections and leave out others, according as they themselves judge good or opportune. They could very well leave out those parts that they think useless, ambiguous, or dangerous. This is not simply a matter of quantity. It is also a question of interpretation. What the readers of the text choose to share is determined very much by their own judgment, interests or objectives. The illiterate hearers have very little scope of judging for themselves. Therefore their understanding of God's Word and their capacity to reflect on it and use it for their own lives are to a large extent controlled by others.

When, then, we discuss the importance of the Bible for doing theology in Africa, we are raising some vexing questions. This theology is meant to be a liberating tool, especially for those who are underprivileged or oppressed. In our developing countries the illiterate are surely among such disadvantaged people. What possibility is there for them to take an active and fair part in hearing the Word of God and reflecting on it in the light of their own experience? Are they reduced to having others do theology for them? Such questions are of special relevance in a continent like Africa.

Literacy and Illiteracy in Africa: Example of Malawian Catholics

It is important to remember that, in general, Africa is largely non-literate. In more than half of the countries less than half of the population above 15 years of age know how to read and write, and in about all the countries literacy among the female population is far below that among the male.[4] Let it be said in passing that this last fact is,. as far as religion is concerned, of tremendous consequence since in general the more active and practising members in any community are often women. And in many communities, especially among matrilineal people, the female role (mother, sister, grandmother) is most decisive as far as religious development and practice are concerned. It is legitimate, therefore to assume that African life is, in general, less literate and more oral, auricular and visual.

Christianity would normally be expected to be influenced by this factor. Only where literacy has been seen as in some way a precondition for

---

[4] Cf. *1987 Britannica Book of the Year,* Chicago, Encyclopaedia Britannica, 1987, pp. 914-919. Of 55 African countries, 30 have an adult literacy of less than 50 per cent. Except for Lesotho (62 per cent male: 84.5 per cent female), in all other countries female literacy is below that of the male, sometimes very dramatically so - for example, Chad, 35.63 per cent male: 0.5 per cent female.

membership in the Church would one expect the majority of believers to belong to the literate sector. This has been the case for most Protestant churches in Africa. If that constitutes an advantage as far as contact with the Bible is concerned, it also spells out the danger of a serious constraint in evangelization: only those with a certain degree of education will feel at home in the Church. In other words, conversion and fidelity to the Christian faith would be conditioned by acceptance of modern culture. That certainly leaves out a large part of the African population, those people who for one reason or another have not had the chance of a meaningful education and live largely within the confmes of traditional life. This is the case for many people in the rural areas; and even in urban and semi-urban areas the proportion of people who live a: non-literate culture is greater than one might be led to imagine.[5]

I am less acquainted with communities where literacy is preponderant, and where therefore the use of the Bible as written word presents no special problem. My experience has been mainly with communities for whom reading and writing were peripheral in daily life: in acquiring and communicating knowledge and in passing on information. Among them there were admittedly persons who had been to school and could read and write more or less fluently. One hoped that more schooling would become available to them; and indeed heroic efforts in education were being made in these areas. Still, for the time being, their ordinary way of life was not dependent on literacy. When we imagine such people using the Bible for their Christian life, for "doing theology at the grassroots", are we just dreaming? Is there no way these people can come into real contact with the Scriptures?

I shall take the case of my own country: Malawi; and more precisely, I am thinking of the Catholic population there. Although statistics

---

[5] D.B. Barrett (cf. *Schism and Renewal in Africa,* Oxford: Oxford University Press, 1968) has rightly established, in the case of Africa, a correlation between literacy and availability of the Scriptures in the local language on the one hand and the growth of Church independency on the other. But he surely did not imply that all meaningful contact with the Bible is through direct reading of the Book. The question, then, of liberative or non-liberative use of Scripture is not exactly the same as that of the growth of independency.

indicate that 49.9 per cent of the population above 15 years of age are literate,[6] among Catholics this percentage would be too high. For reasons that are due mainly to history, the Catholic Church in Malawi has been successful mainly among the more traditional and less Westernized communities. As Linden pointed out: "On the whole their (Catholic missionaries') converts came from the edges of African society, the marginal men and late-comers to Nyasaland (former name of Malawi) like the immigrant Alomwe and Sena."[7]

A large proportion of Malawian Catholics are therefore either illiterate or semi-literate, and belong to the oral tradition rather than the literary one.

As such, the Bible as written word still remains unfamiliar and marginal to their life as believers. When you watch Catholics going to church or to other services, very few will be carrying literature of any kind. A few may be bringing along their hymn-and/or prayer-books, or perhaps a catechism or some devotional book. But hardly any will be carrying the Bible, not even the New Testament text! They know in advance that the standard Catholic service does not require the general faithful to read written texts for themselves. Why is this so?

The historical fact of a majority of non-literate members has been reinforced by what seems to be traditional Catholic practice. In standard Catholic ideology the faith expression of believers and their practical response to God's Word do not derive directly from the Bible, but from the teaching authority of the Church: the *magisterium.* It is understood, of course, that the *magisterium* itself is informed by the Scriptures, and to that extent the faith of the believers rests in the final analysis on the authority of the Bible. But the Bible is read and interpreted, not necessarily by each individual believer, but within the "Tradition" of the Church. Sometimes this ideology has been unfairly and incorrectly expressed as though for Catholics the faith derives from two distinct sources: the Scriptures *and* Tradition. The more correct way of putting the matter is this: Faith derives from God's revelation, and this revela-

---

[6] Cf. *1987 Britannica Book of the Year*, ibid.

[7] Ian and Jane Linden, Catholics, Peasants, and Chewa Resistance, p. 8.

tion reaches us through the Bible within tradition. Vatican Council II, in its Constitution of Divine Revelation, has attempted to express more satisfactorily the relation between these two complementary aspects of God's revelation. "Sacred Tradition and Sacred Scripture", it says, "make up a single deposit of the Word of God, which is entrusted to the Church".[8]

Whether or not this Constitution has succeeded in shedding new light around the Reformation contention about *Sola Scriptura is* a different matter which is not our direct concern here. What comes out clearly, however, is the crucial importance of two elements: Tradition and Community. The need for Catholics to read Scripture *within Tradition* makes this Tradition the *practically* decisive hermeneutical authority. If this principle is taken to its bitter logical conclusion, it would be quite normal for the believers to be satisfied with Tradition's presentation of the Scriptures without the necessity to read and examine personally the letter itself of the Bible. The biblical witness, content, selection and interpretation would come to them through the various organs whereby Tradition addresses itself concretely to the believer. Such are, for example, the catechism, the pronouncements of the *magisterium* (Pope, Councils, Bishops, Synods, etc.), the liturgy (including rituals, preaching, hymnody, iconography) and indeed also popular piety and devotions. Here lies the special power of Catholic faith, but also the source of problems which we shall need to examine later on.

Until quite recently direct contact with the Bible was a rare phenomenon among Catholics, certainly among the ordinary faithful in Malawi. Since Vatican II things have begun to change, and it is fair to say that heroic efforts are being made to bring the scriptures to the people.[9] Since the coming of the use of vernacular languages in the

---

[8] "Dogmatic Constitution on Divine Revelation", no. 10; Cf. A. Flannery (ed.), *Vatican Council II, vol.* I, Northport: Costello Publishing, 1984, pp. 755.

[9] Many new translation of the Bible or portions thereof in African languages have been made or are in progress (cf. John S. Mbiti, *Bible and Theology in African Christianity,* Nairobi: Oxford University Press, 1986, esp. pp. 22-25). The Catholic Symposium of Episcopal Conferences in Africa and Madagascar (SECAM) has set up a biblical apostolate centre in Nairobi with the objective of promoting Bible knowledge among Catholics in Africa.

liturgy, more and more biblical texts are heard by the faithful at Mass and other services. In many areas, as complete Bibles or portions of Scripture become available to the faithful, suggestions for daily Scripture readings are being proposed, often with accompanying aids of an exegetical or spiritual nature. The possibility, then, for a widespread contact with the Scriptures is now there in Malawi.

The Crucial Problem: Bringing the Bible to Non-literate People

But does this solve the problem of the use of Scripture among our Catholic faithful? Not automatically. The crucial point is that even here the methods being used assume largely a literary culture which the majority of the people are not accustomed to. For a people of a non-literate way of life, the mere availability of the written Word is not enough to bring the Scriptures into their life. The Word of God must first become "incarnated" in their own specific way of hearing and responding. In other words: the Bible needs to come to them in non-literate ways.

In communities where reading and writing are marginal ways for learning, communicating, assimilating knowledge and values and expressing them, there exist other media which are, for those people, much more familiar and effective. *Hearing* appropriately formulated inputs and *seeing* cultural adapted messages take the place of reading as means for taking in and assimilating information and knowledge. To match the value of the ever-present written text (to which the readers can always return if they forget), non-literate people employ mnemonic devices like *repetition* or *variation* of analogous visual aids. In order to interpret and apply to life what is being taken in, they have such potent tools as *acting, retelling* in their own words, or *responding* through gestures or emotion-filled expressions. Through these appropriate methods, messages and instructions are passed around, selected, interpreted and evaluated, and then assimilated so that they influence people's lives.

There is no reason why the Bible could not be made to reach the non-literate through these ways with the same efficacy that the written word reaches the literate. If all of them cannot read the Bible text for themselves, they surely can hear it read to them, provided care is taken to make this reading as effective as possible. In a community of mostly illiterate folk there might be two or more who are able to read. By reading out the text to the group these few would enable their brothers and sisters to hear the Word ("Faith cometh by hearing, and hearing by the word of God", Rom. 10:17). Reading out or "proclaiming" the Scriptures could thus become a valuable ministry for the few literates among our people. If need be, the readers would be requested to repeat the text or parts of it for the benefit of the audience. In our modern times when such technical instruments as tape-recorders are no longer rarities even in the remote villages, much use can be made of recorded biblical tapes. Our Muslim neighbours know this only too well: have you not heard hoisted loudspeakers blaring out recorded Qur'anic surahs from up the mosque tower in the market-place? Christians could learn to make such a resourceful use of these modern devices.

Reading out biblical texts could very easily become a new version of the traditional art of the story-teller. Our people do enjoy story-telling: children and adults alike. In all sorts of formal (ritual, courts) or informal occasions people are ever eager to hear *nkhani* (story or narrative). They crowd around the public place where cases are being tried; they surround the newly arrived visitor who brings fresh news and messages from relatives or friends, or who simply describes the wonders of faraway places and peoples; they regale one another with wise sayings, parables, fables or riddles. The spoken and heard word is very central. It fulfills the functions of newspapers, reviews, books or advertisements in literate communities. That is why the radio has become a favourite toy in the villages. The Bible would come effectively to the non-literate if the skills of the spoken word were used judiciously, and if the power of this word were put at the service of the Scriptures.

The role of music and singing in non-literate societies is likewise great. Often the song accompanies dancing, but it should not be thought of simply as a means of entertainment. Singing serves to express interior sentiments, to underline and reinforce values, to praise or to ridicule, to exalt or to debase. In ritual and religion, singing is often used as a means of arousing and communicating appropriate attitudes of mind and soul. As with the spoken word, so also the incantation has effective power. The song is also a vehicle of information and teaching, all the more effective because it is easy to remember and to reproduce. In traditional rituals singing was a favourite tool for instruction, for admonition and for passing on traditional lore: history, customs or the art of living.

With a bit of imagination, singing could be used for bringing the Bible to the people. A lot of the Scripture text was originally for singing - for example, the psalms and the numerous canticles and hymns which scholars discover in various books of the Bible (Revelation seems to be full of them). Our hymn-books offer quantities of fme hymns. Some of them are more or less directly biblical in origin and inspiration. But a large number are not. This is principally because in standard congregational practice the hymns are simply a commentary on, or an accompaniment or reinforcement of, the Bible text that is supposed to be read during the service. But where reading is not possible, or is marginal, why should the song itself not replace the reading of the written word?

Important texts would be put to music (e.g. the Beatitudes, the Sermon on the Mount, the parables). Thus the singing itself could constitute a direct contact with God's Word, thus abolishing the unfair discrimination whereby the Bible is unduly restricted to the literate. In sessions for Christian instruction, and even in Bible discussion groups, the song could thus serve as the Scripture text. There are enough gifted people in the local congregations for whom composing tunes is not a problem. All they need is to be given the Bible text. One can imagine a special ministry for such people whereby they could gradually build up a home-made repertoire of biblical portions in local music.

The part played by the *visual media* in non-literate societies should also be taken into account. Much information and many important messages circulate through what people are able to see and to handle. Students of the so-called African art are wont to say that the objects that Western sensibility classifies as "art" are actually very functional tools in the society, be they sculptures, paintings, pottery, vestments and "ornamentation", architecture, and even weapons and utensils. They are not there simply as an embodiment of the aesthetic spirit. First and foremost they are saying something and are meant to produce useful results for the needs of the community. As with the gestures and words that are usually associated with these objects, we are dealing here with "symbols", understood in the strong sense of conventional signs which are meant to effect what they signify. Symbolism is a central force in non-literate societies. The visual object, by virtue of the evocative and associational power of its shape, design, texture and colours, becomes a medium for expressing values, recalling stories, fables or parables, and often also for evoking meaningful history.

Christian churches still need to learn to exploit the vast resources of our people's visual media in the religious field. The schools, especially at the primary level, have always recognized the importance of visual aids. Just as much contact with the Bible can be established through hearing (e.g. tapes), so also can the eyes capture what the Scriptures are saying through words. A picture depicting a biblical scene is able to bring the message quite powerfully to those who are unable to read. Often the illustrations in a book convey the essential points on the text. Paintings, sketches, statues or artistic arrangements in the place of worship have been used traditionally for more than mere decorative purposes: they were often the text-book of the illiterate. How much biblical instruction could be done with the help of slides, videos or films for non-literate audiences! In recent years catechetical centres have been providing material of this kind. The biblical apostolate should make more use of such visual aids.

Exploiting Local Resources

There is, of course, the objection that this type of material is often prohibitively expensive, and in many cases there is need for sophisticated equipment which simple people would neither possess nor be in a position to handle efficiently. And again, some material is foreign and ill-adapted for use among Africans. That is sometimes true. Well-meaning people, when they set out to meet the needs of non-literate communities, tend to introduce resources that have to be sought from outside. This is not helpful: it simply prolongs, often even aggravates, the dependence of these disadvantaged people on outside help.

But there is no reason why locally available resources should not be exploited. Simple ordinary material, which the people use in their daily life, can be easily turned into effective illustrations for biblical communication. The people are able td attach didactic value to what they possess. They do not need exotic equipment for that. They can resort to the various symbols in their culture which express values and meanings in line with the biblical message: symbols of birth, life, death, purifycation, joy and humility. These can be used anew to stand for one or the other biblical message.

In this connection the symbolic value of colours, insignia or ritual objects come to mind. If the people themselves establish this connection between their culture and the Bible, there can slowly grow up an inventory of visual symbolism through which the Bible message can be interpreted, evoked and made use of. At any rate, it is counterproductive to create the impression that progress is being made because the local needs are being met with "modern" means.

How to Interpret and Apply the Biblical Message

Through auditory and visual media, biblical material is able to be taken in by people who are not of a written tradition. The objective, however, is not simply to receive and take in what Scripture offers. As they receive the Bible message, the people should at the same time have the capacity *to react* to the input, to *interpret it,* that is: give it their own understanding, and then to *apply it* to their life as believers. This is a decisive stage, for it is only in this way that the non-literate actually do their own theologizing with the means that are familiar to .them. They allow the Word of God to meet and challenge their ordinary experience. In ways and idioms proper to their culture, they take the initiative to reflect on this Word, asking themselves what it means to them. They evaluate its significance and relevancy to their lives, and then apply it.

There are several ways whereby non-literate people appropriate and interpret inputs. One of these is *repeating in their own words* what they hear, see or experience. The exercise of re-telling or putting in one's own words forces the person to say what in the input was worth retaining. It is therefore an exercise in personal *selection* of the meaningful: for in a given input not everything is equally relevant to everyone. By the same token it is an exercise in *interpretation* and assessment of value: for one remarks and retains only those points that are significant for one (personal) reason or another.

The value of re-telling is enhanced when several people *exchange and discuss* what they have retained singlely. By so doing they enlarge the extent of the meaningful, one person's points being enriched by points from the others. At the same time this makes possible mutual challenges and criticism. Questions will come as to whether one heard correctly or missed out on an important point. There will be questions about the real meaning of this or that word or expression. And then there is the wider area of discussion about how the biblical message applies to individual or common living. By engaging in a discussion of this type the group is actually constructing their "theology": a reasoned reflection on their experience in the light of God's Word.

Another powerful means of selecting, interpreting and applying inputs is what we may call *drama* or re-enacting. When the audience proceeds to act out what they have taken in, they inevitably select what struck them, and automatically express *why* and in what way it struck them. By reproducing it through drama they are also applying the meaning to their familiar world in familiar idiom. Even when only one part of the community does the acting, while the others look on, there is possibility of mutual exchange and "discussion". The reactions of the onlookers can be affirmative, interrogatory, encouraging, reinforcing (e.g. through applause), or, on the contrary, cool, disapproving or indifferent. It has been said that the preaching in some churches, where the congregation is expected to manifest its response, is a version of this kind of drama. It is not the preacher alone who interprets and expresses the message. Through their responses and reactions, "the audience" take part in directing the content, affecting the flow of delivery, and giving it shape. This too is a group-type of theologizing.

In this context of a religious gathering, another effective way of interpreting and applying God's Word is *prayer.* When people pray after hearing the Word of God, they automatically express what meaning the Word has for them, and usually they go on to apply it to their lives. The Word will have enlightened them, questioned their assumptions, rebuked their conduct, or given them guidance and encouragement. All this usually transpires through prayer, which then becomes a response to the challenge of God's Word. We know how enriching shared prayer can be. Different members simply say aloud what the Word has done to them; and as diverse responses flow into one another the assembly shares in an ever-enriched pool of understandings and applications.

In some congregations there is the practice of *testimony*. Here individuals attempt to put in communicable words their experience of God's activity in their lives. Often these testimonies are veritable biblical commentaries made in simple terms by ordinary people. We can see, then, that much scope exists even for the non-literate to receive the biblical message, to interpret and apply it, even if they do not themselves read the written text.

A Liberating Theology From the Underside of History

What is the point in all this discussion about the Bible and non-literate people? Our concern is for the integrity of the kind of Third World theologies which our Ecumenical Association of African Theologians has been attempting to formulate and promote in the past ten years of its existence. In numerous discussions and exchanges, the gist of which can be found in the written works produced by both EATWOT and EAAT, several basic characteristics of this type of theology have emerged.

I would like to recall three of them. First, it is a committed and liberating theology, as was stressed at the very inaugural assembly of the Ecumenical Association for Third World Theologians (EATWOT):

> We reject as irrelevant an academic type of theology that is divorced from action. We are prepared for a radical break in epistemology which makes commitment the first act of theology

and engages in critical reflection on the reality of the Third World.[10]

Second, this liberation must be achieved ultimately by the oppressed themselves, and not on their behalf, even though others will join them in this commitment. The Asian theologians expressed this felicitously when they said:

> To be truly liberating, this theology must arise from the Asian poor with a liberated consciousness. It is articulated and expressed by the oppressed community using the technical skills of biblical scholars, social scientists, psychologists, anthropologists, and others. It can be expressed in many ways, in art forms, drama, literature, folk stories, and native wisdom, as well as doctrinal-pastoral statements.[11]

Third, the basic source of this liberating theology is the Bible.[12] If the Bible is the source of liberating theology, those who would engage in doing such a theology must have the Bible realistically available to them, and they must be in a position to reflect on it, not by procuration, but in their own right. Clearly this poses a question for those who cannot read and write, since the Bible offers itself to us today primarily as a written text. Normally only those who are literate will be able to study it directly and base their reflection on this Word of God. Those who are unable to read are in the unenviable position of depending on others.

Unless there is a radical change in methodology, it is not realistic to expect such people to take a creative part in doing theology. Their knowledge of the Scriptures risks being from mere hearsay and to consist only of bits and pieces that are kindly made available to them by those who can read. As we said, the interpretation itself is affected by

---

[10] Torres and Fabella (eds.), *The Emergent Gospel*, pp. 269.

[11] Fabella (ed.) *Asia's Struggle*, pp. 156-157.

[12] Cf. Note 1.

this dependence. The non-literate would not have full confidence in their own understanding of the Bible, as they would not know whether or not they had all that was required for an informed interpretation. Those who have direct access to the Scriptures would always be tempted to act as judges, with the very real risk of presenting their own interests and viewpoints as the only valid and correct norm of God's Word. The literate would thus have a decided advantage over the non-literate as far as the Bible is concerned.

In the present situation in the Third World, literacy is a key for access to resources of knowledge, power and wealth; and inversely, illiteracy usually bars people from all thee. It is natural, therefore, that, all things being equal, the non-literate will tend to be among the less advantaged, among the powerless and those most likely to be oppressed and exploited. If then, they are incapable of taking an active part in reflecting over the Bible; the project of a liberating theology is largely in vain. There is the frightening possibility that theology, dominated by the more advantaged, will not be really for the liberation of those on the underside of history.

Conclusion

The gravity of this situation becomes evident in the case of a continent like Africa where illiteracy is so high. And taking the example of Malawi, we saw that the predicament of the Catholic population was quite tragic. The conclusion seems to be, then, that a major concern for those interested in developing an effective theology in Africa should be to make sure that literacy is not the only condition for access to Holy Scripture.

This paper attempted to suggest how this could be done: how the Bible could very well become accessible to non-literate people through the media adapted to their way of life. It does not pretend to offer elaborate recipes or ready-made prescriptions. All we are saying is that there is need to liberate ourselves from the idea that only those who have the advantage of modern education can take part in developing the kind of liberating theology that Africa needs today.

9 Spirituality in the African Perspective

Originally this essay was commissioned, along with other contributions from several African theologians, by Rosino Gibellini of the Italian publishing house: Editrice Queriniana of Brescia. Gibellini 'S intention was to introduce the Italian theological readership to various themes of present-day African theologies. Consequently the article first appeared in an Italian translation as: "La spriritualità in una prospettiva Africana" in Rosino Gibellini (ed.), Percorsi di teologia Africana, Brescia: Editrice Queriniana, 1994. But almost simultaneously an English version was published by Orbis as Paths of African Theology (Rosino Gibellini (ed.), Maryknoll: Orbis, 1994,), and the essay was included with the above title. In 1996 the article appeared in the British review Monastic Life.

In the African context, it would be both misleading and inadequate to discuss theology without dealing with the question of spirituality. The reason is simple. One of the basic characteristics of African culture is its holistic and integrating nature. Thus it would be distorting African theology if it were treated merely as a theoretical enterprise, without taking into account the fact that the ideas and theories being discussed are merely extrapolations from a way of life that consists first and foremost in concrete attitudes, relationships and practices. African religion is essentially a way of living in the visible sphere in relation with the invisible world. This relationship pervades the whole of life, of individuals as well as of the community - or rather, of individuals in the community.

Spirituality has been described generally as "those attitudes, beliefs and practices which animate peoples' lives and help them to reach out toward the super-sensible realities".[1] It is the relationship between human beings and the invisible, inasmuch as such a relationship derives from a particular vision of the world, and in its turn affects the way of relating to self, to other people, and to the universe as a whole. In this

---

[1] Gordon S. Wakefield, *A Dictionary of Christian Spirituality*, London: SCM, 1983, p. 549.

sense, spirituality is not restricted to any one religion, but can be found variously in all religions and cultures. It is determined in the first place by the basic world view of the persons or people concerned. It is also shaped by their life context, their history, and the various influences that enter a people's life.

This essay starts from the conviction that there exists a particular brand of spirituality that can be called, in a general way, African. In a general way, because on the one hand there should be no pretension to claim that what constitutes such a spirituality is exclusively African, and on the other hand, we are not affirming that all Africans necessarily live this spirituality. For, as a matter of fact, many do not, and those who may be said to do so vary considerably in the measure in which they conform to the rather idealized model that I shall present. These caveats are so evident as to need no further discussion; still, in a study such as this, it is not superfluous to formulate them clearly at the outset. The integrity of the very exercise depends on them. As I proceed to describe what this special African perspective is and how it is both a challenge and a contribution to spirituality in general, the value of the claims would be compromised if they were on carelessly overstated. I may, then, just as well start by clarifying the points in these cautions.

How "African" is African Spirituality?

Does it make scientific sense to speak about African spirituality? The African continent is so vast and diversified. It consists of such a variety of ethnic groups, each with its own customs, history, and ways of life, that sweeping generalizations about things African are always dangerous and risky. Serious scholars of African traditional religion, such as E.G. Parrinder[2] or J.S. Mbiti[3] preface their studies with a wise warning against treating religious practices in Africa as if they were uniform in every detail, a temptation that in the past was not often avoided by those who loved to tell exotic tales about Africans. E. Bolaji

---

[2] E.G. Parrinder, *African Traditional Religion*, London: Sheldon Press, 1962, p. 10.

[3] Mbiti, *Introduction to African Religion*, p. 3.

Idowu himself, as he set out to present his pioneering study of African traditional religion, had to admit that "African traditional religion with reference to the whole of Africa, as a subject of study, is an impossible proposition",[4] but he added the precision "where detailed study and thoroughness are concerned". Here, I think, is the crucial point.

Whether or not it is legitimate and meaningful to make some generalization in this area of religion depends very much on the level at which such generalizations are made. Although there is such a diversity in details, there is, however, an astonishing convergence in African cultures and religion when one considers the deeper, underlying outlook, values, and attitudes. This is what gave courage to D. Zahan to pursue his research into *The Religion, Spirituality and Thought of Traditional Africa*. He writes:

> The diversity of African ethnic groups should not be an obstacle to such an undertaking since the variation in religion has less to do with the ideas themselves than with their expression by means of dissimilar elements linked to the occupations and the flora and fauna of the area.[5]

What I shall attempt to propose here is precisely that complex of spiritual outlook and values that seems to undergird the various expressions of African religion.

There is, however, a more practical problem that has to do with culture change. The African way of life, which is the background against which spirituality needs to be examined, is not something static. Over the centuries, African societies have been in constant transformation, mainly due to interactions with the outside, but also due to changing conditions of life, new needs, development of ideas, and modification of techniques and values. Such changes are often gradual, hardly noticeable except over long periods. But at other times they are sudden, violent or revolutionary. Such dramatic changes have certainly

---

[4] Idowu, African Traditional Religion, p. 105.

[5] Zahan, The Religion, Spirituality and Thought, p. 2.

occurred in the past century due mainly to the exposure of Africa to the powerful modernizing influences of the Western world: colonialism, industrialization, new religions, especially Christianity. Because of these new influences, the former traditional ways of life have been modified; they are taking new shapes and configurations. But these changes are not uniform everywhere. While in some areas and for certain groups the former traditional ways of life are still operative to a greater or lesser extent, for other individuals and groups, especially those in the urban context, the influence of modernity is more profound and revolutionary.

The question then is: Where do you go in order to discover the African culture today? Where is African spirituality to be captured? Is it among those who are still influenced by traditional cultural values and customs? Do we have to discard, as irrelevant or inauthentic, the more complicated modern developments, while attempting to recapture an idealized past state of traditional culture?

This is indeed an important question, one that cannot be brushed aside or answered in a simplistic way. If, indeed, spirituality is an aspect of human culture, it can only be discovered authentically where people's actual way of life is going on. And so, African spirituality today should be examined within the complexity of present culture change, and not in some romantic and artificial reconstruction of traditional life that is no more really there. This makes the task much more difficult, because it is not possible to present a coherent cultural picture out of the divergent and fluctuating manifestations of the present process of culture change. But this should not mean that there is no way of discovering a sufficiently identifiable pattern of spirituality or spiritualities in today's Africa.

Even in the midst of the most confused culture revolution, it is possible to isolate some basic trends and orientations that form the deeper underlying foundations against and over which the on-going transformations are struggling. These are the result of past decisions and customs that have marked the life of a people over a long period; they are also the effects of past and present responses to decisive historical events that people continue to carry along even as they move forward developing new ways of living. At any one moment, a people never exists as a *tabula rasa*. It always carries the baggage of its past as a resource for interpreting and dealing with new experiences. What I seek to investigate here as African spirituality is the sum total of this past configuration of values and orientations together with the new trends resulting from responses to modern experiences. Even if this is not a simple exercise, it is nevertheless quite possible.

Finally, a possible misunderstanding needs' to be cleared up. When I discuss African spirituality, I do not intend to imply that each and every African individual or group lives that spirituality in the same way or to the same extent as the ideal form. That is certainly not the case. The model presented here can only be a theoretical extrapolation, logically structured from diverse elements deduced from observations. In real life, individuals and even groups may correspond to fewer or more of those elements, depending on a never-ending variety of configurations to which individual situations and histories give rise. The validity of this extrapolation is tested only by the plausibility of verification as concrete individuals or groups are examined against the ideal model. Some will be found to correspond to a number of elements, while others will demonstrate a different pattern, or even prove to be aberrant in that their way of life follows a totally different model. But this does not necessarily prove the model false. I shall base my reflections mainly on my acquaintance with my own people, the Achewa/Ngoni of Malawi.

Where Do We Look for African Spirituality?

In principle, the answer should be easy. If, as I have said, spirituality is an aspect of the total culture, we look for it by examining the African way of life and following up "those attitudes, beliefs, and practices that animate people's lives and help them to reach out toward super-sensible realities", since this is what we chose as a working description of what spirituality is. For Africans, life is a totality; culture is holistic. What one might isolate as the spiritual dimension is embedded in the whole of the people's way of living. It may be valid to distinguish different aspects, such as the economic, social or political spheres, or again the individual and community aspects. One may consider occupational and leisure activities as distinguished from one another, or isolate the legal system from that of belief and ritual. But in real life all these are held together and given shape by an underlying spiritual outlook, which is what we would like to discover.

In conformity with my reflections in the introductory discussion, it will be helpful to search from two sides of African life today: first from what comes from the past, and then from what results from more recent influences. The underlying contention is that the shape of African spirituality today is a result of the interaction between these two. And yet the first is certainly the more determinant. I will start from there.

The most obvious place to search for spirituality is in the context of traditional religious practice: in worship, ritual and prayer. Here the shape of a people's spirituality becomes easier to grasp, for their deepest aspirations are made manifest and their underlying outlook on the world of realities is revealed, not in theories or formulas, but in practical attitudes. Two collections of prayers from African religious life appeared in 1975, one by an African[6] and the other by a European.[7] These collections are an important indication of African spirituality as it manifests itself through traditional culture. There is need, however, for some caution here. Collections such as these are a personal undertaking whose demonstrative value depends very much on the answer to such obvious questions as: Who did the selection? From what source were the prayers taken? What were the guiding assumptions and preoccupations in that selection? And to what extent do these predetermine the end result?

It can be argued, for example, that the preponderance given to prayers to the Supreme Being ("Most of the prayers are addressed directly and specifically to God ... A few, not more than 10 per cent, are addressed to divinities, spirits, the living dead and personifications of nature"),[8] is mainly due to the fact that the sources from which these prayers were taken had been preoccupied with demonstrating that Africans, contrary

---

[6] John S. Mbiti, *The Prayers of African Religion,* Maryknoll: Orbis, 1975.

[7] Aylward Shorter, *Prayer in the Religious Traditions of Africa,* London: Oxford University Press, 1975.

[8] Mbiti, *The Prayers of African Religion,* p. 3.

to adverse prejudice, did have a clear notion of the Supreme Deity. And so the selection of the recorded prayers was heavily in favour of those addressed to God. In the real life of many of the ethnic groups mentioned, perhaps the proportion of prayers to the other addressees was more than that meager 10 per cent. But this is a minor point that does not really affect the revelatory value of these collections.

The prayers and the spirituality they reveal

The first indication is given in the answer to the question: To whom is prayer addressed?[9] The prayers are made to the Supreme Deity, but also (whatever the relative proportion) to other spiritual realities such as divinities, spirits, the living dead and personifications of nature. All these can be subsumed under the notion of "the invisible" or "the other-world spiritual realities". Prayer is based on the view that the world of realities consists of two interrelating spheres, the visible and the invisible, of which the visible is in some ways dependent on the invisible. The project of human living, both individual and communitary, consists mainly in an on-going interaction between these two spheres. What goes on among the living in the visible sphere cannot be fully accounted for solely from a consideration of the palpable processes of the visible or physically observable realities, for there is a mystical interaction of forces and wills between the two spheres. African traditional spirituality is based firmly on this premise.

There is thus a basic cosmology that underlies many of the traditional myths, stories, beliefs, customs and practices. God, or the Supreme Deity, is all-encompassing as creator and sustainer, up above heaven as down below the earth. This omnipresent Reality "in whom we live and move and have our being" is so much taken for granted that the Supreme Deity often is not mentioned explicitly and is rarely (in many ethnic groups) offered sacrifices and the customary ritual worship: the Supreme Being is above it. Some observers, intrigued by this, have concluded that the Supreme Being is a remote, even "otiose", deity, indifferent to his creatures. This is a gross misunderstanding, although

---

[9] Ibid., pp. 2-16; Shorter, Prayer in the Religious Traditions of Africa, pp. 8-13.

we have to admit that taking God's presence for granted in this way does create the danger of doing as if God does not count very much. But then, it is important to understand the significance of this "distance".

It is not absence by any means, for, as it is often repeated, the presence of God is so obvious that you do not have to convince people about it. Rather, it is a special type of presence: a presence that operates concretely through mediation. *God's presence asserts itself through the interaction of heaven and earth, the visible and the invisible.* God is like the paramount chief in the tribe or nation. God's will and authority pervade the whole of life, but in the working-out of events and relationships, the normal processes on the lower levels must be respected; only when these fail or are inadequate is recourse to the higher instances in order. What the family can deal with, for example, should be left to the members and elders of that family. Appeal will be made to the village head or to the chief only if the matter is beyond the competence of the family.

In theological terms, an important assumption is being made - *the absence of a radical dualism.* Good and evil, life and death, love and hatred, justice and injustice, good luck and misfortune - all these are, indeed, the two opposing camps in the drama of the cosmos. But God is not involved on one of the two sides in such a "partisan" way that another agency (Satan or some such) would be on the other side as an equal opponent. On the contrary, God is above this drama and is there to act as the ultimate arbiter. But, of course, God is ultimately the champion of good, life, love, justice and harmony, so there is always, even in the midst of the worst developments, an underlying optimism that in the long run God will triumph. This, I think, is the real explanation of that kind of optimism that seems to rule traditional life and expresses itself in a kind of "resignation" even when things are really unbearable. Some observers have interpreted this as the effect of belief in determinism or blind fate, and think this is how you can explain the astonishing capacity of African individuals and communities to take in a lot of suffering and pain without apparent bitterness or despair (think only of the long centuries of slavery, colonialism, and now neocolonialism and the accumulated misfortunes visited on modern

Africa). I rather think the explanation is in this cosmology that places God and God's basically good intentions above, below, and in the whole of the world.

Humanity (individuals and community) is at the centre of consideration. African spirituality is based on this centrality of human beings presently living in the concrete circumstances of life this side of the grave. It consists of their attitudes, beliefs and practices as they strive to reach out toward the super-sensible realities: God, the spirits, and the invisible forces in the universe. The central concern is how to make sense of this life and ensure that it is meaningful, harmonious, good and' worth living. The outcome of the project of life depends on how successful and beneficial the relationships are between the living and the invisible world.

But for traditional Africans, humanity is first and foremost the *community*. In the first place is the extended family based on blood kinship or on affm-ity through marriage, and then the clan, the tribe or the nation. Kinship and affinity create a special kind of bonding within which mutual rights and duties are exercised unconditionally. Individuals acquire their basic identity through these relationships, and they enjoy the feeling of security in life as long as the exchange of these rights and duties is guaranteed. It has often been said that where Descartes said, "I think, therefore, I am" *(cogito ergo sum)*, the African would rather say, "I am related, therefore, we are" *(cognatus ergo sum)*.[10] In African spirituality, the value of interdependence through relationships comes high above that of individualism and personal independence. By the same token the practice of cooperation is more relied upon than competition.

There are positive consequences of this exigence for kinship and community solidarity. Among them is hospitality. Members of the same family or clan exchange hospitality as a matter of course. But it is also extended to outsiders, though here it is first necessary to make sure that the stranger is not an adversary. The bonded kinship community does have its boundaries: they exclude the enemy and the totally

---

[10] Pobee, Toward an African Theology, p. 49.

unknown incomer who might be a potential danger to the community. Any stranger, therefore, is first required to become known as *bona fide*. Only then is she or he accepted, and becomes an honorary kinsperson.

The community solidarity tends also to create requirements of sharing and redistribution of resources, so that no individual accumulates and hoards resources that become unavailable to others when they need them. Hence, the fear of anyone who surpasses others too obviously in wealth, power or influence. The underlying fear is that such persons become a public danger and are likely to use their surplus for selfish purposes over against the others. Only those whose role is that of centres of redistribution (such as heads of families or chiefs) have surpluses of any kind. Any breach of this requirement of basic egalitarianism creates jealousies and ill feelings.

There is also a great dread of those who renounce the duties and rights of solidarity: those who are notoriously cruel, quarrelsome, egotistical, unforgiving or unkind. They attract the suspicion of being witches or eaters-of-human-flesh. The widespread fear of witchcraft, and consequently the frequency of beliefs and accusations about witchcraft and sorcery and practices to counter it, are signs of the central importance of kinship solidarity. M.G. Marwick and other scholars have demonstrated that witchcraft and sorcery are really about feelings of a breakdown in family and community sense of solidarity.[11]

The primacy of community and cooperation may be related to the fact that, in general, traditional African life was based on a simple technology with a minimum of "scientific" knowledge of and mastery over the rest of the universe. We should perhaps state it more clearly. The relationship between the human community and the rest of the universe was not conceived of as a project of struggle where human beings would look at the world as an object or an adversary whose nature and working should be investigated and reduced to formulas so as to master and exploit it. Rather, the universe is seen as a common heritage, its diverse components as potential partners in the shared

---

[11] M.G. Marwick, *Sorcery in its Social Setting*, Manchester: Manchester University Press, 1965; M.G. Marwick (ed.), *Witchcraft and Sorcery*, Harmondsworth: Penguin, 1970, 1982.

project of existence. There is, therefore, a feeling of mutual dependence among the different parts: human beings, the animal world, vegetation, the elements, the heavenly bodies, the departed as well as the diffuse forces, visible and invisible, that circulate all around.

Success in living depends very much on how well these different parts interact, by negotiating carefully and "respectfully" the common resources available to all. There is a certain awe, something like a religious attitude, in this interaction: it is as if the whole universe possessed personality, consciousness, sensitivity and "soul". Scholars coming from scientific and industrialized cultures are wont to call this attitude "superstition", and they have coined words like "animism", "fetishism" or even "idolatry". These words, which attempt to make sense of "strange" peoples' religious attitudes, but from the point of view of another culture, are, in fact, more confusing than helpful. I would suggest that the key to a better understanding is to appreciate the full significance of the relationship between the visible and the invisible.

The invisible world

The relation between human beings and the rest of the universe is governed by the distinction between the visible and the invisible. The invisible is not just what cannot be perceived by the human senses, but rather what is beyond the range of ordinary perception. This category of ordinary is not identical with the Western one of natural as opposed to supernatural. These Western categories are based on a particular world-wide view that is the foundation of modern science. According to this world view, the universe is conceived of as being regulated by a set of laws of nature (which religious believers grant were laid down by the divine Creator, while atheists and deists deny or simply do not worry about). Events and processes occur in conformity with these laws, and if something happens outside or contrary to these laws, it is deemed super- or preter-natural. Believers will call it a miracle, while nonbelievers will tend to be skeptical or assume it is the effect of a hitherto unknown natural law. This universe, which is thus regulated by natural laws, is partly visible and partly invisible.

It is not in accordance with such a world view that the cultures we are describing here distinguish the visible from the invisible. The background thinking is rather that the whole world of realities - spirits, persons, objects, words, gestures - are bearers of force and efficacy at two levels: the ordinary one that is perceptible and manageable without special knowledge or power (this is what I call visible), and another that is mystical and can be perceived and handled only with a heightened perception and power. And that is what I call invisible. The whole .idea of force and efficacy has turned into a confused controversy ever since Placide Tempels came up with the idea of *force vitale* as a central element in what he called Bantu ontology.[12] Scholars have had ample occasion to criticize and refute various aspects of that theory.[13] The intention here is not to enter again into this discussion, but simply to remark that the idea of interacting forces is an enlightening intuition for a proper understanding of this question of the invisible.

African spirituality is based on the assumption that life is influenced by relationships between human beings and the visible and invisible forces. These relationships are basically ambiguous: they can be beneficial or harmful, life-giving or destructive, good or bad, reinforcing or weakening, auspicious or misfortunate. At any rate, we cannot account for what happens or can happen simply by considering the visible, since the influence of invisible forces cannot be ruled out as a cause of any occurrence - death, illness, fortune or misfortune, success or failure. Hence, it is crucially important for individuals as well as for the community to have a good knowledge of the invisible and the power for dealing with it.

Specialists of this knowledge of the mystical (diviners, prophets, visionaries, interpreters of omens and dreams), and medicine practitioners who have powers to deal with the visible as well as the invisible are a crucial category in society. The frequent sessions and rituals of divination, ferreting out evil influences and dealing with them, are more than mere cultural practices; they are elements of the people's

---

[12] Placide Tempels, *La Philosophie Bantoue,* Paris: Presence Africaine, 1949, pp. 33-47.

[13] Henri Maurier, *Philosophie de l'Afrique noire,* St Augustin: Anthropos, 1985, pp. 58-59.

spirituality. Medicine is a central part of this world view. A medicine is not, as in the West, simply a substance imbued with natural powers for healing. It is anything that activates the visible and invisible forces and enables human beings to deal with them for good or for ill. Since objects, as well as words and gestures, can be repositories of both visible and invisible forces, they are potential medicines for all sorts of effects. Medicine people know of these forces, more or less, and are capable or using them. The notion and practice of medicines is thus an important aspect of African religion. By the same token, belief in and practice of magic cannot be excluded from the wider ambit of religion, since in various ways the working of the mystical and the unusual is part of religious practice. In Christian parlance, we can put it this way: the miraculous or the preter-natural is essentially part of African religious consciousness.

The world of the invisible is indeed quite wide. It includes, first of all, the heavens where God resides. It also includes divinities and nature spirits for those cultures whose world view reserves a place for them.[14] And almost everywhere in Africa the spirits of the dead (especially the dead ancestors) are the central area of the invisible, as I shall demonstrate presently. But other parts of the universe are also potential fields for the invisible: animals, vegetation and other objects.

Spirits of the dead

The centrality of the conception of the spirits of the dead follows logically on the fact that African spirituality assumes that the centre of consideration is the community of those presently living. This community is seen in terms of kinship and affinity relationships, on which even the wider expressions of neighbourhood, clan, tribe or even nation are modelled. That is why marriage, as the foundation of the family, is so important. As Mbiti has so aptly expressed it:

---

[14] v.g. in Western African, cf. Idowu, *African Traditional Religion*, pp. 165-173; Mbiti, *Introduction to African Religion*, pp. 65-70.

> Marriage is the uniting link in the rhythm of life. All generations are bound together in the act of marriage - past, present and future generations. The past generations are many but they are represented in one's parents; the present generation is represented in one's own life, and future generations begin to come on the stage through childbearing.[15]

The family and the community are thus not limited to those presently alive: they include members of the past and also future members. This link is seen in real terms as a continuing flow of the same life. The life of the present generation is not a novel creation; it is a carry-over from those who preceded us. Even physically we owe it to them, and we cannot understand who we are or what our exact identity is except by remembering them.

In the same way, the present generation does not have to reinvent the rules or the art of successful and harmonious living or take the risk of making fatal mistakes in the process. Its best bet is to interrogate the past and receive the accumulated wisdom of those who have gone ahead. That is why there is much store laid by the traditions of the ancestors, their customs, taboos, instructions and directives. They know better. As the standard African saying goes, these dead are not dead; they are still around and are part of the families and the community. They understand fully what is going on, they share in the preoccupations and projects of the living members, and are intimately interested in what is going on. Thus, those who have preceded us and are now in the spirit world are the models and guides of the present generation. They are also its source of identity. Hence, their importance.

But there is more. Having passed through death, they have become prominent members of the invisible world, whereby they share in mystical powers not ordinarily available to those presently alive. They are nearer to God, the invisible *par excellence,* with whom they are able to communicate and to whom they can present more effectively the needs of those still alive. They are also nearer to the other invisible

---

[15] Mbiti, *Introduction to African Religion*, p. 104.

forces, such as those in the "bush" (animals, vegetation, the landscape, the elements and other forces of nature), and so are in a position to mobilize them for good or for ill toward the living. (Symbolically the dead are usually buried in the cemetery, outside the village, and actually in the bush!)

In this position of special power, the spirits of the dead are natural guardians of their relatives on earth and can act as mediators with God. This is a position of tremendous power. That is why the living cannot afford to _ignore them: the more so as their intervention, although normally beneficial, can also be punitive if the living misbehave or break the basic mies of life (such as the taboos). The living get in touch with the spirits as often as there is need to ask for help or for advice, to seek protection or simply to show them that they are not forgotten. Recourse to the spirits is most likely at important moments of individual or community life, such as initiations, marriage, birth of children, sickness, installation of chiefs, funerals and moments of danger (drought, epidemic, war). This contact is made through prayer and invocation, and often accompanied with offerings of foodstuffs or libations. On their part, the spirits get in touch with the living through dreams, apparitions (visions) or ominous occurrences that are usually interpreted by specialists.

Christians will naturally see a strong parallel between this notion of the spirits of the dead and the belief in the communion of saints. But there are important differences. One is the strange dependence of the spirits on the living, for according to a widespread African belief, the spirits of the dead need to be "fed" by the living through rituals of remembrance. In fact, a spirit remains operative and present as a beneficial guardian and mediator only so long as its memory is kept among the living. If this memory has died out or is deliberately obliterated, the dead recede into the hazy but dangerous zone of ghosts, spirits that have lost their link with the living and can only linger around as restless and frustrated beings prone to mischief and harm.

I think this indicates the function of this belief in spirits in the philosophy of the people – both why they are important and how they relate to God, the real invisible. I suggest that the notion of spirits serves as a practical way of handling the problem of divine transcendence and immanence. As I indicated above, God's transcendence is safeguarded through the respect of God's distance from the living. Contact with God is maintained through the mediation of the spirits. In a way, the spirits render the transcendent immanent, but in such a way that the transcendent becomes "tamed", manageable and even negotiable. The remembrance of the spirits assures the benefits of care, protection and involved interest from the invisible. But there remains the possibility of rendering the invisible humanly manageable, since the living have some grip over the spirits. Thus, there is an intrinsic danger when religion is centred too much on the remembrance of the spirits: it tends to lower religious practice down to a humanly manageable enterprise. But this should not make us forget the positive advantages of such a spirit-centred religion.

What is the Content of African Spirituality?

I have attempted to describe the world view on which the African spirituality is based, and the various parts of the universe around which this spirituality evolves. Let us now try to see it at work.

A useful way of doing this is to go back to the collections of prayers we examined earlier, to see what is asked for in these prayers. One thing seems to be common in the list of things that make up the object of prayer.[16] They are things that are basic to the very existence of individuals and the community or to survival: things like children, rain (against drought and famine), abundant food, success in hunting or gathering expeditions, protection or healing from sickness and epidemics, aversion of war or success in its reconciliation and peace, detection of evil (witchcraft, sorcery, adultery, breaking of taboos, curses) and its defeat. On the one hand, people ask for what they need in order to survive and live well, and on the other they seek to be protected from evil.

---

[16] Shorter, Prayer in the Religious Traditions of Africa, pp. 4-15; Mbiti, The Prayers of African Religion, pp. 16-18.

If, as we said, spirituality is the complex of beliefs, attitudes and practices that animate people's lives and help them to reach out to the supersensible realities, we can see the orientation of this spirituality. It seems to be based on the conviction that the community of tile living is involved in a dramatic struggle between life and death, and that the outcome of this struggle depends on how successfully the human community can avail itself of the help of the invisible world. Two elements, then, animate African spirituality: first, the consciousness that individuals and the community are committed to an ever-present struggle against menacing evil if life is to be worth living; and secondly, that in this struggle the decisive key is the availability of assistance from the invisible.

Furthermore, there is the conviction that this struggle is not pursued by individuals alone in isolation, but that it is in and through the community that the fight can be carried on effectively. African spirituality relies on the spirit of community, on cooperation rather than open competition, on sharing and distribution, rather than on 'accumulation or individualistic hoarding. This community is conceived of in terms of "family", that is, in terms of kinship and affinity relationships whereby ideally duties and rights are exchanged unconditionally. This type of relationship offers a greater feeling of security at the same time as it builds up a strong sense of identity and belonging. The success of individuals and the community in attaining a good life is predicated on the smooth working of all this, and "death" is bound to ensue when these relationships are denied or threatened.

The list of things asked for in prayer also indicates a marking characteristic of people's life in general. Since in Africa there was little advance in technology and in the mastery over nature, most of the time of individuals and communities was taken up in activities of sheer subsistence and survival. The overarching preoccupations were about existing; hence, the importance of family and marriage, children, health and sickness, security and danger of death. Most activities focused on ensuring life and survival in the face of all sorts of menaces and dangers.

There was also the constant struggle to produce sufficient food; hence, the preoccupation with land (a basic commodity that should not be subject to individual possession), with rain, the weather, cultivation, harvesting, storage and appropriate distribution and consumption of foodstuff. In this struggle for survival, the people were only too conscious of the tremendous odds they were up against: possibilities of drought, famine, failure of crops. Human beings on their own were open to tragic failures, and so they had to rely on the succour coming from "above", from alliance with the invisible. Such failures were a common occurrence. People expected them and had grown accustomed to hardship and suffering: sickness, accidents, misfortunes, even death. It is impressive to observe the calm and courage with which people faced such trials of life, taking them almost in their stride and maintaining a sense of equanimity, even a defiant response in humour and sane *joie de vivre*. It is as though, faced with constant death, they responded with optimism and a refusal to be broken. Such people are masters in frugality, "poverty of spirit", and simplicity of life. It has been observed how, in the face of tremendous odds, Africans have developed a spirituality of joy: the song, the dance, the celebration.

There is danger in romanticizing all this and thinking that the African is a naive, childish and carefree individual, perhaps insensitive to human misery. In actual fact, the general lot of African people's lives was a tragic experience. One also has to admit that this capacity for suffering patiently, without rebellion or desperation, was not the case of everyone. There are sufficient cases of psychological and even physical breakdowns, instances of heart attacks and suicides, to prevent us from painting too rosy a picture. Moreover, it must be admitted that this kind of resignation is basically a weakness: it prevents people from organizing a real struggle for improvement. This failure to be assertive; the too-ready acceptance of events as if they are inevitable; the reluctance to exhibit openly impulses of individualistic ambition, aggressiveness, and self-interested acquisitiveness - all this adds up to a recipe for easy defeat in the face of determined aggression. These traits of African spirituality may help explain why historically it has been easy to enslave and keep in subjection whole groups of African peoples. And yet one must still appreciate the power and beauty of this spirituality of realism and humanity. It calls to mind the kind of sane spirituality proposed by the Book of Proverbs, where the supreme ideal is expressed in these words:

> Remove far from me falsehood and lying; give me neither poverty nor riches; feed me with the food that is needful for me, Lest I be full, and deny thee, and say, "Who is the Lord?" or lest I be poor, and steal, and profane the name of my God.[17]

Modern experience: African spirituality put to the test

The foregoing discussion has attempted to examine the kind of spirituality that one can deduce from African traditional culture. But as I pointed out at the beginning, my interest is not really with such a spirituality extrapolated from a past culture that is no longer there. In the past two centuries or more, Africa has been forced into a rapid and radical culture change, due mainly to its contact with the Western world. The results of this culture change must be taken into account in order to understand the present state of African spirituality.

Evidently such a summary exposition as this 'does not allow for an extensive and discriminating analysis of this contact with the outside - in the first place with Asia, and then with modern Europe and America. I can only mention its main manifestations insofar as they are of significance for this discussion. Three such manifestations deserve particular attention, namely slave trade, colonialism and neocolonialism. With these we should include the introduction of new religions: Islam and especially Christianity, since these religions coming from outside have confronted more directly the indigenous religion and spirituality. For the purposes of our discussion, these contacts introduced a different and thus alternative world view. They also disturbed the balance and coherence of those cultural values on which the people's spirituality was based. And so this spirituality has been put to a severe test.

---

[17] Proverbs 30:8-9.

Slave traffic for the purposes of a foreign economic system provoked, on the surface, a disturbance of family, tribal and indigenous national security surpassing by far the effects of even the most devastating local wars. It instilled a traumatic sense of insecurity enhanced by the feeling that, while it was a human-made disaster, the usual mechanisms of self-defence and redress were totally inadequate. But even more critical was its radical questioning of the basic understanding of the human person, for here the human being was treated as a thing, an object of mere utilitarian transaction.

Colonialism, on the other hand, inflicted a loss of independence on the native cultures. New norms and customs were imposed on the people in such a way that they had to live and act in conformity with a foreign world view. It was continually impressed on them that their own culture was not valid: it was primitive, pagan and retrograde. If they wanted to move forward, then they had to abandon it and adopt the civilized way of life of the West. Clinging to their own traditional culture was going to keep them backward and incapable of functioning successfully in the modern world.

Given the circumstances, the adoption of new ways was not really a matter of choice, for colonialism was an imposition by force. And yet the means of enabling people to adapt to these new ways and to function successfully within the new context were in no way equally available to everyone. Modern education and training, unlike traditional methods, reach individuals and communities in a highly selective manner, and the conditions for obtaining them are not totally in the hands of the people themselves, but dependent on the good will of the colonial powers and their successful allies. Success in the modern world is dependent mainly on the individual's own efforts and personal ambition, rather than on community cooperation and sharing. It is a world view that puts a premium on aggressive and self-interested competition.

The result of colonialism has been that only a relatively few Africans have managed to acquire the tools needed to have access to power, wealth and success in the modern context. The large majority are still left behind, trying to cope with the new situation as best they can. They struggle to assure a measure of survival with the help of some remnants of the traditional culture that are still familiar to them, and bits and pieces of the new system that they are able to take hold of. But they are at a disadvantage, and end up being at the mercy of those who are more successful. In general the process has been one in which more and more people are becoming poorer and more and more powerless in the face of modern forces. The real tragedy is that traditional culture has been practically discredited. Everyone is fascinated by the power and promise of modern life and secretly hopes somehow some day to become part of it. Even those who have to fall back on traditional culture do so only as a measure of desperation. There is very little else they can do. If it were possible, they would exchange places with those who are making it in the new world.

To begin to appreciate what a severe testing traditional spirituality is undergoing as a result of colonialism, we should consider what is actually taking place, now that colonialism is officially over in most African countries and African societies are now developing into independent, self-governing nations. In the early years of independence, there was much hope and enthusiasm for development and progress. After several decades of sincere efforts, what do we see? A kind of development has surely been taking place in most nations: fantastic urban growth, modern industries, and agricultural projects resulting in higher gross national products (much wealth being produced), better infrastructure (for communication and transport), and social and health services. But why is it that this development has not been sustained? And why have only relatively few benefited from this wealth, while the majority become poorer each day? How was it that almost immediately internal power struggles started, resulting in tribal and regional wars, oppressive military regimes, corruption, bribery, nepotism, land-grabbing, extortions, exploitative and unfair labour practices, displacement of whole populations (refugees, expulsions, asylum seekers), imprisonments, tortures and executions? How does all this tally with traditional culture and spirituality?

This question becomes all the more pressing when we consider the present situation of neocolonialism. Neocolonialism is a shorthand designation of the fact, processes and consequences of the relation between the developed and industrialized nations (the North) and the less developed and poorer nations (the South) to which Africa as a whole belongs. The decisive point in this relationship is that the South is in practice the dependent and servant member. Its economy is basically subsidiary to the North, which explains why the South is less powerful and consequently exploitable and poor. But when you consider the actual situation in the nations of the South, not every individual or group is really powerless or poor. You often see concentrations of power, wealth and privilege in sections of these poor nations, side by side with extreme poverty and disadvantage. Not that in traditional society there was no poverty, injustice, jealousy or suffering. There certainly was. But there is a radical difference, nonetheless, a difference not simply of magnitude, but rather of basic structure and orientation - a difference in spirituality.

I submit that the key to a proper understanding of what is going on is to realize that contact with the outside has introduced a new, alternative spirituality based on a world view quite different from the traditional one and governed by a different set of values and priorities. This new spirituality is humanly more powerful and imposing. It promises attractive, immediate and palpable results and has the capacity to validate these promises by offering samples of success that are hard to ignore or pass by. Central to this spirituality is the supremacy of the value of acquiring, possessing, multiplying and enjoying material goods by individuals. This value precedes all others and should not be necessarily restricted by other values, such as the consideration of other people's needs and feelings.

Traditional African spirituality (ideally, though perhaps not always in fact) would rather consider as primary the value of good and harmonious human relationships, and esteem that material goods, however desirable, should not take precedence over these. But it is not so with this new spirituality. On the contrary, the pursuit of individual ambition and self-interest through fair competition is a *positive* value. Traditional African spirituality had an almost superstitious fear of such open self-interest, unless it could be justified as serving the purpose of the group. There is a lurking suspicion that such a competition is never really fair: The playing down of personal ambition and the strictures induced by the need to consider the interests of the group tend to make the task of achieving success or acquiring personal wealth much more inhibited and less effective. Likewise, the high value placed on cooperation and the sharing of resources puts a brake on the instinct of acquisition and hoarding. But new spirituality releases people from such restrictions and thereby liberates the powerful drives of self-interest and individual acquisitiveness. Those who manage to get the chance can now go ahead and become powerful, rich and successful without feeling bad about it or being bothered by the obligation to share their good luck with other people.

In all fairness, we should recall that another side of the contact of Africans with the outside has been Christian evangelization, which in some cases *preceded* colonialism, and in many others came together with it. The Christian message is, by and large, in opposition to what we proposed as the "spirituality" of colonialism. It is centred on love of God (not mammon) and love for neighbour. Although it seeks to promote human development and well-being, at the same time it warns against the danger of riches. It proclaims the sacred value of the human person and yet castigates self-centred individualism by exalting the value of community. In fact, there are many similarities between the values Christianity preaches and those I have pointed out as belonging to African spirituality. There are, of course, radical differences between the two, which it is not my intention to explore here. But the haunting question is this: Has Christian spirituality recognized African spirituality as a potential ally in the struggle against the worst aspects of colonial and neocolonial infection?

The answer cannot be a simple yes or no. Christianity came to Africa in many shapes and models, and so its encounter with African cultures has not been the same everywhere. Two contrasting attitudes can be distinguished, one of opposition and rejection and another of openness and dialogue. In some cases, Christianity regarded traditional culture and religion with suspicion, even hostility. It was seen as the work of the devil: a backward and pagan way of life that must be destroyed totally if the pure religion of Christ is to be preached successfully to the people. And yet often, after this destruction had been achieved, what was proposed to the people instead was very much like the colonial spirituality. In other cases, Christian evangelists were able to recognize valid and positive elements in the traditional way of life side by side with other negative ones that the gospel would have to destroy, as has been the case with every human culture where the Christian message has been preached. In deciding between the two attitudes, Christians have tended to seek guidance from Holy Scripture. This procedure is not only legitimate, but the only sure way. The problem, however, is that it is not simply a question of discovering some isolated texts in the Bible and then coming to this or that conclusion. Rather the whole trend of God's dealing with humanity as revealed in the Scriptures needs to be taken into account. After all, the decisive question is this: In the development and functioning of human cultures and spirituali-ties, such as the African one, has the God of our Lord Jesus Christ been totally absent? Is it possible that God was at work with the Spirit, inspiring and promoting positive values for the guidance of God's people, even if human sinfulness always tends to put obstacles in front of God's saving work?

Conclusion

When considering African spirituality as we have done, these questions are extremely important. For if it is true that "God did not leave himself without witness" (Acts 14:17), then whatever is true, honorable, just, pure, lovely and gracious in what God has done among the nations has to be respected and used with gratitude. God loves to "choose what is foolish in the world to shame the wise ... (God chooses) what is weak in the world to shame the strong ... what is low and despised in the world, even things that are not, to bring to nothing things that are, so that no human being might boast in the presence Of God" (1 Cor. 1:27-29). In our present world, cultures of greed and violence are creating death while people long for peace, security and joy. It may be that simple spiritualities, based on more human and humane values, like those coming from the weak and poor nations of the world, are the hopeful reserves for humanity's future survival.

Bibliography

Idowu, E.B., African Traditional Religion: A Definition, Maryknoll: Orbis, 1975.

Marwick, M.G., Sorcery in its Social Setting, Manchester: Manchester University Press, 1965.

Marwick, M.G. (ed.), Witchcraft and Sorcery, Harmondsworth: Penguin, 1970, 1982.

Maurier, H., Philosophie de l'Afrique noire, St Augustin: Anthropos, 1985.

Mbiti, J.S., The Prayers of African Religion, Maryknoll: Orbis, 1975.

Mbiti, J.S., Introduction to African Religion, Maryknoll: Orbis, 1975.

Parrinder E.G., African Traditional Religion, London: Sheldon Press, 1962.

Pobee, J.S., Toward an African Theology, Nashville: Abingdon, 1979.

Shorter, A., Prayer in the Religious Traditions of Africa, London: Oxford University Press, 1975.

Tempels, P., La Philosophie Bantoue, Paris: Presence Africaine, 1949.

Wakefield, G.S. (ed.), A Dictionary of Christian Spirituality, London: SCM, 1983.

Zahan, D., The Religion, Spirituality and Thought of Traditional Africa, Chicago and London: University of Chicago Press, 197

Index

Abidjan 38
Abraham 15, 49, 115, 118
Academic ministry 8, 39f
Acolyte 18
Acts of the Apostles 70
Ad Gentes (A.G.) 45, 56, 112, 122
Africa 8f, 11f, 19, 21-25, 27, 29, 38, 40f, 54, 78, 83, 86-89, 91, 95, 97, 99, 101, 105f, 109, 123, 126f, 131f, 143ff, 149, 153-157, 159-163, 169, 182f, 185, 187, 190, 192, 194ff, 201, 206f, 209, 218f, 221ff, 225f, 228, 232, 235f, 238, 241f
Africa Report 88, 96, 105
African Christian theology 161
African Church 33, 86, 88, 164
African Independent Churches 139, 165
African languages 131, 209
African liberation theology 144
African National Congress (ANC) 163
African Protestant theologians 160
Africanization 30f
Afrikaner Nationalist Party 163
Afrikaners 162
Akan culture 159f
  chief 160
Algeria 15, 19, 21, 24
  War of Independence 24
Algiers 21, 24, 81

Alomwe 208
American Dream 147
  history 148
Anglican Church 159
  African theologians 160
Angola 20
Animism 78, 230
Anthropological poverty 145, 161
Anthropologists 174, 217
Apartheid 163, 167ff
Apostles 52, 119
Apostolic Church 25, 107
  ministry 21
  of Christ 55
  preaching 100
Apostolic Nuncio 37
Apostolicam Actuositatem (A.A.) 45
Arabs 24
Arkansas 151
Asia 41, 144, 149, 153, 174f, 177, 199, 217, 238
Asian theologians 174, 217
Association of Member Episcopal Conferences of Eastern Africa (AMECEA) 38f, 54, 74, 100, 105, 109, 127, 143
Asylum seekers 240
Atheism 78
Balasuriya, Tissa 175, 177, 198f
Champmartin, Fr J.B. 14

Banda, Dr H. Kamuzu 26, 33, 183
Bantu cultural identity 168
   ontology 231
Bantustans 168
Baptism 47, 57, 70, 201
Basic Christian Communities 70, 104
Beatitudes 212
Beira 20
Belgians 22
Bembeke 29
   Parish 29
   Teacher Training College 30
Berkeley 12, 39
Berlin Wall 143
Bible 29, 32, 47, 51, 100, 112f, 124f, 146, 150f, 166, 196, 203-219, 243
Biblical scholars 174, 217
Biblicum 27
Birmingham 39, 126
Bishop of Lilongwe 19, 33, 39f, 90
Bishop of Rome 52
Black Americans 145
Black churches 167
   church leaders 148f
   communities 147, 149
   feminsim 149
   ghettos 147
   religion 148, 149
   theologians 143, 145
   theology 143, 145, 148-152, 162, 164, 165, 167, 168

Black Consciousness Movement 164
Black Messiah 150, 167
Black Power movement 148
Blantyre 21
Blyden, E.W. 153
Boesak, Allan Aubrey 165, 167, 168
Book of Ruth 115
Bribery 240
British 22, 220
Brown, Kelly 153
Buddhism 78
Buku Lopatulika 30
Buthelezi, Bishop Manas 165, 168
Calvinist Dutch Reformed Church 167
Calvinistic faith 162
Camden Town 53
Canadians 22
Canon Law 18, 33
Cape Maclear 11
Caribbean 41, 153f
Carmelite Brothers 91
Carmelite Fathers 89, 91
Carmelite Sisters 91
Carmelite Sisters of Luxembourg 89
Carmelite Sisters of Spain 89, 91
Carthage 23, 25f
Catechetics 18, 31
Catholic Bible 30
Catholic Church 12, 14, 46, 64, 88, 97, 107, 111, 208
   African church 89

ideology 208
missionaries 40, 128, 208
missions 10f, 13
Catholic Church of Malawi 29
Catholic diocese of Zambia 30
Catholic Institute of Higher Religious Studies for Anglophone Africa 38
Catholic Institute of Lovanium 155
Central Region 33, 37, 89
Césaire, Aimè 154
Chamgwera, Allan 18
Chewa 10, 12, 33, 126, 208
Chichewa 30, 32, 44
Chikwawa 34
Chipata 18
Chisendera, Bishop G. 16
Chitsulo, Bishop Cornelius 29
Christendom 116
Church elders 67, 71
Church History 109
Church in Africa 33, 84, 86, 88, 197
Church of Christ 55, 72, 100, 107
Churches in Europe 88
Churches in North America 88
Churches in South Africa 154
Civil Rights movement 148
Clergy 33, 58f, 66ff, 72, 89, 101-105
Cold War 143
College of Bishops 52
Colonialism 24, 96f, 145, 153f, 157, 181, 183f, 223, 227, 238ff, 242

Communalism 201
Communism 37
Cone, Cecil 153
Cone, James H. 146, 148, 150, 152
Confirmation 14
Constitution of Divine Revelation 209
Corruption 159, 190, 240
Cosmology 226, 228
Council of Trent 25
Covenant 118, 120
Crusades, the 116
Dar-es-Salaam 41f
De Gouveia, Cardinal 20
Deacon 18, 58
Decolonization 108
Dedza 28, 40, 128
district 11, 16
Dependence 103, 107f, 190f, 195, 198f, 214, 218, 230, 234
Descartes 141, 228
Despotism 162
Developing nations 41, 206
Diaconate 17
Dickson, Kwesi 156
Diocesan mini-synod 36
Diocesan Pastoral Plan 34, 44, 55f, 58, 63
Discrimination 143, 146, 153, 162, 164, 166, 212
Dogmatic theology 17
Drama 174, 201, 215, 217, 227
Dubois, W.E.B. 147, 153
Dutch 22
immigrants 162

Reformed Church 11, 128, 167
Duval, Cardinal 81
Eastern Africa 33, 74, 100, 127
Eastern and Central Africa 30
Ecclesiology 37, 157
Economics 31, 36, 169
Ecumenical 13, 26, 32, 127, 149, 159, 176
Ecumenical Association of African Theologians (EAAT) 156, 165, 203, 216
Ecumenical Association of Third World Theologians (EATWOT) 42, 144, 149, 150, 152, 165, 172ff, 178, 204, 216
Ecumenical Centre for African Students and Pilgrims 39
Ecumenical Centre for Black and White Christian Partnership 39f
Ecumenical Centre of Tantur 39
Ela, Jean-Marc 156
Elite 175, 181, 183, 186
England 39
English-speaking Africa 38
Episcopal College 52
Episcopal Conference 29, 34, 37, 74
 of Malawi (ECM) 54, 74
Episcopal conferences 33, 38, 54, 74, 79, 100, 209
Eternal City 51
Ethiopia 33
Eucharist 53, 55, 70
Europe 25, 40f, 87, 97, 100, 108, 116, 127, 140, 154, 183, 195, 238

European languages 131
 influence 11
Evangelization 21f, 75, 78-86, 88, 94, 96f, 134, 154, 181, 207, 242
Exile 8, 15, 39, 40
Exorcist 18
Exploitation 42, 144f, 162, 168f, 181, 187, 191f, 199, 204
Fady, Bishop Joseph 19, 33, 89f
Faith dialogue 22
Family Movement 68
Famine 162, 235, 237
Fashole-Luke, E. 87, 152
Federation of Rhodesia and Nyasaland 26
Fetishism 230
First Communion 14
FLN 24
France 25
Freire, Paulo 199
French 19f, 22ff, 154
 -speaking countries 38
Funerals 234
Gaudium et Spes (G.S.) 45
Generalate 21, 28, 39
Genesis 50, 118, 120
Geneva 159, 173
Gentiles 114f, 118ff
Germans 22
Goba, Bonganjalo 165
Golah 114
Grant, Jacquelyn 153
Grassroots theology 172, 175, 178, 199f, 202
Greeks 120

Gregorian 26
  University 26
Gutierrez, Gustavo 173
Harding, Vincent 153
Harlem 53
Hastings, Fr A. 62
Hinduism 78
Hispanics 149
Holland 167
Holy Childhood 93
  Scripture 18, 26, 31, 218, 243
  Spirit 22, 28, 32, 45, 53, 55, 72, 74f, 78, 86, 168
Idolatry 78, 114, 230
Idowu, E. Bolaji 222
Ignatian spirituality 21
Inculturation 30, 161, 169
Indians 149
Industrialized nations 41, 240
Initiations 234
Inter-faith 13
Islam 78, 83, 117, 131, 238
Israel 118, 120f
Italians 22
Ivory Coast 38
Jerusalem 8, 39, 119
Jesuits 21, 27
Jewish 116, 123, 125
  nation 121
John the Baptist 115
Jos 87
Judaism 78, 114f, 118
Justice 35, 50, 125, 143, 162, 168, 227

Kabasele, F. 156
Kachebere Major Seminary 15, 17, 31, 40
Kachindamoto, chief 11
Kaffirs 162
Kairos Document 166
Kalilombe, Pierre Mangulenje 10
Kanchamba village 10
Karonga paramountcy 11
Kasina Minor Seminary 14, 16
Kenya 33, 74, 100, 109
Kingdom of God 22, 34, 50f, 122, 146
Kinshasa 38, 109, 155
Kinship 54, 129, 131, 133, 140, 152, 180, 188, 190f, 201, 228f, 232, 236
Kipalapala 17
Kirk Range 11
Kwacha (Malawian) 92
Lake Malawi 11
Land-grabbing 240
Latin 16, 30
Latin America 37, 41, 144f, 149, 192, 197
Latin American liberation theologies 144
Lavigerie, Cardinal Charles A. 21
Law 54, 70, 230
Lay apostolate 68f
Lay Movements 68f
Lay people 59, 66, 69, 101
Lector 18
Legion of Mary 68
Legon 159

Leprosarium 11
Letters of St Paul 70
liberation theology 149, 204
Life President 36
Likuni 44
Lilongwe 8, 33ff, 37f, 40, 44, 47, 52, 54ff, 65, 71, 73, 87-90, 94, 99, 102
Limpopo 143
Lincoln, G. Eric 153
Linden, Ian 12, 208
Lisbon 20
Literacy 206f, 218
Liturgy 17, 29f, 57, 70, 209, 210
Livingstonia Missionaries 11
Livulezi 11
Local priests 14, 56, 58, 91, 94f
Long, Charles 153
Lourenco Marques 20
Lumen Gentium (L.G.) 45, 49, 57ff, 122
Lusaka 18
Luxembourg Carmelites 89
Magisterium 208f
Maimela, Simon 165
Mainline Christian tradition 148
Maison-Carrée 19, 21
Major Orders 18
Malawi 8-12, 15-18, 26, 28, 30f, 33, 35, 37, 39ff, 44, 54, 74, 89f, 94, 100, 126, 183, 207, 209, 218, 224
Malawi Congress Party 33, 183
Malawian Catholics 206, 208
Malembo 11

Malembo Oyera 30
Mankhamba 11
Maputo 20
Maravi 11
Marist Brothers 90, 91
Marriage 138, 140, 160, 228, 232ff, 236
Martinique 154
Marwick, M.G. 229
Marxism 37, 166
Mau-Mau 20
Mazombwe, Archbishop, M. 16
Mbiti, J.S. 131f, 152, 209, 221, 225, 232f, 235
Medicine 231f
Mesters, C. 203ff
Milingo, Emmanuel 16, 18, 158
Militarism 162
Mini-Synod 34f, 37, 44, 90
Minor Orders 18
White Sisters 12f, 89
Missionary 11f, 19, 21f, 24, 28ff, 33, 40f, 56ff, 62, 88f, 91, 94-101, 108, 110f, 113, 116, 118, 127, 130, 137, 154, 159
Mofokeng, Thakatso 165
Montfort Fathers 11
Moral Theology 17
Mosque 211
Mother House 21, 93
Motlhabi, G.M. 165
Mozambique 16, 19ff, 95, 126, 182
Mtakataka 11, 14f, 29, 128
Mtulo 64

Mua 10-14, 29, 128
Multi-racial Britain 153
Muslim 21, 24, 81, 128, 211
Mvera 11
Mzifei, Helena 10
Nairobi 38, 74, 100, 127, 209
Namaacha Seminary 20
Nationalist movements 183f
    parties 184
    struggle 184
Nègritude movement 154
Negro Spirituals 146
Neocolonialism 145, 227, 238, 240
Neophytes 62
Nepotism 190, 240
New Testament 53, 115f, 119, 122, 208
New World, the 240
Newbigin, Lesslie 176
Ngoni 11, 126, 224
    chieftaincy of Kachindamoto 11
Nicaragua 200
Nicaraguan revolution 200
Niebuhr, H. Richard 151
Non-Christian religions 78, 81, 85, 112, 116, 120, 122, 125
Non-ordained ministries 59f, 102, 105
North Africa 15, 18, 81
North African Muslims 22
North America 42, 144f
North American black theology 152
North, the 143f, 163, 168, 240f
Northern Rhodesia 17

North-South relations 169
Novitiate 18-21, 23f
Ntcheu 11
Nyanja 30
Nyasaland 12, 17, 19, 20, 25, 183, 208
Nzama 11
One-party system 36
Oppression 42, 51, 77, 143f, 150, 153, 166, 168f, 191, 194, 196, 199, 203
Original Sin 79
Ottawa 89, 91, 167
Oxford 143, 159, 165, 207, 209, 225
Pacific, the 153
Pagans 113ff, 120, 123
Pan Africanist Congress (PAC) 163
Pan-African Catholic consciousness 89
Pan-Africanists 153
Papacy 28
Parables 211ff
Parrinder, E.G. 221
Pastoral ministry 31, 33
    theology 17f
Patriarchates 54
Peasants 188, 191, 193
Peltier, Fr Beltrand 19
Philosophy 18, 154f, 182, 234
Phiri/Maravi groups 11
Pieds Noir 24
Pious Associations 67
Pobee, John S. 156, 159, 228
Political freedom 143

Politics 169
Pontifical Biblical Institute 26
Pontifical Urbanian University 27
Poor Clares 89, 92
Pope John XXIII 28, 83
Pope Pius XII 28
Porter 18
Portugal 19f, 116
Portuguese 20
Post-independence politics 184
Prayer 17, 59, 75f, 90, 101, 200, 208, 215f, 225f, 234ff
Prein, Fr 20
Pre-independence political movements 184
President Bourguiba 25
Priesthood 14, 16, 58
Propaganda Fide 97
Propagation of the Faith 93
Prophet Jonah 115
Protestant 29, 87, 146, 160
  Christians 128
  churches 207
Proto-Chewa Banda clans 11
Proverbs 160, 201
Psychologists 174, 217
Qur'anic surahs 211
Reformation, the 209
Refugees 162, 240
Regional Minister 37
Regionalism 190
Religious Brothers 91
  Sisters 91
Rift Valley 11

Ritual 30
Roberts, J. Deotis 152
Roman Catholics 13, 29
  Congregation 97ff
Roman universities 27
Romans 114f, 119, 123
Rome 15, 19, 21, 26-29, 31, 33, 37, 39f, 63, 74, 87, 89, 93
Sabbatical 39
Sacred Congregation for the Evangelization of Peoples 39, 87
Salvation 34, 47ff, 51, 60, 66, 75, 77, 83f, 109-112, 114, 118, 121f, 124, 129f, 160f, 197
Sangu, Bishop J. 87
Satan 113, 227
Scholasticate 23
Schools 11-14, 27, 63, 90ff, 95, 147, 154, 213
Scriptures 8, 74f, 112ff, 116, 121, 123ff, 146, 160f, 179, 196, 199f, 203ff, 207-211, 213, 217, 243
Secularization 78
Segregation 147
Seleucids 114
Self-ministering 34, 57ff, 62, 65, 101f, 106
Self-propagating 34, 57, 62, 65, 101ff
Self-supporting 34, 57, 62f, 65, 92, 103, 106
Selly Oak Colleges 39, 126
Seminaries 24, 94, 149
Sena 208
Senegal 154

Senghor, Léopold 154
Sermon on the Mount 212
Setiloane, Gabriel 165, 168
Seventh-Day Adventist Church 128
Sharpeville 164
Sickness 15, 129, 157, 234-237
Sinai 118
Sisters of Charity of Ottawa (Grey Nuns) 89
Slave trade 238
Slavery 60, 145ff, 152f, 157, 227
Small Christian Communities 35, 36, 105, 158, 201
Social anthropology 31
Social restructuring 162
Social scientists 174, 217
Society of Missionaries of Africa 19
Sociologists 188
Solentiname 200
Songs 121
Sorcery 229, 235
South Africa 143f, 153f, 162-169
South African black theology 145, 169
South African Student Organization 164
South, the 11, 147, 151, 163, 241
Soweto 164
Spain 89, 116
Spanish 22, 91, 200
Spark, the 18
Spirituality 9, 17, 21, 32, 72, 220-243
St Augustine's Association 27

St Peter Apostle 93
Stories 146, 174, 201f, 213, 217, 226
Sub-deacon 18
Subdiaconate 17
Sub-parishes 55
Subsistence economy 188
Sudan 33, 95
Superstition 123, 230
Swaziland 20
Swiss 22
Symposium of the Episcopal Conferences of Africa and Madagascar (SECAM) 38, 54, 209
Syncretism 161
Synod of Bishops 22, 74, 80, 87f, 105
Taboos 233ff
Tanzania 17, 33, 100, 182
Taxes 92, 189
Tempels, Fr Placide 154f, 231
Teresian Sisters 89, 91
Thibar 23ff
Third World 39-42, 143ff, 150, 153, 159, 163, 165, 172ff, 176ff, 192, 195, 203f, 216ff
Tlhagale, Buti 165
Tonsure 18
Traditional authority 188
  culture 13, 35, 134, 154, 160, 223, 225, 238ff, 242
  customs 168
  religion 13, 126ff, 130f, 133ff, 140, 161, 181, 221f

societies 188
spirituality 226, 240
theology 149, 173
Tshibangu, Bishop T. 155
Tunis 23
Tunisia 15, 21, 24
Turner, Bishop Henry M. 147
Tutu, Archbishop Desmond 165
Uganda 33, 88, 95, 100
Ujamaa 182
Underdeveloped nations 41, 192
Uneversity Christian Movement (UCM) 164
Union Theological Seminary 151
United States of America (USA) 8, 39, 41, 143
Universal Church 47, 97f
Universities 27, 149, 155f
University of California 12, 39
University of Ghana 159
Vanneste, Canon A. 155
Vatican I 25
Vatican II 26, 32ff, 37, 44ff, 53-56, 58, 66f, 110ff, 122, 209
Venn, Henry 34
Vicar Apostolic 19
Vicariate 17, 97
Wach, Joachim 134f
War 23ff
Washington Jr, Joseph R. 148
Washington, Booker T. 147

Weber, Max 135
West, Cornel 153
Western Christian thinking 154
Western culture 97, 116, 126, 156
  civilization 25, 97, 116, 154
  education 181, 186
White churches 148f
  church theology 149
White Father Brothers 91
White Fathers 11, 13, 15, 19, 21f, 24, 29, 31f, 39, 89, 91
William Paton Fellow 39
Williams, Delores 153
Wilmore, Gayraud S. 148f, 153
Witchcraft 138, 229, 235
World Alliance of Reformed Churches 167
World Council of Churches 159
World War II 23, 25
World-wide Catholic communion 52, 97
Yahweh 34, 46, 114, 118, 121, 167
Yao 11
Young Christian Students (YCS) 68, 179
Young Christian Workers 68, 179
Zahan, D. 127, 222
Zaire 38, 155
Zambia 16ff, 30, 31, 33, 100, 126
Zion 121
Zobue 20

www.ingramcontent.com/pod-product-compliance
Lightning Source LLC
Chambersburg PA
CBHW021351300426
44114CB00012B/1181